The Scientific Study of Abnormal Behavior

The Scientific Study of Abnormal Behavior

Experimental and Clinical Research

James Inglis

Routledge
Taylor & Francis Group
LONDON AND NEW YORK

First published 1966 by Transaction Publishers

2 Park Square, Milton Park, Abingdon, Oxfordshire OX14 4RN
711 Third Avenue, New York, NY 10017

Routledge is an imprint of the Taylor & Francis Group, an informa business

First issued in hardback 2017

Library of Congress Catalog Number: 2007021130

Library of Congress Cataloging-in-Publication Data

Inglis, James, 1927-
The scientific study of abnormal behavior : experimental and clinical research / James Inglis.
p. cm.
Originally published: 1966.
Includes bibliographical references and index.
ISBN 978-0-202-30986-6
1. Psychology, Pathological. I. Title.

RC454.152 2007
616.89—dc22 2007021130

ISBN 13: 978-0-202-30986-6 (pbk)
ISBN 13: 978-1-138-53846-7 (hbk)

TO M. B. SHAPIRO

WHO PIONEERED THE WAY

WE GIVE THE NAME OBSERVER TO THE MAN WHO APPLIES *methods of investigation, whether simple or complex, to the study of phenomena which he does not vary and which he therefore gathers as nature offers them. We give the name experimenter to the man who applies methods of investigation, whether simple or complex, so as to make natural phenomena vary, or so as to alter them with some purpose or another .... In this sense, observation is investigation of a natural phenomenon, and experiment is investigation of a phenomenon altered by the investigator. We shall see that this distinction, apparently quite external and depending simply on a definition of words, still supplies the one meaning with which to grasp the important difference separating sciences of observation from sciences of experimentation or experimental sciences.*

CLAUDE BERNARD

FOREWORD

THERE WAS A TIME when books on abnormal psychology were primarily descriptive, theoretical, non-experimental, and qualitative. In recent years description and theory have given way to scientific models and the testing of their hypotheses by experimental methods. Even descriptive approaches have focused on objective measures of patient behavior rather than case histories or clinical interpretations of these behaviors. As a result the scientific literature of abnormal psychology has grown tremendously and, today, one textbook cannot contain all the findings except in an abstract encapsulated form. Such texts, however, important as they are as handbooks, do not serve the purpose of instruction. An instructive textbook must indicate why certain problems are important, what research methods have been developed for attacking them, what success has already been attained, and what problems are still to be solved. This, of course, forces the author to select from the vast amount of material available. The reader of this book will find that the selections made by the author are most fortunate, since they deal with urgent problems now in the forefront of research.

This book points up the essential differences between the clinical and the experimental approaches to psychopathology and their interdependence. If one were to choose a single characteristic that differentiates the two, I would recommend that it should be the tendency for self-reference in judgment. The clinician tends to depend heavily on intuitive, subjective self reference in arriving at his judgments. His own feelings, experience, and emotions constitute an important basis for his conclusions. For example, some clinicians report that they rarely make a diagnosis of schizophrenia (or dementia praecox) unless they experience "that praecox feeling" while examining the patient. The experimentalist tries his utmost to free himself from these self-referred moorings and appeals instead to external criteria whose objectivity, reliability, and validity are demonstrable operationally. These external criteria can not replace clinical judgment, but they can buttress it and confirm or disconfirm it. In this way the experimentalist can provide a bridge between the clinician's intuitions and the verifiable aspects of patient behavior.

One of the difficulties of crossing such bridges is that the other side may have symbols and signs that are in a foreign tongue. Students of abnormal psychology will find that this book, steeped as it is in both clinical and experimental knowledge, attempts to provide them with easy passage between the two fields and with a common vocabulary that will permit them to get acquainted with both sides of the river. How well this has been accomplished may safely be left to the reader to decide.

JOSEPH ZUBIN
Chief of Psychiatric Research (Biometrics)
New York State Department of Mental Hygiene

PREFACE

THE AIM OF this book is to consider some applications of the scientific principles of psychology to the field of abnormality, exemplified by selected studies involving the measurement and the manipulation of disordered behavior.

There has, in the past, been an unfortunate tendency for books about abnormal psychology to be written as if they could best be conceived as mere diluted textbooks of psychiatry. Much emphasis has usually been placed upon psychiatric nosology and psychiatric theory. More recently, however, many psychologists interested in abnormal behavior have begun to address their problems by methods derived from their own discipline rather than by techniques borrowed uncritically from the medical arts. It is to be hoped that eventually, through a consideration of the procedures and findings of a number of different examples of the scientific study of abnormal behavior, some general principles may emerge that will show how these methods might profitably be extended to cover the whole field of behavioral disorder.

Most of the material that describes what has already been achieved by the behavioral attack upon psychiatric problems is still widely scattered throughout the literature. This, of course, vastly increases the difficulty of assessing any general implications. There seems, in fact, to be a need to have at least some of these studies gathered together in order that their findings may be more universally known; then, if the beginnings of a larger plan exist, these rudiments might rapidly be developed into an even more active strategy. Attempts have already been made on this problem by the compilation of handbooks and selections of readings; for some purposes, however, the former may be too diffuse and the latter too narrow. Another approach is required so that the student may assimilate the relevant information without being either swamped by or confined to detail. It seems that this end can be served by a concise overview of a number of different topics, each having its tentative place within a broader scheme.

When it came to the matter of selecting the particular topics to include for that purpose in this book, it was evident that several criteria might be invoked. After careful consideration, it seemed better to select studies mainly for the relevance of their content rather than solely for the sophistication of their design. It also seemed preferable to look at investigations that have produced positive and promising results rather than at those of only negative outcome. Often enough, the principal use of the latter studies has been to refute notions that were not worth putting forward in the first place.

In the field of abnormal psychology, it is only too common to find that data are mainly collected and presented in terms of, or in relation to, some overall "theory of behavior," which they are then used to support or disprove. Although such systems must often deal with findings that are important in their own right, these data are nevertheless mainly used to buttress or to undermine the theory, which remains the real focus of interest throughout. An attempt has been made here to reduce this kind of bias. This is not to maintain that theoretical issues should be avoided completely. Some kinds of data may be conveniently subsumed within a miniature system but still resist inclusion within any all-embracing scheme.

Having settled on a few of the criteria for the kind of investigations to be considered, it remained to decide how these studies should be presented. It would, for example, have been possible to carry out a broad, critical review of each of the areas chosen—an approach that can make for a useful source book but one that certainly makes for congested reading. It seemed better to try to deal with the work of individuals, or of small groups of investigators, whose main concern has been systematically to initiate inquiries and to elucidate problems related to very circumscribed topics in the field of abnormal behavior. Another writer might have chosen different examples, and therefore the choice represented here must be regarded as idiosyncratic rather than comprehensive.

The following chapters, then, contain an account of the work of a few investigators, and try to show how their techniques, procedures, and findings have gradually emerged and evolved over a number of years. The concern, therefore, will not be simply with their most recent results but with the steps through which some of these results came to be secured. The arrangement of the chapters, it is hoped, will provide one possible scheme for the conceptual ordering of various kinds of psychological inquiry related to behavior pathology.

Whatever merit attaches to this way of looking at the study of abnormal behavior derives mainly from the work of others. I owe most to M. B. Shapiro, who has, for some twenty years, expounded and exemplified the scientific approach to abnormal psychology to graduate students at the Institute of Psychiatry of the University of London. I hope that this book reflects, without too much distortion, something of what he has taught and practiced.

Of the other colleagues and friends who have given me invaluable help and advice, I should like, in particular, to thank Robert W. Payne, H. Gwynne Jones, Dugal Campbell, and Victor Meyer. It has also been my great good fortune to collaborate with a number of psychiatrists whose understanding, cooperation, and scholarship have put me very deeply in their debt; among these I am especially grateful for the interest and encouragement accorded by R. Bruce Sloane, Samuel George Laverty, and Felix Post.

I should also like to take this opportunity to thank those agencies that have financed the research of my own that is mentioned in this volume. Grants have, at various times, been provided by the Research Fund of the Board of Governors of the Bethlem Royal Hospital and the Maudsley Hospital, by the Canadian National Health Grants Administration, by the Ontario Mental Health Foundation, and by the Nuffield Foundation. My greatest debt, however, is to the Foundations' Fund for Research in Psychiatry, which for three years provided an Interdisciplinary Teaching Award to finance my appointment in the Department of Psychiatry at Queen's University, Kingston, Ontario. This Fund donated much more than money by giving me the time and the impetus to consider a wide range of psychological researches relevant to psychiatric problems, some of which are described in this book.

Only those who have ever been blessed with a perfect secretary can appreciate how fortunate I am to have been granted three such secretaries in succession; Valerie Howell, June Payne, and Ilene Fainberg have been paragons.

I have now thanked some of those who have made my task possible, but my greatest gratitude is to those who have made it worth while, my wife and daughters: Lily, and Jane and Katrin.

James Inglis

ACKNOWLEDGMENTS

THE FOLLOWING publishers and publications have most kindly given their permission for the use of various figures, tables, and quotations throughout this book.

American Medical Association
American Psychiatric Association
American Psychological Association
Appleton-Century-Crofts: Fig. 6.1 in this volume is reproduced from Fig. 10 of:

Cumulative Record by B. F. Skinner, enlarged edition, copyright © 1959, 1961, by Appleton-Century-Crofts, and is reproduced by permission of Appleton-Century-Crofts.

Association for Research in Nervous and Mental Disease
Barnes and Noble
Basic Books: Permission was granted for quotation from the *Handbook of Abnormal Psychology* edited by H. J. Eysenck, by Basic Books, Inc., Publisher, New York, 1961
Behavior Research and Therapy
British Journal of Educational Psychology
British Journal of Medical Psychology
British Journal of Psychiatry and Journal of Mental Science
British Journal of Social and Clinical Psychology
Canadian Journal of Psychology
Comprehensive Psychiatry
Diseases of the Nervous System
Dover Publications
Gerontologia
Grune and Stratton: Material has been used by permission of Grune and Stratton from the following sources.

Cohen, B. D., Luby, E. D., Rosenbaum, G., & Gottlieb, J. S. Combined sernyl and sensory deprivation. *Comprehensive Psychiatry*, 1960, I, 345–348.

Lindsley, O. R. Free-operant conditioning and psychotherapy. In J. H. Masserman (Ed.), *Current psychiatric therapies*. (Vol. III). New York: Grune and Stratton, 1963.

Truax, C. B., & Carkhuff, R. R. Significant developments in psychotherapy research. In L. E. Abt and B. F. Riess (Eds.), *Progress in*

clinical psychology. (Vol. VI) New York: Grune and Stratton, 1964.
Harvard University Press: Tables, figures, and quotations have been reprinted, by permission of the publishers, from Philip Solomon, Philip E. Kubzansky, P. Herbert Leiderman, Jack Mendelson, Richard Trumbull, and Donald Wexler (Eds.), *Sensory Deprivation,* Cambridge, Mass., Harvard University Press, copyright © 1961 by the President and Fellows of Harvard College.
Houghton Mifflin
Hutchinson Publishing Group
International Universities Press
Johns Hopkins Press
Journal of Clinical Psychology
Journal of Counseling Psychology
Journal of Neurology, Neurosurgery and Psychiatry
Journal of Psychiatric Research
Journal of Psychosomatic Research
Lea and Febiger
McGill University Press
Oxford University Press
Pergamon Press
Pitman Medical Publishing Company
Psychological Reports
Routledge and Kegan Paul
Scientific American
Charles C. Thomas: Figs 3.3 and 3.4 in this volume are reproduced from Figs 3 and 4 in James Inglis, "Immediate Memory, Age and Brain Function," A. T. Welford and J. E. Birren (Eds.), *Behavior, Aging and the Nervous System,* courtesy of Charles C. Thomas, Publisher, Springfield, Illinois.
John Wiley and Sons
Williams and Wilkins

The author is also very grateful to those editors who have allowed him to republish some of his own work that originally appeared in the following journals.

British Journal of Psychiatry, part of Chapter 5
British Journal of Psychology, part of Chapter 3
Canadian Psychologist, part of Chapter 10

Grateful acknowledgement is also due to the following individuals, who kindly gave their permission for the use of their material.

S. G. Armitage, W. H. Bexton, J. P. Brady, N. A. Cameron, R. R. Carkhuff, B. D. Cohen, B. K. Doane, H. J. Eysenck, D. H. Ford, F. A. Gibbs, J. R. Graham, W. Heron, R. C. A. Hunter, D. D. Jackson, D. Kimura, L. Krasner, P. H. Leiderman, O. R. Lindsley, V. Meyer, B. Milner, P. E. Nathan, R. W. Payne, C. R. Rogers, G. Ryle, K. Salzinger, M. B. Shapiro, B. F. Skinner, P. Slater, C. B. Truax, P. Solomon, and H. B. Urban.

CONTENTS

Foreword vii

Preface ix

Acknowledgments xiii

1 INTRODUCTION—*Content and Method* 1

PART I Observation and the description of abnormality 15

2 THE STUDY OF *Thought Disorder* 17

3 THE STUDY OF *Memory Disorder* 41

PART II Experiment and the alteration of abnormality 69

4 THE EFFECTS OF *Neurosurgery* 71

5 THE EFFECTS OF *Sensory Deprivation* 101

6 THE EFFECTS OF *Reinforcement* 129

7 THE EFFECTS OF *Reinforcement on Verbal Behavior* 163

8 THE EFFECTS OF *Psychotherapy* 179

9 THE STUDY OF *The Single Case* 205

10 CONCLUSION—*Description and Change* 229

References 233

Index 251

1

INTRODUCTION
Content and Method

THIS BOOK IS dedicated to the view that abnormal human behavior is now, and will increasingly become, a proper subject for scientific inquiry. In order to support this contention about abnormal psychology, it is first of all necessary to describe the place of scientific inquiry in the study of *normal* behavior.

For students whose knowledge of science is founded upon instruction in its physical or biological branches, the notion of a "science of psychology" is not always easy to accept. Some of this reluctance to enroll psychology among the other sciences seems to be due, in part, to a misunderstanding of the nature of its actual content. Other difficulties derive from misconceptions about the nature of the methods appropriate to psychology.

So far as the content or subject matter of psychology is concerned, when we first address ourselves to the question of what it is exactly that psychology is *about*, we may be very dissatisfied with the answers initially offered. The questions dealt with by psychology may seem rather nebulous compared with the problems, say, of organic chemistry. The subject matter of many of the other sciences somehow seems to be much more "real." We can see, and sometimes even handle, many of the materials with which the chemist, for example, deals. The data with which he is involved are "out there," outside the investigator, who can, so to speak, take the substances dealt with by his science and push and pull them about. By contrast, the content of psychological inquiry, at least apparently and at first sight, may seem to be intangible and in some way, therefore, "unreal."

This is, of course, an error, but it is one that has deep historical roots. It springs from a misconception that is perpetuated by the definitions of the word "psychology" given by almost every English dictionary. These definitions commonly state that psychology is that branch of science that deals with the nature and functions of the human mind. If we accept this kind of definition, then of course the subject matter of psychology does indeed seem to be relatively nebulous and insubstantial, because the notion of "mind," as commonly understood, excludes the possibility of its external observation or manipulation by any set of concrete operations. What must be emphasized, however, is that this definition of psychology is one that describes the historical beginnings of the discipline rather than one that designates its contemporary interests. Most modern psychologists would prefer to define psychology as that branch of the biological-social sciences that studies *behavior.*

The difference between these conceptions of the nature of psychology, trivial though it may seem at first sight, is crucial to an appreciation of how abnormal behavior can be made the subject of scientific inquiry.

The traditional definition, which represents psychology as the study of the mind, assumes a form of dualism. This hypothetical split between mind and body has perhaps been best described by the philosopher Ryle in his book *The Concept of Mind* (1949). In terms of this kind of hypothesis, Ryle says

> There is thus a polar opposition between mind and matter, an opposition which is often brought out as follows. Material objects are situated in a common field, known as "space," and what happens to one body in one part of space is mechanically connected with what happens to other bodies in other parts of space. But mental happenings occur in insulated fields, known as "minds," and there is, apart maybe from telepathy, no direct causal connection between what happens in one mind and what happens in another. Only through the medium of the public physical world can the mind of one person make a difference to the mind of another. The mind is its own place, and in his inner life each of us lives the life of a ghostly Robinson Crusoe. People can see, hear and jolt one another's bodies, but they are irremediably blind and deaf to the workings of one another's minds and inoperative upon them. (1949, p. 13)

In the days in which a view of this sort was accepted, even by psychologists, there was—by definition—a complete division between psychology and the other sciences that was based on the nature of their subject matter. This acceptance of a fundamental dualism could be caricatured as the "vertical" view (see Figure 1.1) of the relation between psychology and the other sciences, in which, again by definition, there could be no common ground between material and so-called mental phenomena. An impenetrable barrier is created between mind and matter because each of these "aspects of existence" is conceived in such a way as to exclude any possibility of the interaction of one with the other. Although this duality is now accorded

Mental Events

Impenetrable Barrier of Mutually Exclusive Characteristics

Material Events

Fig. 1.1. Diagrammatic representation of the "vertical" view of the mind-matter dichotomy.

very little attention in general experimental psychology, it still, nevertheless, bedevils much of abnormal psychology. Such terms as "mental illness," "mental disease," and even "psychosomatic disorder" epitomize this dualism. It is therefore necessary to ask how the difficulties reflected in such terms may be resolved.

By the first decade of this century, experimental psychologists had come to see, and suffer from, the sterility of this kind of definition of their science. As will be emphasized later, some of the main essentials of scientific method are provided by the processes of measurement and manipulation. If, however, the content upon which these operations should be conducted has already been defined as insusceptible to these very procedures, the investigator finds himself in a very frustrating dead-end. It is probably just this irritating kind of impasse that has led, and indeed still leads, some skeptics to the belief that psychology can have little (if anything) in common with the other sciences. In other words, major and apparently insoluble difficulties arise if we accept this mental-physical division. It becomes impossible to see how one agent can act upon another if the nature of each is defined so as specifically to exclude the possibility of interaction.

This doctrine has been criticized by Ryle (1949) as involving the fallacy of the "ghost-in-the-machine." It is a doctrine whose explicit or implicit acceptance has led some psychologists in the abnormal field to concern themselves only with the vicissitudes of the ghost, and others to concern themselves only with breakdowns in the machinery of behavior. Most modern experimental psychologists, however, have been fairly successful in by-passing this dead-end simply by redefining their area of interest. Experimental psychology is now usually held to involve the study *not* of "mind" but of *behavior*. It will be argued here that abnormal behavior can also best be studied in these same direct terms.

Two questions might immediately be raised at this point. In the first place, it might be asked how this reformulation can, in itself, help to relate psychology more usefully to other topics of scientific inquiry. In the second place, it might be asked if there are any good grounds for the belief that abnormal behavior can even hopefully be regarded as a proper subject for scientific inquiry.

To tackle the second problem first, it seems that the best answer to this question is a pragmatic one: we have to try to see. Only with the benefit—and acuity—of hindsight can we guarantee that any phenomenon whatever may be dealt with in a "scientific" fashion; we cannot be sure that *any* problem can profitably be made the subject of scientific inquiry until after the attempt has been made upon it. It is the purpose of this book to show that a scientific approach to the problems of abnormal behavior does indeed show both present profit and future promise.

How, then, it might be asked, can a simple redefinition of the content of psychology help to relate the subject more closely to other topics of scientific inquiry? One possible answer to this question is that it places psychology in a "horizontal" relation to the other sciences, as compared to the "vertical" relation that has already been discussed.

This horizontal relation is determined by the view that the various scientific disciplines may be distinguished, one from the other, in terms of the "size" of the basic unit of their discourse. This unit, which each discipline is concerned to observe, measure, and manipulate, tends to differ in magnitude from one discipline to the next, and a rough representation of the relations between the sciences—expressed in this way—is shown in Figure 1.2.

Broad Fields: Physical Sciences Biological Sciences Social Sciences

Disciplines: Physics ⟷ Chemistry ⟷ Biochemistry ⟷ Physiology ⟷ Psychology ⟷ Sociology

Unit Size: Molecular ⟶ Molar

Fig. 1.2. Diagrammatic representation of the "horizontal" relation between scientific disciplines.

According to this view, psychology is bounded on its molecular side by physiology, and on the other, molar, side by sociology. Thus we move from the study of the behavior of parts of organisms, through the study of organismic behavior, to the study of the behavior of groups of organisms. The two-headed arrows between the disciplines serve to emphasize that the areas occupied by the adjacent sciences are not to be regarded as fixed, segregated, or sealed. These subdivisions, on the contrary, are bounded by permeable regions, and are, so to speak, always engaged in a kind of cultural osmosis.

It is also worth noting that the direction in which the interchange of fresh ideas and new knowledge may take place is not always from the molecular to the molar levels. Often enough, the movement is in the opposite direction, the molar sciences providing conceptions and findings that may be taken up and further explored by the more molecular sciences. Thus newly discovered physiological processes may later be formulated in the language of biochemistry, which in turn may eventually be described in terms of physical principles. At no stage in this sequence of events, however, would it be profitable to insist that discoveries at the molar end of the continuum must of necessity wait for developments at the molecular end. We must advance where we may and translate when we can.

Hebb (1958a) has provided an illuminating analogy relating to this kind of progression. He has pointed out that engineers were successfully building bridges, and in this sense developing scientific techniques relating to the larger components of bridges—such as beams and ties—long before there was any systematic knowledge of the molecular principles underlying stress and strain phenomena.

This way of conceiving the relations between the sciences also serves to protect us from the fallacious belief that the disciplines with the more molecular units somehow deal with "realer" entities and events than do the molar sciences. This fallacy is expressed in the belief that physiology, say, is a "more real" science than psychology. This is not, of course, to deny that physiology may presently be the more advanced and exact of the two disciplines; it is simply to reject the notion that all psychology is "really" a kind of physiology—a contention that would make no more and no less sense than would the claim that all physiology is "really" a kind of biochemistry. Each domain, in fact, is entitled to deal in its own terms with its own subject matter, although this may overlap with the content of adjacent, or even more distant, disciplines.

The boundaries between disciplines, then, are not hard and fast, or water-tight, limits; they involve, rather, zones or areas where the concerns of the sciences overlap. They are, in fact, more like areas of climatic influence than like national frontiers. For this reason it would be misleading to try to be too exact about the precise size of the basic, defining unit with which any particular scientist deals. Roughly speaking, the physiologist, on the one hand, is commonly interested in unlearned bodily events; the psychologist, on the other hand, is usually concerned with learned organismic activity. The difference between them might therefore be held to lie in the transition from the unconditioned to the conditioned reflex; the interests of many workers will, however, coincide when such a limiting size of unit is defined. There is, in other words, no need for any discipline or any scientist to "stake a claim" on a particular piece of "territory" since all areas will contain a variety of problems that may be tackled in many different ways.

It is also essential to note that our horizontal, two-dimensional figure gives a very much oversimplified picture of the relations between the disciplines. A more realistic description might be given only by a multidimensional, non-linear scheme, which would show, quite rightly, that the relations between psychology and the other disciplines are complex and complicated. Even the simple horizontal view, however, is certainly not as misleading as the vertical conception of the relation of psychology to the other sciences. The former contains within itself the fruitful possibility of interaction, the latter only the sterile certainty of separation.

So much, for the moment, for the definition of the subject matter of psychology. The qualifying term "abnormal" reflects the fact that one branch of the discipline concerns itself mainly with the study of deviant behavior. Some of the kinds of behavior with which it deals will be considered later in terms of actual examples.

As the quotation from Claude Bernard (1957) at the beginning of this text states, there seem to be two main aspects to scientific method, both of which may be discerned in the activities of psychologists as scientists. First, there are those studies that are principally concerned with the description and measurement of behavioral characteristics. Second, there are those studies that are more concerned with changing or manipulating behavior. It must be emphasized, of course, that these are not by any means hard and fast categories; in many studies the two procedures of measurement and manipulation must inform and complement one another. It would be impossible to engage profitably in any attempt to change behavior unless it were also feasible to define, describe, and, if possible, accurately measure those characteristics of behavior that we intend to change. Important differences can, however, be traced between those kinds of study in psychology that are mainly concerned with observing and measuring and those that are mainly concerned with producing changes in behavior.

One of the first attempts at the former kind of study began in the field of educational-developmental psychology. In these investigations the behavior observed by the psychologist is usually produced by his subjects in response to a fixed set of standard stimuli, which often take the form of items in some kind of test. The familiar intelligence test provides a well-known example. The notion that underlies this kind of testing is, of course, that individual differences exist in the behavioral as well as in the physical sphere of human organization. Thus, while we can talk about some people being heavier than others, we may also talk about some people being brighter than others. An intelligence test, however, is not a kind of psychic light-meter that can give an unequivocal estimate of the absolute amount of such "brightness"; it is, rather, a way of conveniently comparing a given individual with a particular reference group so that we can determine his status on the test in relation to the performance of others in the group.

The hope is that his group status, as defined by the test results, will be correlated with some other, usually more broadly defined, kinds of performance that it would be inconvenient or impossible to examine directly.

Test behavior, in fact, is useful only insofar as it enables us to predict the relative status that an individual will maintain in his performance in a criterion situation. We may try to establish the propriety of this kind of inference in a number of ways; for example, through the estimation of concurrent validity or through the estimation of predictive validity. These kinds of validation procedures may be represented as in Figure 1.3, which, however, shows only the special case of perfect correlation. This diagram illustrates the fact that the inferences that can be drawn from tests are valid to the degree to which their results are mirrored in criterion situations.

In the fields in which such testing was first developed, these situations were usually educational or vocational. Some intelligence tests, for example, are validated in terms of their ability to predict later educational achievement, and others relate more immediately and directly to current social adjustment or to vocational attainment. This kind of test may also, therefore, find some direct application in the study of abnormal behavior;

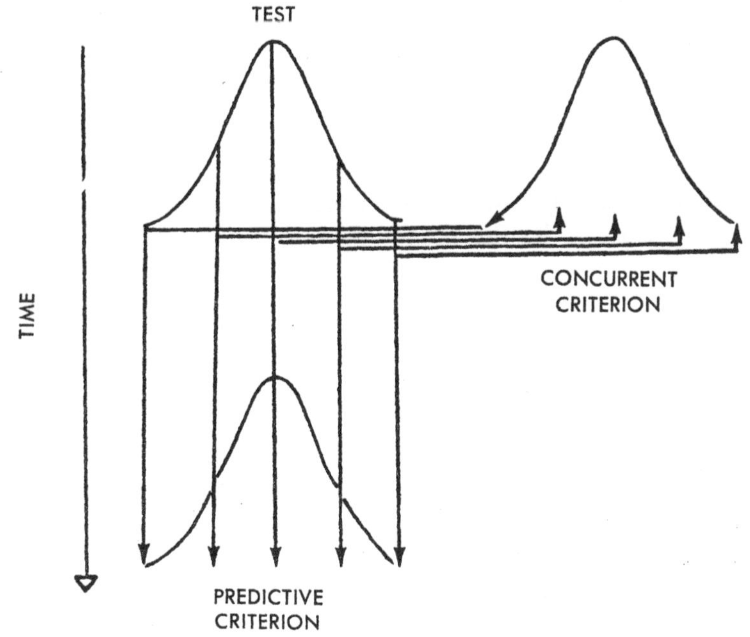

Fig. 1.3. Illustration of two types of validation procedure.

for example, in the determination of intellectual defect. A very low test score may be, within limits, predictive of poor future educational and poor social adjustment.

A more ambitious and perhaps an even more common use of psychological tests in the field of abnormal behavior, however, has been concerned with their so-called "diagnostic" function. This application of psychological techniques of measurement seems to have been based on the hope that they could provide a means for the detection of psychiatric disorders analogous to those physiological and biochemical techniques which may help in the identification of physical diseases. Just as the Wassermann test can discriminate between patients infected with syphilis and others free from this disease, it has been hoped that tests could be designed that would discriminate between psychiatric syndromes and normality, or between one disorder and another. Unfortunately, however, such attempts have so far met with remarkably little success. Some likely reasons for this failure have been ably dissected by Payne (1958a), who has pointed out that "diagnosis" in psychiatry is almost entirely a matter of labeling. Few investigators, however, are interested in the disease label for its own sake. It is useful only insofar as it carries with it certain fairly specific implications. These are commonly fourfold.

(1) *Descriptive implications* are those parts of the labeling system that give a shorthand description of the presenting abnormalities, or symptoms, or signs to which the psychiatrist or clinical psychologist accords importance.

(2) *Prognostic implications* refer to the natural history, the likely course, and the outcome of the disorder in question.

(3) *Aetiological implications* are the elements that give some indication of the likely cause of the disturbance.

(4) *Therapeutic implications* are the indications given by the label as to what may be done about the disorder.

When the psychologist investigates disorders of behavior and builds his study upon psychiatric labeling, it is usually one or another, or all, of these implications that he has in mind, and not the label per se. But the dangers of fallacious inference in this process are great, and they deserve more attention than they have usually been given. If we look at only the descriptive implications, we must first consider the possible relations that can exist between the label, these descriptive implications, and the results of any psychological test performance.

The criterion groups (which may be labeled in such terms as "organic," "functional," "demented," "depressed," or the like) are usually chosen because the individuals whom they comprise show certain supposedly characteristic clinical abnormalities of behavior. Any attempt to secure test-performance variables that will also be characteristic of such groups must be informed, however, by the knowledge that a psychiatric label can itself correlate both with the behavior abnormalities—toward which the attention of the psychiatrist or clinical psychologist has been directed—and with the selected test results, *without the abnormalities and test results being correlated with one another.*

This fact can be very simply illustrated, in a geometrical diagram, because the size of the correlation between variables is equivalent to the cosine of the angle between the vectors representing them. It can be seen from Figure 1.4 that unless the correlation of each of two variables with a third is greater than .70, these two need not correlate with each other. Because the reliability of psychiatric diagnosis itself probably seldom exceeds .70, it cannot itself correlate with any other variable to a greater degree than this. Hence psychological measures validated against diagnosis as such need never necessarily relate to any of the descriptive implications that the label itself may possess.

It is to be feared that the results of some of the apparently successful attempts that have been made to relate such labels, their descriptive implications, and test performance have been spurious, frequently having been due only to a lack of adequate control over those variables, other than

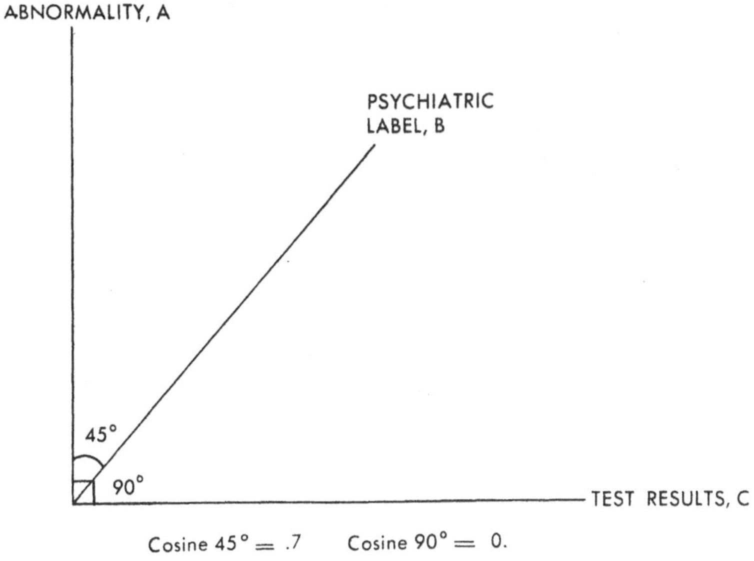

Fig. 1.4. Diagram to show that if A correlates with B, and B with C, this does NOT necessarily entail a correlation between A and C.

pathology, that may produce differences between groups. One of the less obvious faults in this kind of study may spring from criterion contamination of one kind or another.

Direct criterion contamination takes place when the performance under investigation is itself used as one of the criteria for sorting the groups—against whose behavior the relevance of these results is being evaluated. This kind of contamination can be seen, for example, in one study of Rorschach responses in old age. The investigators in this case set out to discover what might be the effect of chronological age on performance on this test, and they examined elderly individuals in decade groups from sixty to one hundred years of age. When their test protocols were grouped in this way, they did *not* show marked differences between the different age groups. These investigators then sorted the groups differently, *in terms of their test results*, and discovered that this method produced more significant differences. It would indeed have been surprising if they had then failed to find significant differences, because the data had been deliberately biased, and thus "contaminated."

More often, however, contamination enters such studies more subtly, in the form of what has been called "indirect contamination." This can take place in the following way. Suppose it is to be discovered if the presence of characteristic *X* (say, memory disorder) has any relation to the existence of condition *Y* (say, organic brain lesions). A study of this problem would first require that we secure at least two groups: a group having condition *Y* (group *Y*+) and a group not having condition *Y* (group *Y*−). It can be seen that, even if direct contamination were excluded, should the person originally sorting individuals into groups *Y*+ and *Y*− use his own judgment of the presence of *X* as one of his criteria for putting an individual into group *Y*+, and his judgment of the absence of *X* as one of his criteria for putting another individual into group *Y*−, and, further, if his judgment of the presence or absence of *X* were good, it follows that any objective measure of *X* subsequently given to these individuals would inevitably show that characteristic *X* was possessed more frequently by the members of group *Y*+ than by the members of group *Y*−. But it can also be seen that the initial question asked about the association of characteristic *X* with state *Y* remains unanswered, and *can* be answered rigorously only when groups *Y*+ and *Y*− are initially sorted *without* any reference to *X*.

Even if we take care of this problem, another possible difficulty must be borne in mind. Suppose that, for the purpose of defining groups *Y*+ and *Y*−, characteristic *X* was *in fact* one of the most important criteria. To deny the person who sorted the groups even his judgment of this variable might be to deprive him of a crucial item of necessary information and thereby dilute the adequacy of the criterion groups eventually chosen.

How, then, it may be asked, can we legitimately pursue the relation between aspects of disturbed behavior to which psychiatric labels appear to refer and objective estimates of performance? One answer, of course, is that the investigation of such relations may be pursued *directly*.

This suggestion simply serves to turn the attention of the psychologist back where it belongs, back to the abnormal behavior that is the core of his problem. After all, diagnostic labels in psychiatry are often only unvalidated (but not necessarily invalid) hypotheses about relations between different kinds of deviant behavior, their antecedents, and their consequences. These hypotheses are certainly not so well supported by evidence that their validity can be taken for granted. It has, indeed, been shown that there is not even a very satisfactory level of agreement between psychiatrists on what may be the best diagnostic hypothesis to use to subsume the behavior of a given patient (Matarazzo, 1965). This being the case, the psychologist may be able to do better by reexamining the basic data of behavior than by continuing to examine only what are, as yet, unproven diagnostic hypotheses. As the history of physical medicine shows, received ideas have often directed attention away from the observation of relevant variables. Immorality and poverty were held to be factors that explained the incidence of puerperal fever—even after Semmelweis, for example, had shown the relevance of the physician's own hygiene to this disease. It may be that if the psychologist were to make a direct attack upon the description and measurement of some of the implications of diagnosis, rather than to persist in an indirect attack via diagnosis, he could make a greater contribution to the study of abnormal behavior than has yet been made—for example, by the fruitless multiplication of so-called "diagnostic tests."

The next two chapters, Part I of this text, will deal with studies in which the main emphasis has been placed upon just such a direct description of particular behavior abnormalities. In these chapters, and all subsequent chapters, the material considered will derive mainly from the work of a single investigator and his associates. These studies have been chosen because they have, on the whole, been data-oriented rather than technique-oriented, and problem-oriented rather than theory-oriented. The aim of each has been to explore a mystery rather than to support a dogma.

The second, and perhaps the most important, aspect of the scientific method in psychology is concerned with the manipulation of behavior, the kind of manipulation that Claude Bernard conceived as the defining characteristic of the experimental method in science.

It would seem obvious that the psychologist whose concern is with abnormal behavior must also be interested in trying to create changes in behavior. Too often, however, he has been concerned merely with "diagnosis." It would also seem evident that the psychologist who wishes to change behavior should be familiar with a wide range of independent variables that may produce measurable variations in response. More often than not, however, he has concerned himself with only a single technique, psychotherapy, whose efficacy has been judged by rather coarse and unsatisfactory criteria, such as ratings of improvement.

It would appear that the range of choice of possibly relevant independent variables is wider than the common concentration on verbal manipulation, or psychotherapy, would make it seem. There are, in fact, studies in the field of abnormal behavior that show the power of a whole range of independent variables, from the more concrete to the less tangible, over specific, behavioral, dependent variables. In the present state of our knowledge it certainly cannot be definitely stated that any single independent variable is the only one whose effect it is permissible for the psychologist to examine. As long as the system we use can successfully and precisely describe the phenomena of behavior, can relate these phenomena together, and can achieve control over them so as to produce testable expectations about specific changes in behavior, we are, so to speak, "in business."

In Part II of this text, then, some studies will be considered whose main concern has been with the production and specification of such changes; but it is necessary to reiterate some general points about work in this category in the abnormal field.

In the first place, the main concern of such studies is with the specification of those variables that may influence, and make detectable changes in behavior. The *source* of the concepts and hypotheses used to describe and interrelate such variables may differ from investigator to investigator: some may prefer to deal with the terms and techniques of physiological psychology, others may prefer the language of social psychology. So long as the system used can describe, relate, and generate testable expectations, it does not matter whether the elements it employs are molecular or molar.

Second, the experimental-clinical psychologist who deals with abnormal behavior may usually try to alter such behavior for the better; this, however, need not necessarily be the case. It is possible that any alteration may be more illuminating than the failure to secure any change at all. The current popularity of so-called "behavior therapy" may, however, turn out to be unfortunate in this regard because it tends to emphasize "cure" rather than the precise control of measured changes.

Third, it is not suggested that techniques of measurement are irrelevant to work directed at the alteration of behavior. On the contrary, adequate measurement is essential for the proper assessment of change. Tests, however, do not in this context provide the sole basis of inference; they are used mainly, when they are used at all, to evaluate inference.

In conclusion, then, we have stated that scientific psychological activities, or methods, that deal with the problems of abnormal behavior seem to fall into two, often complementary categories.

In studies in which the main emphasis is upon observation and measurement, the investigator has often been concerned to define the status of an individual in relation to the performance of some group or groups. When this kind of procedure is based upon diagnosis, the results may not have the value that is often accorded to them by some investigators. The direct observation and description of behavior abnormalities may well prove to be much more profitable.

In studies in which the main emphasis is upon control, the approach is particularly concerned with the specification of variables that may influence and change behavior. Such change may be—but is not necessarily—devoted to the amelioration of disorder. Even when this method of working does not seem to be immediately related to the alleviation of distress, it still has much to offer in the understanding of the disorders of behavior.

PART I
Observation and the description of abnormality

2

THE STUDY OF *Thought Disorder*

THE HISTORY AND the present status of the diagnostic label "schizophrenia" epitomize the difficulties met in creating an adequate and acceptable psychiatric nosology.

Disturbances of the general kind that would today probably be called schizophrenic were once taken to be due to *dementia praecox*, a term whose earliest use, in 1860, is credited to the Belgian psychiatrist, Morel (Zilboorg and Henry, 1941). As the literal meaning of this expression suggests, it was used to characterize a *dementing abnormality*, or one that involved a general falling away from a previously higher level of intellectual and social competence, occurring *precociously*, or, in other words, appearing mainly in young people. This conception was then used by Kraepelin, in the 1890's, to systematize and relate a number of kindred disorders whose principal common characteristic seemed to him to be the early onset of progressive and lasting impairment.

In 1911, however, Bleuler repudiated the use of this term. He believed that it did not properly describe the disorders to which it was usually applied. He pointed out that it was used to refer to disturbances that did not always lead to a state of dementia and that occurred in some individuals later rather than earlier in life. He proposed, instead, the conception of schizophrenia, on the following grounds.

> I call dementia praecox "schizophrenia" because (as I hope to demonstrate) the "splitting" of the different psychic functions is one of its most important characteristics. For the sake of convenience I use the word in the singular although it is apparent that the group includes several diseases. (1950, p. 8)

Bleuler also defined certain disturbances that he regarded as fundamental to schizophrenia, including (1) a loosening of associations in thinking; (2) disturbances of emotion or affect, including flattening of affect and inappropriate affect; and (3) autism, in which there is muteness and a withdrawal from reality and from external contact, apparently into a kind of internal dream world.

Much of the current use of the diagnosis of schizophrenia appears to derive from Bleuler's work, which, however, has also left a certain legacy of imprecision. In the first place, in spite of Bleuler's warning that the term schizophrenia does not comprise a simple, homogeneous syndrome, much of the research in this topic tends to be carried out as if it did. This tendency has been very well described by Jackson (1960), who has stated that

> The concept of schizophrenia as a disease rather than as a group of disorders or as an end state delimited by the capacity of the brain and the shaping of culture, has influenced the majority of investigators. Thus, because most medical diseases have a single aetiological agent, this majority has approached schizophrenia in a reductionist frame of mind, looking for *a* rejecting mother or *a* specific toxin. The human being is relegated to the role of host—much as he is when his lungs harbor pneumonia—and all his supraorganic complexities are ignored. This reductionist, oversimplification tendency leads one to look for the "key to schizophrenia"; and premature claims that it has been found undoubtedly result in the abandonment of promising leads simply because they were not all-inclusive. (1960, p. 10)

In the second place, what Bleuler himself conceived to be the principal defining characteristics of the group of schizophrenias, such as "thought disorder" or "disorder of affect," have seldom been defined in a precise, measurable way. To some extent this failure has been due to the fact that many of the investigators of this kind of disorder have taken the "vertical" view of such processes as thinking and feeling. In terms of this view, as we have seen, such mental events are not susceptible to direct measurement or manipulation; they are regarded as taking place not in a public, behavioral world but in the secret, inaccessible realm of the mind. This, in turn, leads to the belief that their adequacy or inadequacy and their appropriateness or inappropriateness can be evaluated only by intuitive, empathic means. Unfortunately, the freedom accorded to subjective judgment may also provide a license for loose and vague speculation, hence to widespread disagreement about the characteristics being judged, and ultimately to unreliable diagnosis.

In one of his earliest papers, R. W. Payne—whose work in this area will be considered in the present chapter—remarked upon the double-edged nature of these difficulties. He pointed out (Payne, 1953), for example, that diagnostic questions—often posed in such terms as "Is this patient schizophrenic?"—create a kind of problem not necessarily best solved by categorization. Such statements as "Yes, he is" or "No, he is not schizophrenic" could have different implications, depending upon who made the inquiry and who provided the answer, because the term "schizophrenic" is not itself an expression of unequivocal meaning. It is, he argues, more profitable to describe and, if possible, to measure directly what may be regarded as the crucial abnormalities to which such a label is commonly supposed to refer.

Although Payne (1958b, 1960) has recognized the lack, in psychology, of any comprehensive theory of cognitive functioning, he has in practice adopted the view—which is of course also current among other investigators in the field (Bruner, Goodnow, and Austin, 1956)—that some aspects of the cognitive process are open to behavioral description and analysis. This means that some facets of thought and of thought disorder can be specified and examined in terms of objective, public performance rather than in terms of subjective, private opinion.

Payne has therefore chosen to examine a number of the crucial areas of disorder of cognition, and much of his work has been devoted to the exploration of overinclusive disorders of conceptualization. This chapter will deal with the background and results of his investigations into this aspect of cognitive abnormality.

The original conception of overinclusion was developed by Norman Cameron. On the basis of comparative performance on a sentence completion test—given to twenty-five schizophrenic patients (Cameron, 1938a), twenty-two patients with senile psychosis, twenty-nine normal children, and twenty normal adults (1938b)—he concluded that the schizophrenic group behaved unlike either the senile or the normal groups. This meant that their disorders could not be simply characterized as either "organic" or "regressed." The kind of peculiarities shown by the schizophrenic group were instead interpreted as reflecting a kind of "overinclusion," involving, in part, the interpenetration of irrelevant personal themes into impersonal problems.

Cameron further explored this disorder (1939a, 1939b) by means of the Vigotsky (1934) Sorting Test, given to five of the original twenty-five schizophrenics and to six of the twenty-two senile patients. This test requires the subject to sort a number of small blocks into sets of coherent, logical categories. The senile patients failed to grasp the nature of the problem, and behaved in a rigid, inflexible way, whereas the schizophrenics again showed interpenetration of thoughts and an inability to preserve conceptual boundaries. Ideas more or less associated with the appropriate categories became incorporated into them, thus making them far less precise.

Cameron (1963) has provided a graphic illustration of the nature of this disorder by quoting comments made by one overinclusive patient during performance on a block-sorting test.

"I've got to pick it out of the whole room. I can't confine myself to the game.... Three blues—now, how about that green blotter? Put it in there too. (Green) peas you eat, you can't eat them unless you write on it (the green blotter). [Cameron explains that the patient had just come from a meal at which he had eaten green peas.] Like that wrist watch (experimenter's). I don't see any three meals coming off that watch.... White and blue (blocks) is Duke's Mixture. This (pulling out cigarette paper) is white. All this wood and Japan (pulling out match box). There's a man out there with a white tie; that's got something to do with white suits.... To do this trick *you'd* have to be made of wood. You've got a white shirt on, and the white blocks, you have to have them cut out of *you*. You've got a white shirt on. This (white block) will hold you and never let you go. I've got a blue shirt on; but it can't be a blue shirt and still go together. And the room's got to be the same." Contemplating a group of similar white and yellow blocks, he asked, "Are there any Chinese working here? (No.) Only white ones, then you can't put *them* together." (1963, pp. 613–614)

It is easy to see how this kind of defect might lead to the disorganization of behavior. One consequence might be an overloading or flooding of perceptual and conceptual systems. It is possible to imagine that the clinically apparent effect of such excess might be a "blocking" of thought as too many incompatible impulses jostle toward some final common path of expression, or a pathological "pressure of ideas" as these impulses eventually manage to burst forth in some violent, disordered sequence.

Such disturbances are, of course, of the same kind as Bleuler (1950) himself explained on the basis of the primary symptom of loose association.

In the normal thinking process, the numerous actual and latent images combine to determine each association. In schizophrenia, however, single images or whole combinations may be rendered ineffective, in an apparently haphazard fashion. Instead, thinking operates with ideas and concepts which have no, or a completely insufficient, connection with the main idea and should therefore be excluded from the thought process. The result is that thinking becomes confused, bizarre, incorrect, abrupt. Sometimes, all the associative threads fail and the thought chain is totally interrupted; after such "blocking" ideas may emerge which have no recognizable connection with preceding ones. (1950, p. 22)

Payne began his series of extensive and systematic investigations of thought disorder with an experimental investigation of Kretschmer's (1951) theory of "dissociation" (Payne, 1954, 1955), which however produced negative results. He then turned to the examination of overinclusion.

So far as the nature of the overinclusive process is concerned, Payne has put forward two rather different hypotheses, both of which involve the notion of *inhibition.* This concept was explicitly used when he stated that

It is possible to reformulate Cameron's theory of overinclusion in a slightly more general way so that a number of predictions follow from it. Concept formation can be regarded as largely the result of discrimination learning. When a child first hears a word in a certain context, the word is associated with the entire situation (stimulus compound). As the word is heard again and again, only certain aspects of the stimulus compound are reinforced. Gradually the extraneous elements cease to evoke the response (the word), having become "inhibited" through lack of reinforcement. This "inhibition" is in some sense an active process, as it suppresses a response which was formerly evoked by the stimulus. "Overinclusive thinking" may be the result of a disorder of the process whereby "inhibition" is built up to "circumscribe" and "define" the learned response (the word or concept). (Payne, Matussek, and George, 1959, pp. 630–631)

The second, slightly different way of looking at the abnormality seems to be invoked to account for situations in which disorders of overinclusion are immediate rather than developmental in nature. Thus Payne has noted:

The same theory can be expressed in different terms. All purposeful behavior depends for its success on the fact that some stimuli are "attended to" and some other stimuli are ignored. It is a well-known fact that when concentrating on one task, normal people are quite unaware of most stimuli irrelevant to the task. It is as if some "filter mechanism" cuts out or inhibits the stimuli, both internal and external, which are irrelevant to the task in hand, to allow the most efficient "processing" of incoming information. Overinclusive thinking might only be one aspect of a general breakdown of this "filter mechanism." (Payne, Matussek, and George, 1959, p. 631).

The difference between these two formulations seems to involve the kind of distinction drawn by Eysenck (1957 p. 46f.) between the processes of temporal and spatial inhibition. Temporal inhibition is involved in what Hull (1943) called reactive (I_R) and conditioned (${}_SI_R$) inhibition. In the building up of any stimulus response connection over time, a certain amount of reactive inhibition, which may be conceived of as a kind of fatigue process, accrues. When the reinforcement of the *S-R* connection stops, this negative process supervenes, and, together with consequent conditioned inhibition, results in the unlearning or extinction of the habit in question. This process of temporal inhibition has also been held to account for discrimination learning, hence its disruption might account for failure in the formation of concepts.

Spatial inhibition, on the other hand, resembles Pavlov's (1927) conception of negative induction. This notion is held to account for the observation that, when two excitatory stimuli occur more or less simultaneously, one stimulus can inhibit the possibility of response to the other, depending on the amount of energy involved in both. Shapiro (1951a) has argued that a pathological *increase* in negative induction in cases of brain damage accounts, for example, for the fact that such patients may react to only very limited aspects of the perceptual field. Conversely, a pathological *decrease* in this process would result in reactions being made to abnormally wide aspects of the perceptual field, or, in other words, to perceptual overinclusion. These two conceptions of temporal and spatial inhibition have not always been clearly distinguished in Payne's studies, although they might in fact be expected to affect different kinds of performance.

With these conceptions of the nature of overinclusion in mind, consideration may now be given to the investigation described by Payne (1958c), and by Payne, Matussek, and George (1959), which involved the study of eighteen schizophrenic patients (twelve male and six female) and sixteen neurotic patients (seven male and nine female). These two groups were matched in age and intelligence as defined by the Mill Hill Vocabulary Test (Raven, 1958) and the Nufferno Level Test (Furneaux, 1956).

The notion that schizophrenics would prove to be, on average, more overinclusive than neurotic patients was tested by the administration of five tests, as follows.

(1) *Epstein Test of Overinclusion.* This is a test, developed by Seymour Epstein (1953), that consists of fifty stimulus words, each followed by six response words (including the word "none"). The subject is asked to underline all the response words essential to the concept indicated by the stimulus word. Five of the stimulus words and five of the response words are, in fact, neologisms; that is, they are words of no real meaning, of the kind schizophrenics have been said to invent (e.g., "manicron," "topitch," "sountonific").

In his original study, Epstein (1953) found that schizophrenics had a significantly higher score than a normal group on overinclusion because they underlined words that tended not to be used by normal people.

In addition to the score based on unusual words underlined, Payne, Matussek, and George (1959) also scored neologisms. This score was the total number of words (other than "none") underlined in response to the neologisms used as stimulus words, plus all the neologisms underlined as responses to real stimulus words. Because the presence of overinclusion should make this a more complex task, patients in the schizophrenic group were also expected to return longer time scores.

(2) *Payne Object Classification Test.* This is a sorting test, devised by Payne (1962), that involves twelve geometrical shapes that can be sorted in ten different ways, which are labeled "A responses," and in other less rational groupings that are labeled "non-A responses." It was, of course, expected that overinclusive subjects would produce more of the latter but not necessarily fewer of the former. Overinclusion should lead to indiscriminate conceptualization rather than simply to inadequate conceptualization.

(3) *Leiter–Partington Pathways Test.* This test, described by Leiter and Partington (1950), requires the subject, after a demonstration, to

draw straight lines between randomly placed, consecutively lettered or numbered circles drawn on a sheet of paper. Normal people, it has been found, rarely make errors on this test, although they do show differences in speed. It was predicted that overinclusion should make for slowness *and* errors since this disorder would reduce the usual constraints of any "set to respond consecutively" in relation to the required number or letter sequences.

(4) *Benjamin Proverbs Test.* A list of fourteen proverbs that had previously been employed by Benjamin (1946) was used. It was predicted that if the concepts of overinclusive patients are abnormally wide and vague, these individuals would have more difficulty in explaining the precise meaning of proverbs. This should make for a longer "reaction time," defined in terms of the interval between the presentation of the proverb and the beginning of a response. It was also expected that overinclusion should make for longer answers, taking more time to complete.

(5) *Goldstein–Scheerer Tests.* Both the Color-Form and the Object Sorting tests from Goldstein and Scheerer's (1941) battery were used. An overinclusion score was obtained from the Object Sorting test, as follows. From among the common objects (pipe, spoon, etc.) that make up this test, the subject was required to select one; and he was then asked to "hand over" to the examiner all the objects that might be grouped with it. It was anticipated that overinclusion should increase the number of objects grouped together and "handed over."

Both the Benjamin Proverbs and the Goldstein–Scheerer tests, incidentally, enabled the investigators in this study to test the notion that schizophrenics are more "concrete" in their thinking, a view of their disorder that has, for example, been held by Goldstein (1939). This characteristic has never been so specifically defined as has overinclusion, but Payne (1960) has suggested that it usually may be taken to mean an inability to form concepts or to produce abstract generalizations. As an additional index of concreteness, a test devised by Feldman and Drasgow (1951) was included that requires subjects to sort three of four objects in two different ways.

The results of the five tests used to detect overinclusion may be brought together as in Table 2.1. This table shows that nine of the thirteen measures used to test the expectation that the schizophrenic patients would show more overinclusion than the neurotic patients produced significant differences between the groups in the expected direction.

These results support the view that some schizophrenics are more "overinclusive" than neurotics, but, by definition, this means that they have a disposition to over-rather than undergeneralize. If this is so, they would not—at the same time—be expected to be "concrete." The defining characteristics of these two disorders seem to be quite antithetical.

When Payne, Matussek, and George (1959) examined the "concreteness"

TABLE 2.1
Means, Standard Deviations, and the Significance of the Differences between the Schizophrenic and Neurotic Groups on Measures of Overinclusion[a]

	SCHIZOPHRENICS (N = 18)		NEUROTICS (N = 16)			
MEASURES OF OVERINCLUSION	*Mean*	*S.D.*	*Mean*	*S.D.*	*t*	*p*
Epstein Test						
Overinclusion score	56.93	51.21	16.64	16.90	2.80	< .01
Neologism score	6.00	5.05	1.87	1.75	2.97	< .01
Seconds to complete task	1161.07	415.12	761.92	209.96	3.01	< .01
Payne Test						
"A" sortings	2.13	1.77	4.86	1.23	4.78	< .01
"Non-A" sortings	9.53	3.68	2.21	2.01	6.58	< .01
Leiter – Partington Test						
Errors on Path. 1 (Nos. only)	0.00	0.00	0.00	0.00	0.00	n.s.[b]
Time on Path. 1 (seconds)	75.20	29.64	69.29	30.86	0.53	n.s.
Errors on Path. 2 (Letter and Nos.)	7.00	9.75	1.86	3.76	1.90	.05[c]
Time on Path. 2 (seconds)	123.15	62.16	97.00	45.34	1.24	n.s.
Benjamin Test						
Reaction time (seconds)	26.73	19.40	10.93	6.50	2.90	.01
Average No. of words	20.93	7.30	18.07	7.56	1.04	n.s.
Total time (seconds)	68.73	28.60	38.29	14.13	3.60	< .01
Goldstein – Scheerer Test						
Average No. of Objects in "handing over"	11.33	8.44	5.86	1.66	2.46	< .02

[a] After Payne, Matussek, and George, 1959.
[b] n.s.: not significant.
[c] One-tail test of significance.

scores they obtained from the Benjamin, Goldstein–Scheerer and Feldman–Drasgow tests, they found the results shown in Table 2.2. It can be seen that these groups differ on only one measure in five. The investigators argued that even this significant difference on the Goldstein–Scheerer test is more likely to reflect overinclusion than it is to measure so-called concreteness.

TABLE 2.2
Means, Standard Deviations, and the Significance of the Differences between the Schizophrenic and Neurotic Groups on Measures of Concreteness[a]

	SCHIZOPHRENICS (N = 18)		NEUROTICS (N = 16)			
MEASURES OF CONCRETENESS	*Mean*	*S.D.*	*Mean*	*S.D.*	*t*	*p*
Benjamin Test						
No. of "abstract" answers	7.33	4.20	9.43	2.79	1.57	n.s.
Goldstein–Scheerer Tests (Concreteness Ratings)						
Color-Form test	2.57	1.79	1.64	1.15	1.64	n.s.
Object-Sorting test	4.21	0.80	2.79	1.25	3.60	< .01
Feldman–Drasgow Test (Total Abstraction Scores)						
Within the first minute	30.00	4.91	32.46	4.70	1.33	n.s.
With no time limit	31.14	4.67	33.15	4.18	1.18	n.s.

[a] After Payne, Matussek, and George, 1959.

The originators of this test defined "unusual" responses as concrete, but, if concreteness is defined in this way, it may obscure the fact that unusual responses can be due to uncontrolled overgeneralization rather than to an inability to generalize.

This study by Payne, Matussek, and George (1959), then, produced rather consistent results. Schizophrenics, as compared with neurotic patients, cannot be regarded as "concrete" in the sense of being inflexible or of being unable to generalize at all. They tended, rather, to produce—on a number of tests—responses that were based upon unusual, wide, and imprecise generalizations of a kind that may best be described as "over-inclusive."

These results, however, still left a number of problems unresolved. It still remained to be discovered, for example, if these tests of "overinclusion" could distinguish not only schizophrenics from neurotic patients but also the schizophrenic from other kinds of psychotic patients—as well as from normal subjects. Only too often in the history of this kind of investigation has some test been found that will distinguish, say, one group of patients from normal subjects, but which, on later study, completely fails to discriminate between these patients and other psychiatric categories.

In addition, before these tests could reasonably be labeled "tests of overinclusion," it was necessary to find out if they were correlated with one another. Tests that are supposed to measure the same behavioral characteristic must, of course, fulfil this criterion. In the realm of physical measurement, we would certainly expect a group of children, ranked in terms of the characteristic of "height," to maintain the same rank order if we first measured them with a foot-rule and then with a meter-stick. Similarly, two or more measures of overinclusion should rank patients in equivalent order, thus producing high intercorrelations between the tests.

These two problems, then, were among those attacked in a study reported by Payne and Hewlett (1960). The subjects in this study were twenty normal persons (nine males, eleven females), twenty neurotic patients (seven males, thirteen females), twenty depressive patients (seven males, thirteen females), and twenty schizophrenics (ten males, ten females). The neurotic group was further subdivided into twelve "dysthymics" (five males, seven females), suffering mainly from obsessional and anxiety disorder, and eight "hysterics" (two males, six females) who had such disorders as fugue state, psychopathic tendencies, and the like. These criterion groups were matched in terms of age, pre-illness intellectual level (as assessed by the Mill Hill Vocabulary Scale), socioeconomic status, and educational attainment.

The five tests used in the previous study (Payne, Matussek, and George, 1959), and described above, were also used in the Payne and Hewlett study. In some cases, however, other scores were also derived from them. Additional tests, also purporting to be measures of overinclusion, were added to the battery.

(1) *Epstein Test*. As above (p. 22).

(2) *Payne Object Classification Test*. In addition to the "A" and "non-A" sortings previously described (see p. 22), a number of time scores from this test were also taken as indices of overinclusion. Patients suffering from this disorder, it was argued, should think of more classifications and hence should take longer to do the test.

(3) *Leiter-Partington Test*. As above (p. 22).

(4) *Benjamin Test*. As above (p. 23).

(5) *Goldstein-Scheerer Test*. In addition to the use of the "handing over" score (see p. 23), a score was obtained that consisted of the number of "unusual" responses made by each subject.

(6) *Shaw Test*. This is a test of concept formation that is very similar in character to the Payne Object Classification Test, and it has been extensively used and described by Bromley (1955). The test material consists of four wooden blocks that vary in color, height, shape, size, and weight. There are fifteen ways of ordering the material according to "rational" abstract principles ("A" responses). There are also less abstract categories, or "B" responses, followed in turn by "C" and "D" responses, which are even less abstract and rational. Time scores were also obtained from this test, including total time and average response time.

(7) *Luchins Test.* In this test a series of problems is given that requires the subject to obtain a certain volume of water from a combination of jars of different sizes (Luchins, 1942; Rokeach, 1948). In this series, complicated solutions are initially correct (i.e., are "reinforced") in such a way that normal people are expected to have a "set" for using these complicated solutions, even at the end of the series when simple answers would suffice. Because one hypothesis about overinclusion suggests that it prevents the development of such a set, it would be expected that some schizophrenics would behave abnormally on this test. That is to say, they would tend to remain more flexible in the kind of solutions attempted in the later tests because they would be less influenced than the other subjects by the intervening items designed to create a "set." The principal measure obtained was the number of "easy" solutions used after the set had been established and a count of the number of schizophrenics *versus* the number of other groups who remained flexible—who made two or more "simple" responses after the set had been established.

The performance of the five criterion groups on most of these measures is shown in Table 2.3. It should be pointed out that direct comparison of the scores obtained in this study with the scores recorded in Tables 2.1 and 2.2 is not possible because in the Payne and Hewlett (1960) study all the scores were transformed so as to permit their later intercorrelation and subsequent factor analysis.

In this battery of tests there would appear to be fifteen measures of "overinclusion" ("0" measures) that would not seem to be much influenced by other factors, such as speed. Most of these produced mean differences in the expected direction, with the schizophrenics (in the main) making the most extreme scores. Five of these measures produced differences between the groups significant at beyond the one per cent level, while the remainder did not differentiate between the groups significantly. Payne and Hewlett felt justified in concluding, however, that

> On the whole, these findings support the hypothesis that schizophrenics are abnormally "overinclusive." On none of these measures did the other groups show marked differences. There was no evidence that the depressives or the two neurotic groups are abnormally overinclusive. This type of thought disorder is apparently confined to schizophrenic patients. (1960, p. 80)

Twelve measures related to overinclusion, but also presumably influenced by speed ("O + S" measures), were also obtained. The schizophrenic subjects were expected to perform at a slow speed on these measures because overinclusive thought disorder is presumed to increase the complexity of simple tasks. Depressed subjects were also expected to be slow because "retardation" is one of the cardinal symptoms of this disorder. Nine of the twelve items differentiated significantly between the criterion groups. The depressive and schizophrenic subjects tended to be about equally slow on

TABLE 2.3
Means, Standard Deviations, and the Significance of the Differences between the Criterion Groups on Measures of Overinclusion (Transformed Scores)[a]

MEASURES OF OVERINCLUSION	SCHIZOPHRENICS (N = 20)		DEPRESSIVES (N = 20)		DYSTHYMICS (N = 12)		HYSTERICS (N = 8)		NORMALS (N = 20)		F	p	TYPE OF TEST[b]
	Mean	*S.D.*[2]	*Mean*	*S.D.*[2]	*Mean*	*S.D.*[2]	*Mean*	*S.D.*[2]	*Mean*	*S.D.*[2]			
Epstein Test													
Overinclusion score	4.45	10.05	4.25	6.51	3.92	6.63	3.25	4.79	3.05	4.37	0.97	n.s.	O
Neologism score	0.80	1.64	0.20	0.17	0.33	0.42	0.13	0.12	0.25	0.30	2.08	n.s.	O
Seconds to complete task	5.06	5.82	4.06	4.31	2.45	2.87	1.83	3.37	2.55	1.42	6.65	< .01	O + S
Payne Test													
No. of "A" sortings	2.80	5.12	3.15	4.24	4.00	2.73	3.38	2.84	4.20	2.59	1.76	n.s.	O
No of "Non-A" sortings	2.05	3.63	0.60	2.46	0.33	0.24	0.13	0.24	0.20	0.27	6.85	< .01	O
Total time	5.95	3.00	4.45	3.84	4.42	1.72	3.50	2.57	3.95	1.84	5.15	< .01	O + S
Average response time	5.35	3.17	5.15	3.27	4.67	2.61	3.75	3.07	3.95	2.79	2.56	< .05	O + S
Av. time per "A" response	5.35	3.29	4.25	3.57	3.50	1.00	3.13	1.27	3.15	1.61	6.35	< .01	O + S
Leiter – Partington Test													
Errors on Path. 1	0.25	0.51	0.40	0.78	0.00	0.00	0.00	0.00	0.05	0.05	1.40	n.s.	O
Time on Path. 1	4.68	6.12	4.80	4.17	4.45	0.67	4.13	1.27	3.55	2.68	1.40	n.s.	O + S
Errors on Path. 2	1.40	5.13	0.95	3.10	0.33	0.79	0.38	0.55	0.35	1.40	1.46	n.s.	O
Time on Path. 2	4.84	4.66	5.05	3.10	4.33	2.06	4.25	1.36	3.85	2.56	1.42	n.s.	O + S
Benjamin Test													
Reaction time	3.95	2.50	3.95	4.16	3.50	3.73	2.13	1.84	2.55	3.00	3.08	< .05	O + S
Average No. of words	4.45	5.31	3.00	1.37	3.17	0.70	4.25	2.21	2.50	0.68	5.52	< .01	O
Total time	4.74	2.76	3.35	2.87	3.17	4.15	2.50	0.86	1.80	1.75	8.64	< .01	O + S

Goldstein – Scheerer													
Object sorting Test													
Av. No. of objects in "handing over"	3.75	4.62	2.05	1.00	2.33	1.51	2.88	2.12	2.10	1.78	4.25	< .01	O
No. of "unusual" sortings	1.25	1.46	0.40	0.57	1.00	0.91	1.25	1.07	0.45	0.26	3.64	< .01	O
Shaw Test													
No. of "A" sortings	2.55	5.10	2.30	4.01	3.00	2.73	3.38	1.98	3.80	4.80	1.68	n.s.	O
No. of "B" sortings	0.55	2.05	0.05	0.05	0.17	0.18	0.00	0.00	0.15	0.13	1.25	n.s.	O
No. of "C" sortings	1.25	0.51	0.70	0.33	0.58	0.27	0.75	0.21	0.60	0.47	3.87	< .01	O
No. of "D" sortings	1.50	4.37	1.00	2.53	0.33	0.79	0.63	1.13	0.40	0.67	1.93	n.s.	O
Total responses	3.55	4.79	2.40	1.62	2.75	1.48	2.88	0.48	3.20	1.01	1.75	n.s.	O
Total time	5.70	4.54	5.00	2.63	4.25	3.30	4.63	1.70	4.60	2.25	1.69	n.s.	O + S
Av. time per "A" response	5.35	2.03	5.00	2.32	3.75	0.57	3.75	1.07	3.60	2.78	5.83	< .01	O + S
Av. time per "A+B" response	4.25	3.57	3.75	2.62	2.42	0.81	2.50	0.86	2.35	2.13	5.84	< .01	O + S
Average response time	4.50	3.42	4.65	2.45	3.25	1.48	3.75	1.64	3.15	1.50	3.89	< .01	O + S
Luchins Test													
No. of simple solutions following "set"	1.89	3.99	1.00	3.47	1.33	2.97	1.00	3.71	1.10	3.99	0.63	n.s.	O

[a] After Payne and Hewlett, 1960.
[b] O = overinclusion only = 15.
O + S = overinclusion and speed = 12.

these measures. The neurotic patients tended, on average, to perform much like the normal subjects.

A further examination of the notion that schizophrenics may be "concrete" in their thinking was also made in this study. As in the Payne, Matussek, and George (1959) study, the test scores were again obtained from the Benjamin Proverbs Test and the Goldstein–Scheerer tests already described. The results are shown in Table 2.4.

Although on this occasion all three of these scores differentiated significantly between the groups, Payne and Hewlett (1960) have again argued that the scores made by the schizophrenic group were due not to the inflexibility supposed to characterize "concreteness" but to the tendency to produce unusual responses, itself a reflection of overinclusive thinking.

It seems a pity that in these studies the expectations about concreteness have been cast in such a way that any outcome whatever is held to count against the notion that schizophrenics suffer from this kind of thought disturbance. A more specific test of this view, evidently, must be carried out.

To elucidate further the relationships between all these tests, and hence the functions and dysfunctions underlying performance upon them, Payne and Hewlett (1960) conducted a rather complex correlational analysis of their data (see also Slater, 1960).

If it is claimed that different tests in fact measure a common characteristic, they should correlate with each other to a significant degree. Thus individuals who appear to be relatively high (or low) in terms of their score on one test should maintain a roughly similar status in relation to their group position on other tests of the same attribute. The dimension described by such covariation is held to define a factor. Furthermore, if the factor measured should indeed prove to be one of "overinclusion," scores derived from factorial measures should also differentiate between the criterion groups in the way predicted by the theory.

The actual correlation analyses carried out in this study involved four main stages, as follows.

(1) *A centroid factor analysis.* In this analysis all the groups were combined, product-moment correlations were calculated between all the measures, and the resulting matrix of intercorrelations was analyzed by means of Thurstone's (1947) method for extracting centroid factors. Three factors were extracted, since it was believed that the main sources of covariance in the battery of cognitive tests used would be "overinclusion," "slowness," and "general intelligence." The actual method employed to show that the first three factors extracted (jointly accounting for 39 per cent of the variance) could after appropriate rotation be accorded these labels, involved the procedure used in the fourth stage (described below).

TABLE 2.4
Means, Standard Deviations, and the Significance of the Differences between the Criterion Groups on Measures of Concreteness[a]

	SCHIZOPHRENICS ($N = 20$)		DEPRESSIVES ($N = 20$)		DYSTHYMICS ($N = 12$)		HYSTERICS ($N = 8$)		NORMALS ($N = 20$)			
MEASURES OF CONCRETENESS	*Mean*	*S.D.*^{2}	*Mean*	*S.D.*^{2}	*Mean*	*S.D.*^{2}	*Mean*	*S.D.*^{2}	*Mean*	*S.D.*^{2}	*F*	*p*
Benjamin Test												
No. of "abstract" answers (transformed scores)	2.25	2.51	2.75	1.78	3.17	1.24	4.00	0.86	3.40	1.73	3.36	< .05
Goldstein – Scheerer Tests (Concreteness Ratings)												
Color-Form test	2.35	2.33	1.05	1.42	0.83	1.42	0.88	2.12	0.50	1.05	4.62	< .01
Object Sorting test	2.80	1.12	2.10	1.25	2.25	0.75	2.00	0.29	1.75	0.62	3.31	< .05

[a]After Payne and Hewlett, 1960.

(2) *Discriminant function analysis of the factor scores.* A description of the nature of discriminant functions has been provided by Slater (1960), as follows.

In many psychological experiments the *m* tests are used as a battery in the hope that some linear combination, i.e., weighted summation of them, will provide a reliable estimate of a criterion. For instance, a battery of tests might be tried out in developing a procedure for selecting salesmen. It could be administered to a relatively unselected sample of persons who afterwards pass through a standard training or probationary period. A careful assessment of their success is made; it constitutes the criterion, *Y*. Correlations between the test and the criterion, say,

$$y^1 = (r_{ly}, r_{2y} \ldots\ldots r_{my})$$

could be computed and the multiple regression equation, $Rx = y$, solved to obtain the particular set of values of x, usually denoted $x = \beta$ and described as the partial regression coefficients, by which Y can be estimated with minimum error. A battery of tests of unlimited utility could be related to an unlimited number of criteria in this way, and for each criterion a somewhat different set of β's and a different amount of residual error would be found. The expected value of Y for an individual with a given set of standardized test scores, x_i, would be obtained as

$$y_i = \beta^1 x_i$$

and would provide the basis for a decision about his disposal.

In other investigations the *m* tests may be used experimentally for discriminating between members of two contrasted groups. We might, for instance, contrast people susceptible to an infection with people immune. An appropriate set of measurements could be obtained from a sample of persons all subsequently exposed to the infection, and the differences between the means of the two groups found as

$$d^1 = (d_1, d_2 \ldots\ldots d_m).$$

The analagous equation

$$R_x = d$$

is solved to obtain another particular set of values of x, say $x = \gamma$, generally known as discriminant functions. When substituted in the equation

$$d_i = \gamma^1 x_i$$

they will give a discriminant score for an individual from which he can be allocated to one group or the other with a minimum risk of error. (Slater, 1960, pp. 252–253)

This latter kind of analysis was applied by Payne and Hewlett (1960) to the factor scores on the first three centroid factors calculated for all the groups. By these means a series of questions could be answered.

First, it could be discovered if such an attempt to produce the greatest discrimination between the groups would show the two neurotic groups to be similar to or different from one another. They proved, in fact, not to be significantly different.

Second, the combined neurotic groups could be compared with the normal controls. The difference was again insignificant, and it was therefore concluded that the neurotic group did not differ significantly from the normal group on any of the three centroid factors.

Third, since the neurotic and normal groups did not differ, they were combined to form a "non-psychotic" group and were compared with the combined schizophrenic and depressive patients, who then formed a "psychotic" group. The difference between the "psychotics" and "non-psychotics" was highly significant. In other words, one or more of the first centroid factors could be taken to differentiate the psychotics from all the remaining subjects.

Fourth and finally, the two psychotic groups were contrasted by means of the same technique. The difference between the schizophrenic and the depressive groups was again highly significant. It could therefore be concluded that one or more of the first centroid factors measured some function that separated the two kinds of psychotic disorder.

The results thus far, however, did not tell whether the significant difference found existed in one dimension, as in Figure 2.1a, or in several, as in Figure 2.1b.

The situation represented in Figure 2.1a would suggest that the two psychotic groups had essentially the same "kind" of thought disorder, but that they could be distinguished in terms of the "amount" they possessed, as compared with each other and as compared with the normal and neurotic groups—who in turn did not differ from each other. The differences that are shown in Figure 2.1b, however, exist in two dimensions. It is also conceivable that other dimensions might be involved. The third main stage of the analysis was carried out in an attempt to answer this question.

(3) *Canonical analysis of the discriminants.* This analysis was intended to discover just how many uncorrelated dimensions were needed to account for the differences between the groups on the three factors. Payne and Hewlett (1960) have summarized the technique as follows.

> The procedure employed analyzes the "between groups" dispersion on the three factor scores. A principal component analysis is applied to this "between groups" dispersion to determine how many significant latent roots (with associated latent vectors) can be found in it. In other words, does all the variation between groups lie along the same line (are all the group means in a line in this three-dimensional space?) or are two orthogonal dimensions needed to describe the "between groups dispersion"? (Must two unrelated dimensions be used to describe the positions of the group means in this three-dimensional "factor score" space?) (1960, p. 88)

Analysis showed that there were indeed two significant independent dimensions of variance between the group means. It still remained to identify these discriminating factors in a psychologically meaningful way.

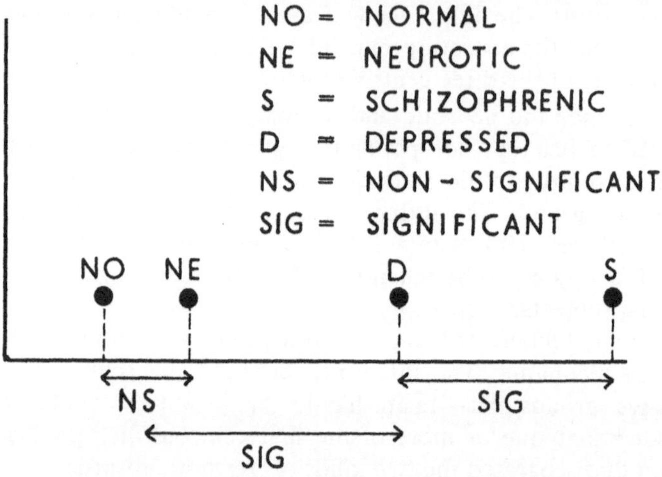

Fig. 2.1a. One possible arrangement of the significant and nonsignificant differences between the group scores, involving only one dimension of difference.

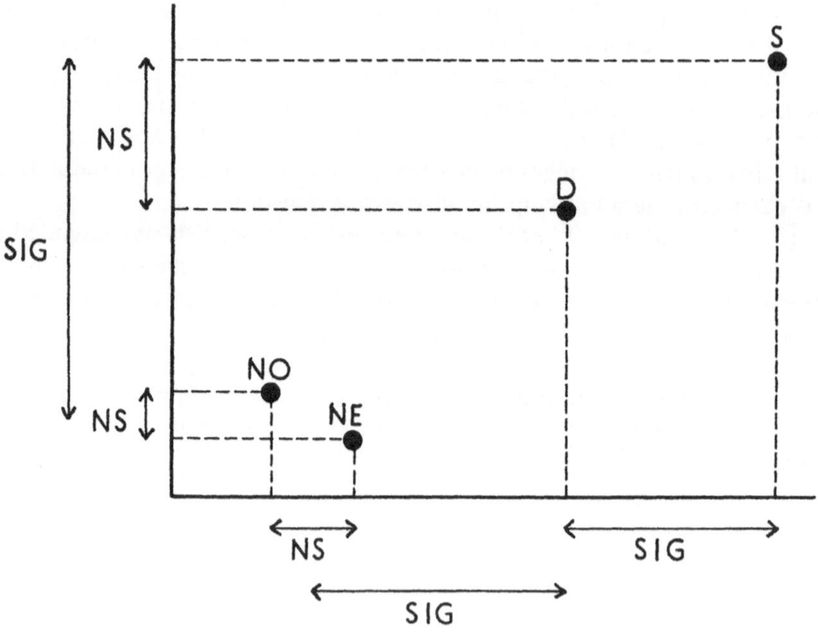

Fig. 2.1b. Another possible arrangement of the significant and nonsignificant differences between the group scores, involving two dimensions of difference.

(4) *Rotation and identification of the factors.* The process of factor analysis (Cattell, 1952) has been developed to enable us to detect how variables can be grouped together in terms of a framework of coordinate axes derived from vectors that represent the correlations between these variables. In other words, factor analysis is a statistical method that aims at the detection of the common abilities that may underlie performance on a number of behavioral measures. Thus if we were to give thirty tests to five hundred subjects and then intercorrelate each test with all the others, we might find that some tests would tend to intercorrelate to a high degree and others to a lesser extent. This would suggest that the former tests defined some common trait or factor. Even after the relevant statistical procedures have shown the extent to which groups of tests belong together, in terms of their position or loading on the coordinate axes mentioned above, the nature of the factor usually remains to be identified and labeled. One possible way of "identifying" factors is to rotate this framework so that the position of the principal axes accords the maximum loading to the "purest" measures of the dimensions likely to be of major importance. This method of rotation was not, however, the one used in the Payne and Hewlett (1960) study, and an alternative one was chosen, which they have described as follows.

> The alternative method is to obtain that factor which maximizes the discrimination between the schizophrenics and the other groups. According to the theory, this should be a factor of "overinclusion," and the theoretically "pure" measures of overinclusion should have the highest loadings on the factor if the hypothesis is correct. It is this method which was used.
>
> The findings described earlier suggested that both the schizophrenics and the depressives were retarded. The schizophrenics, however, were also overinclusive. It was thought that this would prove to be an unrelated abnormality. Therefore, it was predicted that the factor which maximized the discrimination between the depressive and schizophrenic groups, would be a factor of "overinclusion," and that the theoretically "pure" measures of overinclusion would have the highest loadings on it. (1960, p. 89)

It proved to be the case that the factor that differentiated best between the schizophrenic and depressive groups also differentiated the schizophrenics from the normal and neurotic groups. As expected, the tests that had, *a priori*, been selected as measures of overinclusion tended to have the highest loadings on this factor. The dimension on which the two psychotic groups were similar to each other, and together different from the normal and neurotic groups, proved principally to comprise tests of speed; the "non-psychotic" groups being faster.

In effect, the two-dimensional differences between the various groups on these two dimensions could be represented as in Figure 2.2. It is of interest to compare this outcome with the two examples of possible kinds of outcome portrayed in Figure 2.1. It can be seen that it differs from the first of these in

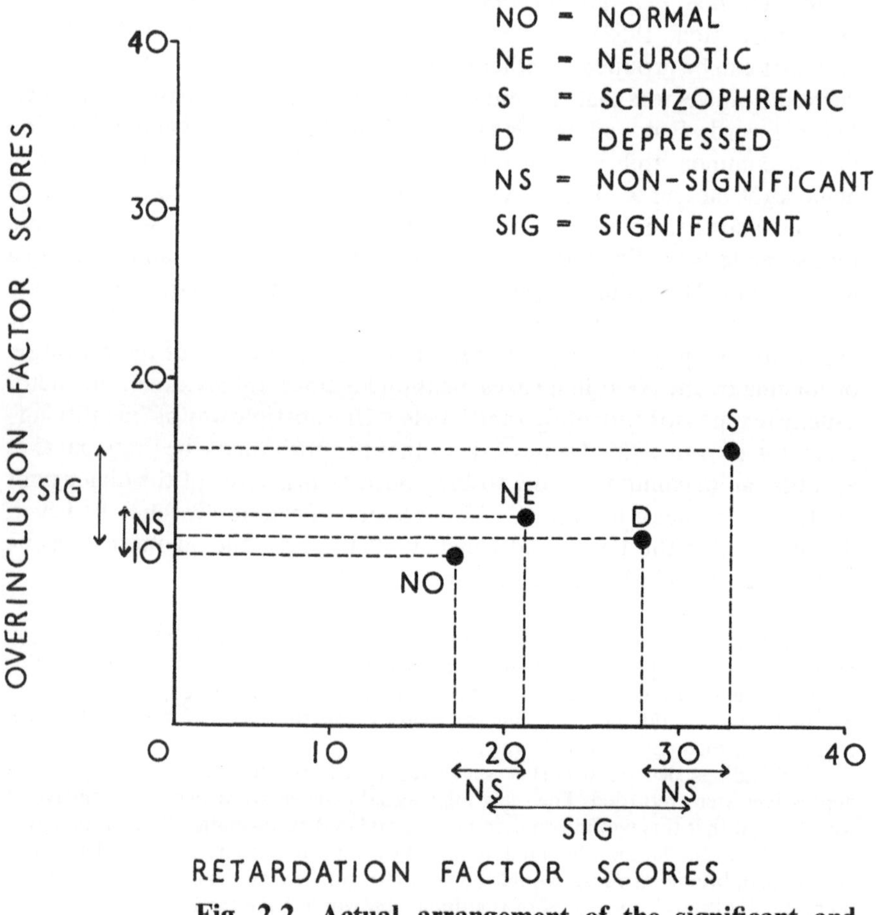

Fig. 2.2. Actual arrangement of the significant and nonsignificant differences between the group scores, involving two dimensions of difference: "overinclusion" and "retardation." (After Payne and Hewlett, 1960)

that more than one dimension of difference is necessary to define accurately the position of the groups. It is unlike the second of these in that the psychotic groups differ from one another on only one dimension, rather than on two.

Payne and Hewlett (1960) have suggested that the third factor extracted by their centroid analysis of intercorrelations was, in effect, one of general intelligence. This, of course, did not discriminate between the criterion groups tested, since they were initially matched in terms of this general ability.

These findings made it possible to come to the following conclusions. Overinclusive thinking may be a relatively specific disorder, independent both of general intelligence and of that kind of slowness or retardation that afflicts many psychotic patients. Overinclusive thought disorder is confined to patients diagnosed as "schizophrenic" and does not seem to occur in other psychotic or neurotic groups. Patients diagnosed as "schizophrenic," however, do not all suffer from this kind of disturbance of thought. Payne (1962) has found that only about half of those patients diagnosed as schizophrenic are abnormally overinclusive. Some so diagnosed may suffer from retardation rather than from overinclusion.

If, however, it is true that by such objective description we can with greater precision specify more homogeneous groups, we might also be able to discover how this disorder relates to other symptoms, to prognosis, and to the effects of treatment.

So far as the relation of overinclusion to other symptoms is concerned, Payne (1961) has suggested that this kind of thought disorder may be associated with, or may indeed even be in part the basis for, the development of paranoid delusions and ideas of reference. He has pointed out that both of these kinds of fixed, false belief may be regarded as founded upon unwarranted generalizations. Patients may develop these symptoms because they perceive relationships where none in fact exist. They may take as evidence for their deluded beliefs information that most people would ignore or regard as irrelevant.

A study of these possible relationships has, in fact, been carried out by Payne, Caird, and Laverty (1964). In this study they selected fifteen schizophrenics with clinical evidence of delusions or ideas of reference, and they compared their performance on a number of tests with the performance of fifteen schizophrenic patients without delusions and fifteen nonschizophrenic patients. These groups did not differ in mean age. Three kinds of tests were used in this study.

First, all the subjects were given the Mill Hill Vocabulary Scale (Raven, 1958) in order to obtain an estimate of general intellectual level. The groups were not expected to differ from one another on this test. Second, measures of overinclusion were derived from the Benjamin (1946) Proverbs Test (see page 23). Third, in order to cover the possibility that the groups would differ in speed of function, three simple psychomotor tests were given. These were taken from the Babcock and Levy (1940) test battery, and involve the speed of writing three separate phrases ("United States of America," "I hope to leave here very soon," and the patient's own name).

The results of this study are shown in Table 2.5. It can be seen from this table that there was, in fact, a significant relation between the presence or absence of delusions and overinclusive thinking as assessed by the Proverbs

TABLE 2.5

Means, Standard Deviations, and the Significance of the Differences between the Criterion Groups in General Intelligence, Overinclusion, and Retardation[a]

	DELUDED SCHIZOPHRENICS (N = 15)		NONDELUDED SCHIZOPHRENICS (N = 15)		CONTROLS (N = 15)			
TESTS	*Mean*	*S.D.*	*Mean*	*S.D.*	*Mean*	*S.D.*	*F*	*P*
Mill Hill Vocabulary IQ equivalents	93.87	5.72	89.53	4.61	90.80	5.39	2.67	n.s.
Benjamin Test								
Reaction time (secs.)	12.43	4.89	11.02	6.34	7.70	3.83	3.37	< .05
Average number of words	33.42	15.42	23.44	22.82	14.48	9.94	4.76	< .05
Total time (secs.)	30.89	11.04	24.91	18.34	14.43	6.59	3.28	< .05
Babcock–Levy Tests								
USA	17.20	4.15	18.60	9.46	15.20	5.13	0.77	n.s.
Sentence	18.13	4.25	20.40	8.70	16.27	5.85	1.18	n.s.
Name	11.60	3.41	11.60	4.99	9.27	3.30	1.07	n.s.

[a] After Payne, Caird, and Laverty, 1964.

test. No relationship was found between delusions and psychomotor speed test results. This shows that it is, in fact, possible to trace relations between one kind of disorder of function, as systematically defined by test behavior, and clinical symptoms.

Payne (1961) has also put forward the view that such test results may be related to the course and outcome, or prognosis, of disorder, and also to the effects of treatment. No completely satisfactory study of these contentions has as yet, however, been reported. Payne (1962) has found that chronic schizophrenics are unlike acute schizophrenics in that the former are no more overinclusive on his Object Classification test than are control subjects. He has argued that this could mean that only schizophrenics who are not overinclusive become chronic patients. This is, of course, a possible but not a necessary implication of his findings.

Thus, if we were to find high fever to be characteristic of recently acquired or acute tuberculosis but fail to find it in chronic tubercular patients, we would not necessarily regard fever as a sign of "good prognosis." It might simply be that the disease goes through different phases from the acute to the chronic stage. A longitudinal study is necessary in order adequately to evaluate the prognostic power of test results. The same kind of objection may be made to similar conclusions drawn by Payne, Friedlander, Laverty, and Haden (1963). In this study, too, it was found that chronic schizophrenics did not show any extreme degree of overinclusion on either the Object Classification test or on the Goldstein—Scheerer Object Sorting test. In this study, a high-potency phenothiazine (*Proketazine*) influenced neither test nor ward-rating results.

In another study of recovered schizophrenics—by Payne, Ancevich, and Laverty (1963)—formerly deluded patients did not differ from controls in the degree of overinclusion shown on the Object Classification test. This led the investigators to state that overinclusive thinking in schizophrenics is probably a symptom of their illness and not a permanent personality characteristic. They infer that this kind of test could therefore be used to assess recovery from such illness. Firm support for this view could, again, be convincingly provided only by longitudinal before-and-after investigations. In the Payne, Ancevich, and Laverty (1963) study, no pre-recovery test results were secured. It is reported by Payne (1966) that a long-term follow-up study of patients with and without thought disorder is currently being carried out.

Payne and his associates (e.g., Payne and Hewlett, 1960; Payne, 1966) have also extensively studied slowness of function, or retardation, as a factor that contributes to the clinical appearance of thought disorder. These studies, some of which have been mentioned in passing, will not be considered in detail here.

The studies of overinclusive thought disorder that have been reviewed in this chapter reflect both the advantages and the disadvantages of the scientific but nonexperimental investigation of one kind of abnormal behavior. Chief among the benefits is the objective specification of the disorder in question. It cannot be too often reiterated that, unless and until we can secure adequate measures of abnormal functioning, we cannot successfully engage in the manipulation of disorder. If we can barely detect change, we can hardly effect change.

Precise description, however, is not enough. Advance seems to be made most rapidly when the scientist begins to gain some degree of control over the phenomena he observes. Research into overinclusion seems, as yet, to have made only very few attempts (Cameron and Magaret, 1949, 1950) systematically to vary this condition. The challenge of experimental work in this field remains to be answered.

3

THE STUDY OF *Memory Disorder*

IT HAS LONG BEEN maintained that one of the hazards of aging is failure of memory. Zilboorg and Henry (1941) have stated that the first modern psychiatric writer to note carefully the mental changes accompanying old age was Esquirol (1838), who described one group of disorders as follows.

> Senile dementia is the consequence of advancing years. As man imperceptibly passes into old age he loses the free exercise of the faculties of understanding before arriving at the last degree of decrepitude. Senile dementia develops slowly. It begins with the weakening of memory, particularly of the memory for recent impressions.*

Like many other psychiatric expressions, however, the term "dementia" has come to carry a number of implications that may not in fact be perfectly related one to the other. As Payne and Inglis (1960) have pointed out, when the psychologist is asked to investigate a "problem of dementia" this inquiry commonly contains a number of different questions that it is usually more profitable to investigate separately. At least two kinds of question can often be distinguished. The first of these is aetiological in nature and refers to the detection of intracranial damage or pathology. The second is more descriptive and is mainly concerned with the estimation of a general or a specific falling away from some previously higher level of ability or attainment. The two are not necessarily best treated as identical problems.

In 1958 the present author (Inglis, 1958) undertook to examine the literature on objective studies of the descriptive aspects of dementia.

---

* Author's translation.

Attention was directed to the efforts that had been made to estimate the abnormal deterioration of general intelligence and to studies of failure of memory, both of which certainly seem to afflict some elderly persons to a pathological degree.

So far as "memory function" in elderly psychiatric patients was concerned, it became evident, upon review, that very few adequate, well-controlled studies had ever been carried out. This lack seemed to be due, in part, to an inadequate definition of the central problem. When the clinician speaks of "memory disorder" he more often than not is referring to a product rather than to a clearly defined process. As Hull (1917) pointed out many years ago, the notion of "memory," as this term is commonly used, is too imprecise in meaning. It directs attention toward a single aspect of output (usually the reproduction of learned material) when, in fact, it is known that the quality of this output may depend on the integrity of a whole series of events that are involved in the learning process. This sequence involves at least the three broad phases of registration, retention, and retrieval. The disturbance of any one of these stages might lead to impairment of the product called "memory." So long as it is borne in mind that, in any experiment, the distinction we make between these different phases is hardly ever absolute (McGeoch and Irion, 1952), it is likely that this kind of description will still prove to be more convenient, and less misleading than the single term "memory" for the analysis of the behavior concerned.

In view of the fact, then, that many old people are said to suffer from "failing memory," and because "memory disorder" may indeed bring some of them into the mental hospital, it appeared worthwhile to investigate the nature of the dysfunctions of the learning processes in the senium.

In the first study (Inglis, 1957), it seemed necessary to use tests that could, in principle, yield simple and objective measures of the main phases of learning. The technique chosen involved the use of very easy paired-associate learning tests (PALT). In the use of this technique it also seemed desirable to take into account a variety of difficulties that might arise; for example, in the learning of material transmitted through different sense modalities (e.g., auditory or visual) or in the different modes of reproduction (e.g., recognition or recall). Four subtests were therefore devised.

(1) *Auditory recall.* This subtest (Inglis, 1959a), as its name suggests, involved verbal presentation and the simple recall form of reproduction of three pairs of stimulus – response words. The patient was given instructions very similar to those for the Paired-Associate subtest of the Wechsler Memory Scale (Wechsler, 1945). He was told:

I am going to read you a list of words two at a time. Listen carefully because after I finish I shall expect you to remember the words that go together. For example, if the words were "East – West," "Gold – Silver," then when I said the word "East" I should expect you to answer "West," and when I said the word "Gold" you would, of course, answer (pause) ..."Silver." Do you understand? Now listen carefully to the list as I read it."

The examiner left an interval of about five seconds between the pair of words when reading the list; after it had been read once, another five-second interval was allowed. The stimulus words were then presented one by one in random order. Thus the examiner asked "What went with Flower?" The patient was allowed about ten seconds to reply, and if his answer was correct the examiner said "That's right." If the answer was wrong, he said "No" and supplied the correct association. If no response was given within about ten seconds, it was also supplied by the examiner.

The material was presented in this way until the patient got three consecutive correct responses for each stimulus word or until each stimulus word had been presented thirty times, whichever was sooner. The acquisition score on this test was the number of times the stimulus words were presented before the first of the three correct criterion trials. For example, the score of the performance represented in Figure 3.1 would be 11, each circled trial before the three consecutive plus signs for each item counting one point. It can be seen that, with this method of scoring, the minimum ("best") score for a test made up of only three stimulus response items is 3, and the maximum ("worst") score is 93.

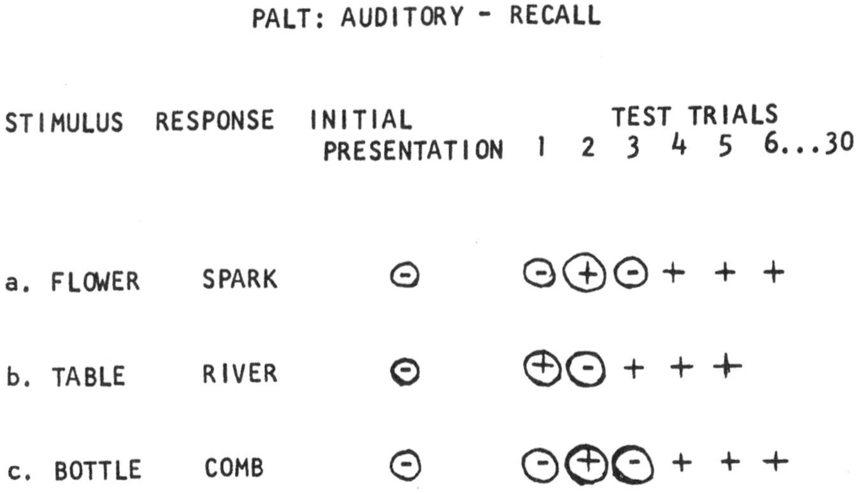

Fig. 3.1. Scoring for the Inglis Paired associate Learning Test (Auditory Recall)

(2) *Visual recall.* In this subtest the three stimulus-response pairs to be learned were simple line drawings on cards. The method of administration and scoring was the same as in the Auditory Recall subtest, except that for the first presentation the cards were shown in pairs from behind a screen. After this, the patient was required to give the name of the response object on being presented with the stimulus card.

(3) *Auditory recognition.* In this test the subjects had to learn to associate another three pairs of words verbally presented. Instead, however, of having to recall the correct response word as each stimulus word was read out, the patient had to choose (i.e., recognize) the correct word from the list of three responses as these were read aloud by the examiner. The criterion of learning and the method of scoring were the same as before.

(4) *Visual recognition.* The stimulus-response items in this subtest were again simple line drawings on cards. After the initial presentation the patient had to recognize the correct response card in the set of three that the examiner showed one at a time. The criterion and scoring of this subtest also remained the same.

In the first pilot study (Inglis, 1957), these tests were given to two groups of elderly psychiatric patients: one group composed of eight patients with, the other group of eight patients without, clinical evidence of memory disorder—as noted by the patients' doctor, nurses, and relatives. The groups were matched in terms of age, Verbal Scale Intelligence (Wechsler, 1944), socio-economic class, and sex (five women and three men in each group). Some of the results of this preliminary investigation are shown in Table 3.1. The significance of the differences between the group means for each variable was assessed by means of Sandler's A-test (Sandler, 1955).

Because age was one of the variables used to match the groups, they were not, of course, significantly different in this respect. They were also well matched on Wechsler Verbal Scale Weighted Scores. Although, in addition, the groups did not differ significantly in their Wechsler Performance Scale and Full Scale Weighted Score, the mean Performance Scale score of the memory-disordered patients was certainly very much lower than that of the nonmemory-disordered control group. The possible significance of this finding may best be considered after the results on the paired-associate learning tests have been mentioned.

It is, of course, possible in principle to obtain scores for both acquisition and retention from any paired-associate learning test. As McGeoch and Irion (1952) have pointed out, it is usual to regard the score obtained in learning up to the criterion as a measure of acquisition, and to take the estimated persistence of these changes (over time) as a measure of retention. These authors have also been careful to point out, however, that, with this kind of test, acquisition *and* retention are involved in every practice trial after the first.

TABLE 3.1
Means, Standard Deviations, and the Significance of the Differences between the Means of the Memory-disordered and Nonmemory-disordered Groups in Age, Intelligence, and Learning Test Scores[a]

VARIABLES	MEMORY DISORDERED		NONMEMORY DISORDERED			
	Mean	*S.D.*	*Mean*	*S.D.*	*A*	*p*
Age	*65.75*	*8.19*	*67.25*	*7.17*	*0.306*	*n.s.*
Wechsler Scales						
Verbal scale, WS	33.88	8.90	30.50	8.42	0.284	n.s.
Performance scale, WS	13.50	13.77	26.50	9.75	0.305	n.s.
Full scale, WS	47.38	18.84	57.00	15.25	0.538	n.s.
VS-PS, WS	20.38	13.53	4.00	9.97	0.223	.05–.02
PALT[b] Scores						
Auditory recall	59.25	23.60	14.13	4.55	0.150	< .001
Visual recall	50.25	29.20	6.63	3.70	0.169	< .01
Auditory recognition	51.88	29.61	7.50	3.42	0.174	< .01
Visual recognition	35.38	22.59	6.00	2.51	0.185	< .01

[a]After Inglis, 1957.
[b]Paired-Associate Learning Test.

In the first study, only measures of the acquisition phase of learning were taken. The significant differences between the groups on all the paired-associate learning tests indicated that the memory disordered group required very many more trials on every test to learn up to the level of the criterion. It may be concluded, therefore, that a defect in the first stage or phase of the learning sequence (that is, in acquisition or registration) is an important factor in the kind of "memory disorder" shown by some elderly psychiatric patients. This disability was found in learning in both of the sense modalities tested, and for both the recall and recognition modes of reproduction.

It is possible that the unexpected, though not unprecedented (e.g., Cleveland and Dysinger, 1944), Verbal – Performance Scale discrepancy in the memory-disordered subjects might also have been due, in part at least, to the registration defect found in these patients. One might, for example, speculate—as others, including Cattell (1943) have done—that in responding to Verbal Scale items the subject is in fact running off sequences of old learning whose initiation does not require him to hold in mind any very complex instructions. In the case of Performance Scale, on the other hand, a fairly long set of instruction precedes each subtest; in addition, more novel response patterns, which may themselves involve learning, are required for the successful solution of the items.

The main finding that emerged from this study was that elderly psychiatric patients suffering from memory disorder have a marked disability in the acquisition phase of the learning of paired associates. This finding might help to explain the often-cited clinical impression that these old people have a "poor memory for recent events," even if they show a fair recollection of events more remote in the past. The test results suggested that there is a faulty registration, or recording of recent events, of which there can therefore be no adequate "playback." More remote events, it may be presumed, were stored before the recording breakdown took place, and they are therefore available for reproduction even when current events can no longer be "held in mind."

Since these initial observations had been made on two very small groups of patients, it seemed necessary to try to repeat, and if possible extend, these findings.

Such an attempt was made in the next study. Inglis (1959b) set out to see if these results could be confirmed in an experiment that used different groups of similar patients. It was further intended to see if an impairment of retention could also be demonstrated over and above the acquisition defect. It was also desired to discover if the acquisition defect would also be elicited on a learning task that was mainly manipulative in nature, as well as on the paired-associate type of tasks.

In order to examine the dependability of the paired-associate learning test findings, the Auditory Recall test alone was given, since there seemed to be a fair degree of equivalence between the four learning subtests previously used. In addition to the acquisition trials, however, this test was given a second time in order to get two scores of retention. These two scores took the form, first, of a relearning score (or the number of re-presentations of each pair necessary—after a filled interval of about half an hour—for the subjects to relearn to the criterion of three consecutive correct repetitions of each pair) and second, a retained members score (or the number of response items correctly recalled on the presentation of the stimulus on the first relearning trial).

The Rey – Davis Test (Rey, 1934) was included as a learning task mainly manipulative in character. Its clinical use, mainly with so-called "organic" patients, had previously been described by Zangwill (1943; 1946). It consists of four 6-inch-square boards, each having three rows of three small pegs. Only one peg on each board is fixed, and it is in a different position on each board. The boards are presented in a regular series. In this experiment the subject was told the position of the fixed peg on the first board and he had to discover the fixed peg on the other boards by trial and error. This test was given either until the patient selected the right peg on each board on two successive series of presentations or until each board had been presented twenty times, whichever came first. This number of presentations was used as an "acquisition" score. A "successes" score was also obtained that consisted of the number of pegs correctly selected on at least two successive occasions.

A number of tests, including these items, were given to ten elderly patients with, and ten without, memory disorder. These two groups were again matched for age and verbal intelligence (Wechsler, 1955).

The means and standard deviations and the significance of the difference between the means of the two groups are shown in Table 3.2. The significance of the differences between the means was again analyzed by Sandler's (1955) A-test.

TABLE 3.2
Means, Standard Deviations, and the Significance of the Differences between the Means of the Memory-disordered and Nonmemory-disordered Groups in Age, Intelligence, and Learning Test Scores[a]

VARIABLES	MEMORY DISORDERED		NONMEMORY DISORDERED			
	Mean	*S.D.*	*Mean*	*S.D.*	*A*	*p*
Age	*70.80*	*5.67*	*71.50*	*5.36*	*2.837*	*n.s.*
Wechsler Scales						
Verbal scale IQ	89.80	8.79	92.50	6.38	1.099	n.s.
Performance scale IQ	78.00	12.40	97.00	8.72	0.136	< .001
Full scale IQ	83.80	10.41	94.30	7.17	0.184	.01
VS-PS IQ	11.80	8.15	–4.50	6.47	0.128	< .001
PALT Scores						
Acquisition	54.80	28.07	10.70	5.16	0.135	< .001
Relearning	56.80	34.93	3.90	3.48	0.136	< .001
Retained members	0.20	0.63	1.30	1.16	0.174	.01–.001
Rey–Davis Test						
Trials	20.00	0.00	7.10	5.40	0.116	< .001
Successes	0.90	0.74	3.80	0.63	0.016	< .001

[a] After Inglis, 1959b.

Previous findings were confirmed by the significance of the Verbal-Performance difference and by the significant difference on the paired-associate learning test acquisition score. The criterion groups on this occasion were also significantly different in their mean Performance Scale scores on the Wechsler Adult Intelligence Scale (WAIS), with the memory disordered group doing much worse than the control group.

It can also be seen from Table 3.2 that the experimental group was significantly inferior to the control group on both the relearning and retained members scores derived from the repetition of the paired-associate learning test. It may therefore be inferred that patients with clinical signs of memory disorder suffer not only from a defect in the registration stage of the learning process but also from a defect of retention once the material to be learned has been acquired. Since only three out of ten of the memory-disordered group failed to reach the criterion of learning in the acquisition trials, this retention defect could not be referred simply to a complete inability to learn.

Results on the Rey – Davis test showed the memory-disordered patients to be significantly inferior both in terms of their acquisition and their successes score. This confirmed that the kind of defect elicited in the verbal paired-associate learning task could also be shown on a different, manipulative test of learning ability.

The usefulness of the simple paired-associate learning test has been further explored by other workers in the geriatric field. Caird, Sanderson, and Inglis (1962), for example, carried out a cross-validation study on sixty elderly patients, thirty with and thirty without memory disorder, and produced results that confirmed the original findings.

Riddell (1962a) carried out a study in which the equivalence of two forms of the auditory verbal recall form of Inglis's (1959a) paired-associate learning test was examined. When the two tests were given to twenty six geriatric patients of mixed diagnosis, the correlation between the two forms of the test was 0.507.

Studies of the "diagnostic" use of this simple test have also been carried out. Riddell (1962b) found tetrachoric correlations of 0.60 and 0.64 between two forms of the test and the "organic" and "functional" diagnoses of twenty six elderly psychiatric patients. Isaacs (1962) gave the test to three groups, comprising fifty normal old persons, fifty elderly patients recently admitted to a geriatric assessment ward, and fifty patients in geriatric long-stay wards. He found that normal old persons performed better than the hospital patients. The patients with clinical evidence of diffuse brain damage did worse than those with focal brain damage; incontinent patients had worse scores than continent patients; and patients who subsequently improved in response to rehabilitation had better scores than those who did not improve.

Isaacs and Walkley (1964) have also reported data, obtained from over five hundred geriatric patients, on slightly simpler paired-associate tests developed by Inglis (1959b). They concluded that the worst performances were found in female patients of age seventy five and over, who had been in hospital for more than six months and in whom a clinical diagnosis of dementia had been made. Similarly, Newcombe and Steinberg (1964) found that this test differentiated significantly between two groups of elderly patients, one with organic cerebral disease and the other with functional psychiatric illness. The rank-order correlation between two forms of the test, given at an interval of three months, was 0.615. The power of the test to distinguish between brain-damaged and depressed elderly psychiatric patients has been further confirmed by Kendrick, Parboosingh, and Post (1965).

The same test was also used in a prognostic study by Sanderson and Inglis (1961). The number of deaths occurring in a group of fifteen elderly psychiatric patients suffering from memory disorder was compared with mortality in a matched group of fifteen nonmemory-disordered patients over a period of sixteen months. There was, in fact, shown to be a closer association between the test scores and mortality than between mortality and initial diagnosis. This finding confirmed an earlier observation made by Inglis (1959c) on the relation between mortality and test scores on the Walton and Black (1957) Modified Word Learning Test.

This kind of paired-associate measure, then, has been shown to produce results of some practical value. It seemed necessary, however, to try to describe more precisely those aspects of the sequence of the learning process that might be the most vulnerable to senility, and possibly even to changes taking place in the normal senium.

In one analysis of the essential aspects of learning and memory function, Welford (1958) has described several critical phases. These comprise perception, short-term storage, the evolution of a durable trace, the endurance of such a trace, recognition, recall or retrieval, and, finally, the use of recalled material. It is evident that if these are several stages of a sequential process, with "memory" as their product, breakdown at any one point in the system could disrupt the whole later succession of the learning chain, and the defective output might then come to be labeled "memory disorder." Welford (1956) has further argued that short-term storage may be the phase most susceptible to breakdown with age and disease.

As a means to permit the closer analysis of one part of the learning sequence, the method of dichotic stimulation developed by Broadbent (1958) seemed to hold much promise. In one experiment Broadbent (1957) showed that when digit-span stimuli were relayed at a speed of two per second through headphones, half of the span to one ear and, simultaneously, the other half of the span to the other ear, the subjects tested under these conditions could reproduce the digits sequentially. Furthermore, in such reproduction, elements from one half of the span were rarely alternated with elements from the other half. The first half-set recalled however commonly contained fewer errors than the second half, producing a kind of serial-order effect.

Broadbent suggested that two kinds of mechanism may underlie such performance on this modified digit-span test. First, there is a "*p* system" that can pass information only successively. Second, there is an "*s* system," or short-term store, that can hold excess information arriving (for example,) when the *p* mechanism is already fully occupied in transmitting information from another channel. In each case the half-set digits recalled first passes directly through the *p* system while the half-set recalled second spends some time in storage.

The method commonly used to record and reproduce such stimuli may be briefly described. Spoken digits are recorded on two channels of a magnetic tape in such a way that different numbers may then be delivered simultaneously to both ears by means of stereophonic playback through earphones. The length of the half-set of digits presented to each ear can obviously vary, as can the period of time between the delivery of successive digits. The technique of dichotic stimulation can be represented diagrammatically, as in Figure 3.2.

In this figure C_1 and C_2 represent two of the separate channels available on stereophonic tape. The digits in the arrowheads represent the simultaneous recording, and hence simultaneous playback, of *different* digits to both ears. The letters t_1, t_2, t_3, and t_4 show the time sequence. In the experimental situation illustrated, the subject first heard the spoken digit *5* read into his right ear at the same time, t_1, as he heard *2* in his left, also at time t_1. Then, after a specifiable interval, at t_2 he heard *6* on the right and *9* on the left, and so on for *3* and *4* at t_3, and *8* and *1* at t_4. It is, of course, possible to vary the length of the strings of simultaneous digits delivered before recall and also to vary the time between the digits in the sequence. As Broadbent found, most subjects will try to recall all the digits presented to one side before trying to recall the other. That is to say, recall by lateral sequence is more common than attempts at alternation. In the case illustrated, the subject would be most likely to recall the digits in the orders 5–6–3–8—2–9–4–1 or 2–9–4–1—5–6–3–8. Furthermore, he would be likely to make more mistakes in the reproduction of the four digits recalled as the second half-span of the total of eight than he would in recalling the first four. This kind of observation led Broadbent to put forward the notion that the digits recalled second in sequence must have been "held" in some short-term store, and have there been subject to some form of trace-decay, during the time it took for recall of the first "half-spans."

The present author (Inglis, 1960a) has suggested that the defect of acquisition found in elderly psychiatric patients suffering from memory disorder might be based upon a breakdown of the kind of short-term storage mechanism postulated by Broadbent. Such patients should therefore show an impairment of recall in those half-sets of digits reproduced second in the dichotic stimulation situation, relative to the performance of a matched group of patients without memory disorder. This expectation was tested by

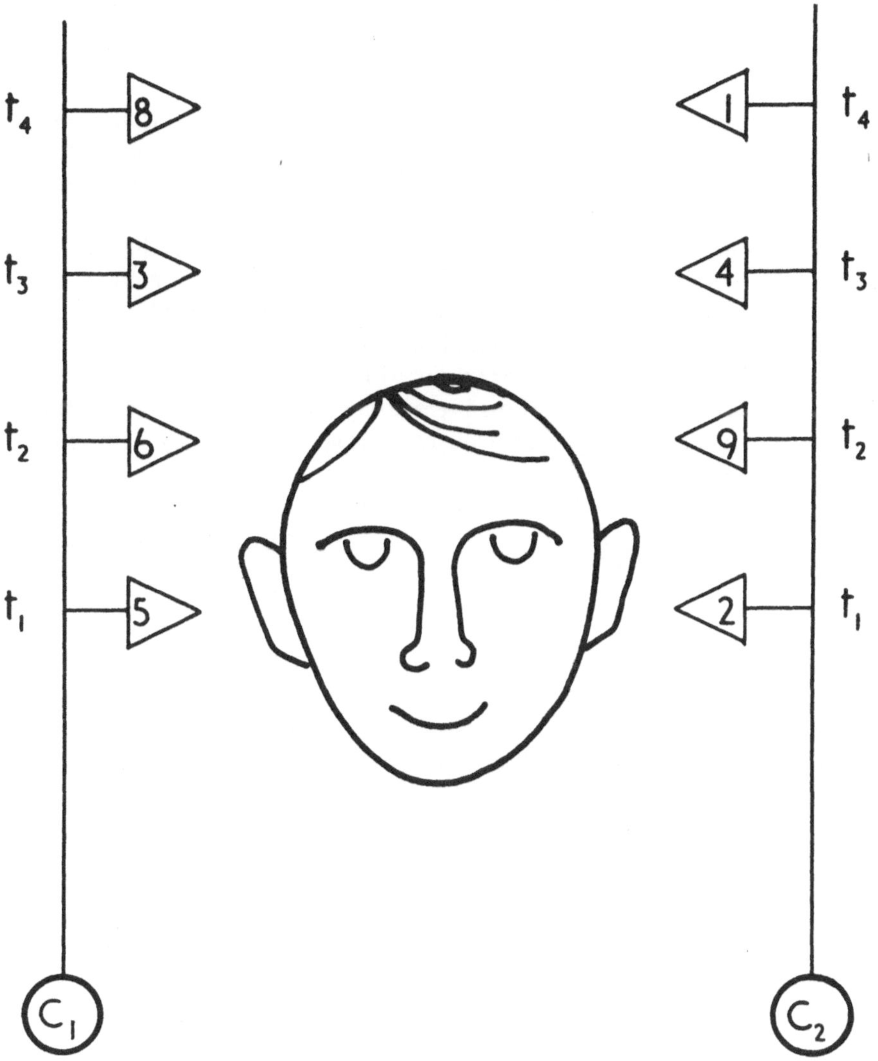

Fig. 3.2. Diagrammatic representation of the technique of dichotic stimulation. (From Mackay and Inglis, 1963)

Inglis and Sanderson (1961) for the case in which the two channels for simultaneous stimulation were the two ears.

In this study, the experimental group comprised fifteen elderly patients clinically estimated to be suffering from undoubted memory disorder. This estimate was made on the basis of a complaint about the patient's memory made by the doctor in charge of the case, by the ward staff, or by both. A control group of fifteen patients without memory disorder was also tested. All the patients (both experimental and control) were cooperative during testing, and none of them suffered any sensory or motor deficit so severe as to interfere with test performance. The experimental group was mainly composed of cases diagnosed as senile dementia, usually having been admitted to hospital for difficulties associated with failing memory. The control group was principally composed of functionally disordered patients diagnosed as cases of depression and paranoid schizophrenia.

The WAIS (Wechsler, 1955) was used for matching the two groups on verbal ability (Verbal IQ) and on average digit span forward. This test was also used to check on the previously observed discrepancy between the Verbal and Performance scales in memory-disordered groups.

The digit stimuli were as shown in Table 3.3, and were delivered at the rate of about one per second. Each subject was first told "You are going to hear a number. Tell me what you hear," The spoken digit *8* was then played on channel 1. If the subject responded correctly, the same procedure was repeated for the digit *5* on channel 2. If the subject failed to respond, or gave the wrong number, the volume was increased until the correct response was made.

Second, the subject was told "Now you are going to hear two numbers together, one in each ear. Tell me what you hear." The two channels then played the spoken digits *8* and *5* simultaneously. If the subject responded with the correct digits (8–5 or 5–8), the experimenter went on to the test series. If not, this item of the practice series was repeated once more.

The foregoing constituted a practice series that served to ensure that any difference found between the groups could not merely be due, say, to sensory differences. It also got the subjects used to the situation.

Third, each subject was told "Now you are going to hear n numbers, $\frac{n}{2}$ in each ear (where n was 2 or 4 or 6 or 8). Tell me what numbers you hear." These instructions were repeated at the beginning of each series of a new length. Between each of the items within a series the experimenter said "Now what numbers do you hear?"

This series of tests was scored as follows. The first correct digit repeated in each series determined which channel was taken as the first for that item by that subject. The score obtained was the average number of correct responses for each half-digit set—with the digit position in the series taken into account.

TABLE 3.3
Digits Used for Dichotic Stimulation Test[a]

	CHANNEL 1	CHANNEL 2
Practice series	8	blank
" "	blank	5
" "	8	5
Test series	6	2
" "	9	7
" "	7	4
" "	5	8
" "	32	94
" "	18	65
" "	37	49
" "	57	86
" "	658	417
" "	432	869
" "	571	243
" "	769	354
" "	6235	1948
" "	4863	2597
" "	2719	8465
" "	9327	6581

[a] From Inglis and Sanderson, 1961.

The means and standard deviations and the significance of the difference between the means of the memory-disordered (MD) and nonmemory-disordered (NMD) groups are shown in Table 3.4. The significance of the differences was estimated by the uncorrelated t test (McNemar, 1949). Previous findings were confirmed by the significance of the Verbal–Performance difference on the WAIS.

The differences between the groups in the dichotic stimulation experiment were significant in the case of the second half-spans recalled for all the lengths of digit series used. This confirmed that the clinical picture of memory disorder in elderly psychiatric patients may be based, at least in part, upon a breakdown of the kind of storage mechanism (*s* system) proposed by Broadbent to account for the capacity of young normal adults to respond successively to information delivered to them simultaneously.

It can also be seen that there were significant differences of lesser magnitude between the groups in their responses to information in the channel recalled first for the two longest half-sets (i.e., three and four digits).

Some of the differences between the accuracy of recall in the first and the second channels within the experimental and control groups were also statistically significant. This confirmed that there is a serial-order effect in

TABLE 3.4
Means, Standard Deviations, and the Significance of the Differences between the Means of the Memory-disordered and Nonmemory-disordered Groups on the Control Variables and on Dichotic Digit Recall[a]

VARIABLES	EXPERIMENTAL GROUP *Mean*	EXPERIMENTAL GROUP *S.D.*	EXPERIMENTAL GROUP *Within-group difference*	CONTROL GROUP *Mean*	CONTROL GROUP *S.D.*	CONTROL GROUP *Within-group difference*	BETWEEN-GROUP DIFFERENCES *t*	BETWEEN-GROUP DIFFERENCES *p*
Age	75.73	4.42		75.00	4.46		0.57	n.s.
WAIS IQ's verbal scale	89.00	9.27		95.40	10.38		1.78	n.s.
Performance scale	72.07	6.43		88.53	11.02		4.99	< .01
Verbal minus performance	16.93	8.29		6.87	8.36		3.27	< .01
Full scale	80.67	7.57		92.07	10.39		3.44	< .01
Digit span forward	5.93	1.44		6.53	0.83		1.36	n.s.
Dichotic stimulation								
1 Digit								
1st channel	0.98	0.14	< .01	1.00	0.00	n.s.	0.55	n.s.
2nd channel	0.47	0.41		0.95	0.44		3.10	< .01
2 Digits								
1st channel	1.83	0.20	< .001	1.95	0.20	n.s.	1.64	n.s.
2nd channel	0.09	0.63		1.80	0.45		8.30	< .001
3 Digits								
1st channel	2.42	0.48	< .001	2.90	0.17	< .01	3.64	< .01
2nd channel	0.05	0.14		2.15	0.67		11.86	< .001
4 Digits								
1st channel	2.82	1.06	< .001	3.63	0.45	< .001	2.72	< .02
2nd channel	0.09	0.63		0.95	0.66		3.55	< .01

[a] From Inglis and Sanderson, 1961.

the recall of the second half of each digit series. This effect appeared even in the shortest series in the experimental group, although it did not appear in the control group until a total digit-series length of six figures was reached. The results of this experiment can be shown even more clearly in Figure 3.3.

A second study (Caird and Inglis, 1961), using different groups of similar elderly psychiatric patients (fifteen memory-disordered and fifteen nonmemory-disordered), produced results in close accord with the initial study, as may be seen from Figure 3.4.

In both these studies, then, the memory-disordered patients showed an impaired ability in the second half-spans recalled, which were, by hypothesis,

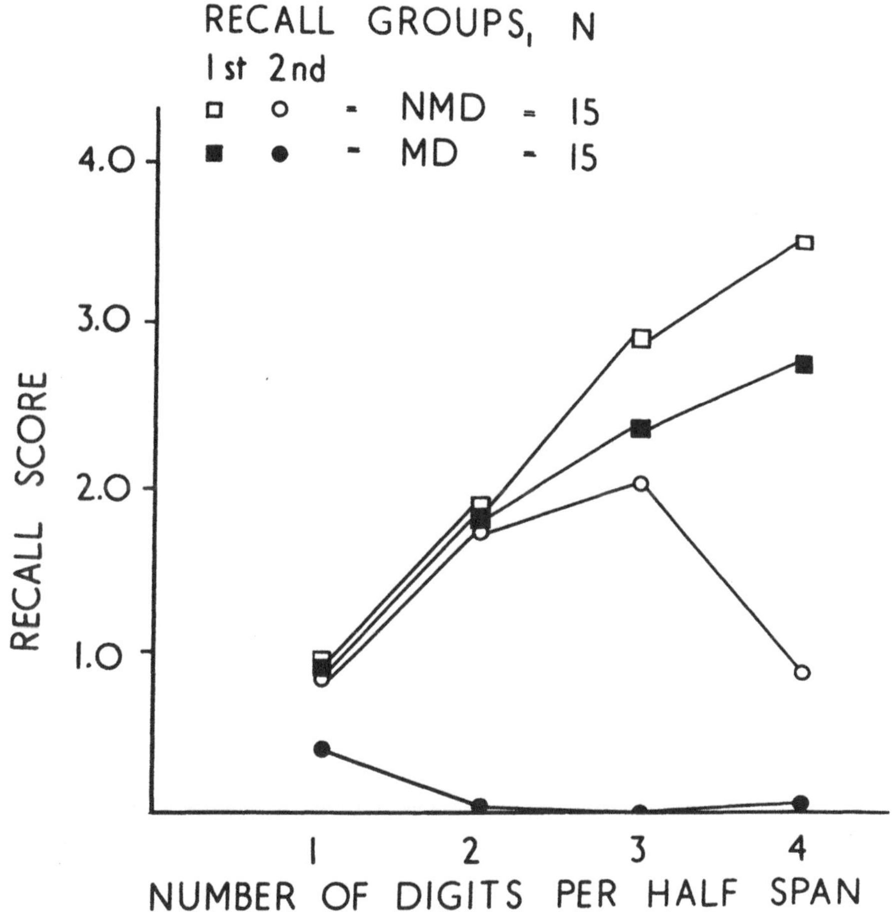

Fig. 3.3. Graph of the scores made by elderly psychiatric patients on the first dichotic listening experiment. (From Inglis, 1965a)

the ones that spent some time in a short-term store. Such findings do not, of course, preclude the possibility that other concurrent but independent functions may also become progressively less efficient, or even break down altogether in senile disorders. The implication of these findings, however, seems to be that the short-term storage process described by Broadbent is an important link in the learning chain. If the chain is broken at this point, the whole sequence of learning may be disrupted with the consequent appearance of the kind of severe memory disorder and disorientation seen in senile dementia.

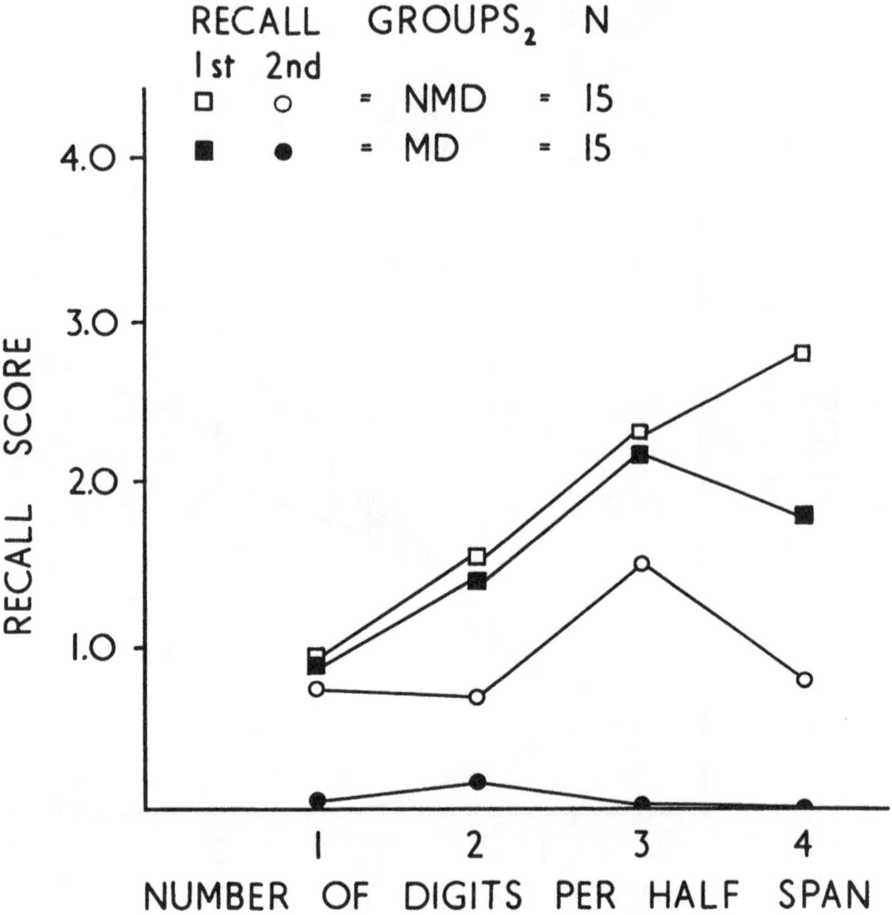

Fig. 3.4. Graph of the scores made by elderly psychiatric patients on the second dichotic listening experiment. (From Inglis, 1965a)

One important characteristic of these differences found between these groups on the dichotic listening task is that they could not be explained away in terms of differences in "motivation." When a senile group performs on some task more poorly than a matched control group it is very often possible to argue that the former just could not be bothered, or were not able to try the test in hand. In the case of the dichotic listening task, however, it was predicted that in one respect the groups would be the same (in recall of first half-spans) and in another respect—gauged at almost the same point in time—they would be markedly different (in recall of second half-spans). It is difficult to see how any general differences in motivation level could account for the appearance of both similarities *and* differences.

This contention, furthermore, led the investigators to the belief (Inglis, 1962a) that the same technique might prove to be a most useful one for the investigation of some of the "normal abnormalities" of aging. Because increasing age in normal individuals also seems to affect learning capacity, and because such impairment may also depend on changes in short-term memory storage, it might be anticipated that responses to dichotic stimulation would show a similar, if not so drastic, change with age. Again, it would be predicted that if age primarily affects storage, the reproduction of the first half-spans recalled should not be affected by advancing years. If the second half-spans recalled must pass through storage, the recall of these digits should be affected by age. Furthermore, if these differences appeared between young and old subjects—on the argument used above—they could likewise not be explained away in terms of any general changes in motivation with age.

In order to investigate these notions, a study was carried out by Inglis and Caird (1963) on one hundred and twenty subjects between the ages of eleven and seventy. There were twenty individuals in each decade group, ten males and ten females. They were presented with the dichotic listening task in the same way as were the psychiatric groups previously described. In this case, however, the digit series went from one to six digits per half-span (as shown in Table 3.5), and were delivered at the rate of about 90 a minute.

The groups were matched on the ordinary digit-span test and the results of an analysis of variance were not significant for this variable. The differences between the groups on the first and second half-spans of the dichotic digits were assessed separately by means of trend analysis (Edwards, 1960), and the results were in remarkably close accord with expectations. These findings may be most clearly depicted by the graphs in Figure 3.5.

These plots very clearly show the effects of increasing age on the dichotic digit half-spans of different lengths. As age increases there was no significant impairment in ability to recall the first half-spans. Progressively greater difficulty was shown, however, in the reproduction of the second half-spans. Furthermore, the longer the span to be recalled the greater the difference, overall, between the first and second half- spans ($p < .001$). These results, however, fitted in so well with what had been expected that it seemed necessary to see if they could be repeated and extended by a different experimenter testing different groups of similar subjects. A study was therefore carried out by Mackay and Inglis (1963) to see if these results were repeatable.

The subjects tested in this latter study were one hundred and sixty persons between the ages of eleven and ninety. None of these was believed to be suffering from any gross mental or physical handicap. There were,

TABLE 3.5
Digits Used for Dichotic Stimulation[a]

	CHANNEL 1	CHANNEL 2
Practice series	3	blank
,, ,,	blank	7
,, ,,	3	7
Test series	5	8
,, ,,	7	6
,, ,,	4	1
,, ,,	6	3
,, ,,	39	72
,, ,,	85	17
,, ,,	38	59
,, ,,	65	28
,, ,,	592	174
,, ,,	793	462
,, ,,	479	836
,, ,,	584	719
,, ,,	5638	2941
,, ,,	9754	8362
,, ,,	6542	7918
,, ,,	9356	4271
,, ,,	81342	96571
,, ,,	74682	31579
,, ,,	57841	29356
,, ,,	38671	15429
,, ,,	251364	746982
,, ,,	984375	753162
,, ,,	451328	238691
,, ,,	438695	965127

[a] From Inglis and Caird, 1963.

again, twenty individuals in each decade group, ten of these being male, ten female. The same dichotic digits were presented in the same way to these subjects. The results were again assessed by means of trend analyses of variance. The findings here may be expressed by the graphs in Figure 3.6.

The results of this experiment reproduced, with some fidelity, the data previously obtained by Inglis and Caird (1963). The effect of testing two older-decade groups (70–80 and 80–90) was to show that the same trend continues as age advances beyond seventy.

Since the findings from these two experiments, carried out on different subjects by different experimenters, proved to be in such close agreement,

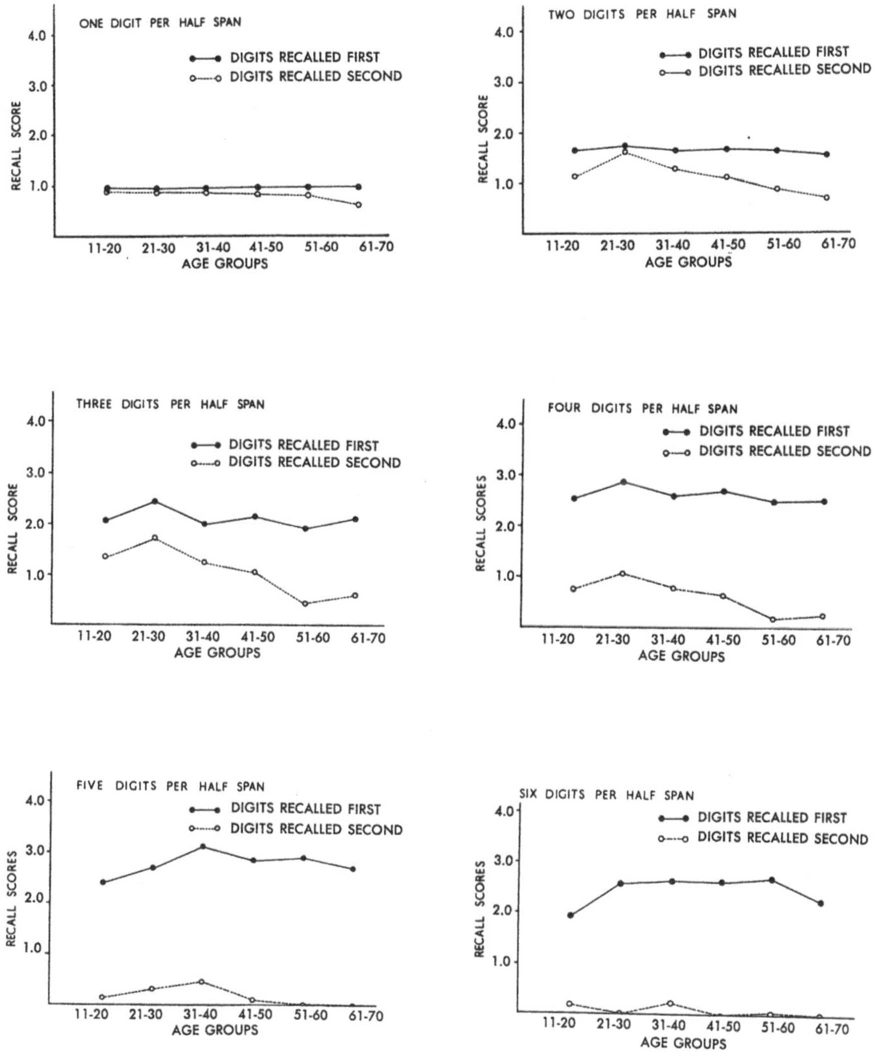

Fig. 3.5. Recall of dichotic digits with from one to six digits in each half-set (free recall condition). (From Inglis and Caird, 1963)

this would serve to increase confidence in the principal conclusions. That is to say, under dichotic listening conditions, and as age increases, there is little or no significant differential impairment in the ability to recall the half-spans reproduced first. Progressively and significantly greater difficulty,

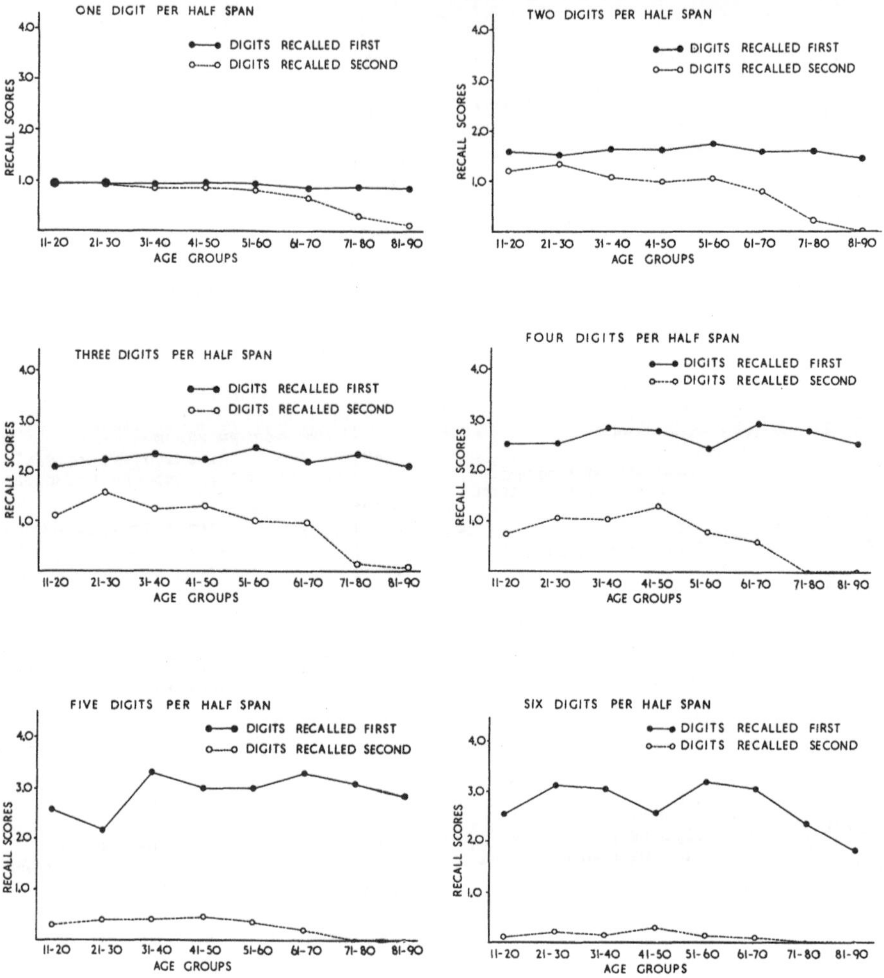

Fig. 3.6. Recall of dichotic digits with from one to six digits in each half-set (free recall condition). (From Mackay and Inglis, 1963)

on the other hand, is shown in the reproduction of the second half-spans as age advances. Furthermore, the longer the span to be recalled the greater the difference, overall, between the first and second half-spans.

These findings make it again seem quite unlikely that differences in motivation can explain such changes in short-term storage with age. It is not easy to conceive how overall changes in motivation as people grow older could make them respond accurately to one ear but not to the other.

It could be maintained, however, that the impairment shown by elderly subjects in the recall of dichotic digits might be due to a failure to hear, or a failure to attend to, the second half-spans on which they showed most errors of report. A further series of experiments (Inglis, 1964a) was therefore designed to cover these objections. This series has been reported by Inglis and Ankus (1965).

One hundred and twenty different subjects, again between eleven and seventy years of age, were tested; and there were twenty persons in each decade group: ten male and ten female. They were required to recall dichotic digits under three separate conditions: (*F*) when the order of recall was left to the free choice of the subject; (*B*) when the ear order of recall was specified before; and (*A*) after these digits had been delivered.

Condition (*F*) was used in order to provide a further repetition of the experiments already described. It can be seen from the previous description of this experimental condition that no control was exercised here over the laterality of the order of recall. The results of this part of the experiment were in accord with previous findings, as can be seen from the graphs in Figure 3.7.

In condition (*B*), the side to be recalled first was indicated by means of a signal panel set in front of the subject, simply bearing the printed words "right" and "left," and a red light was switched on above the appropriate word by the experimenter—in this case immediately before each span of the dichotic digits was delivered. This condition was used in order to evaluate the notion that the changes with age that had previously been shown on this task might be due, for example, to an age-related hearing loss in one ear as compared with the other. If it were the case that as people grow older they tend to suffer such a differential loss in auditory acuity, the apparent deficit in the ear recalled second—under conditions of free response—might be explained by this kind of peripheral difficulty. If, however, an increased order effect were to appear with age—regardless of prior ear-specification—this hypothesis would not be supported.

In this series there were eight sets of each length of span. The subject was signaled to recall the left ear first on half the occasions and the right ear first on the other occasions of the delivery of a given length of span. The right and left signals within each test series were given in random order. Thus there were four of each length of span from one to six digits per half-span, making twenty-four spans in all that required recall from the left ear first ($B-L$), and twenty-four spans with the right ear recalled first ($B-R$). The differences between the groups on the first and second half-spans of the dichotic digits were again assessed separately, by means of trend analyses, for the two subclasses in this section: $B-L$ and $B-R$.

In the $B-L$ condition, the effect of age was again principally on the second half-sets, although in the case of two digits the first half-set was also

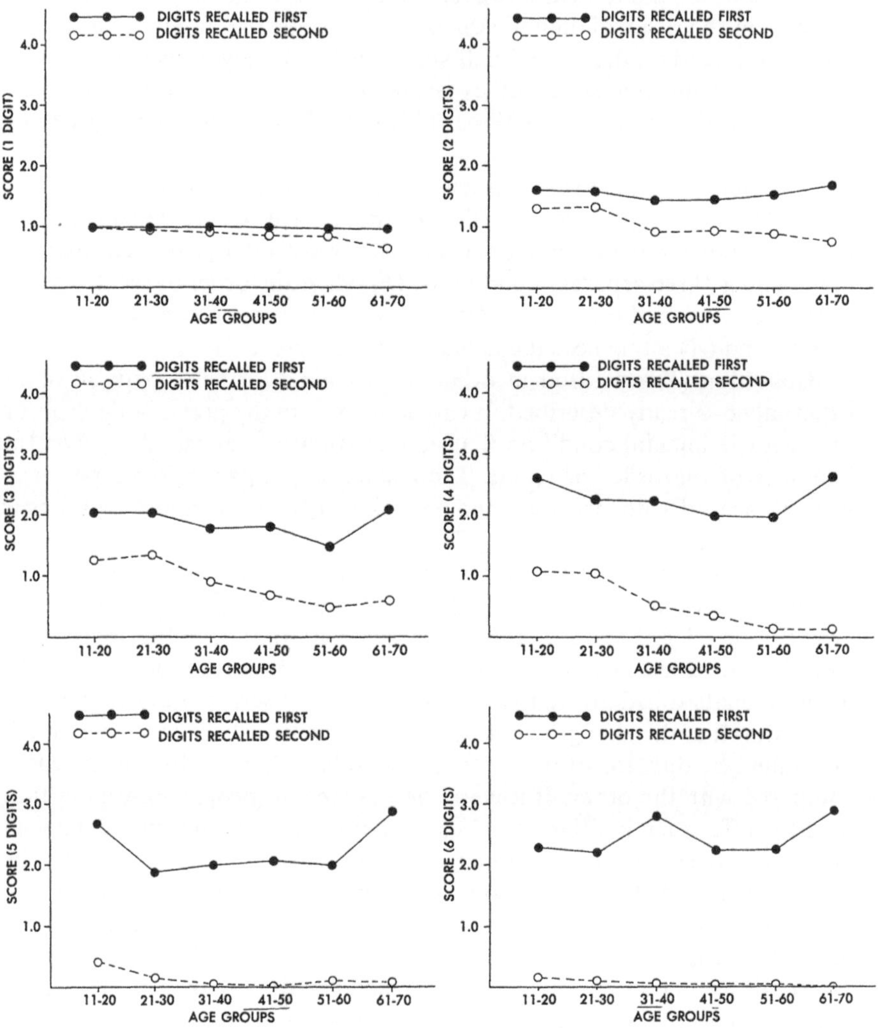

Fig. 3.7. Recall of dichotic digits with from one to six digits in each half-set (free recall condition). (After Inglis and Ankus, 1965)

affected by age. These results (Figure 3.8) bear a striking resemblance to the results secured under conditions of free recall.

The results of the $B-R$ condition were quite similar; they showed an age-related change in four of the six first half-sets as well as in five of the six

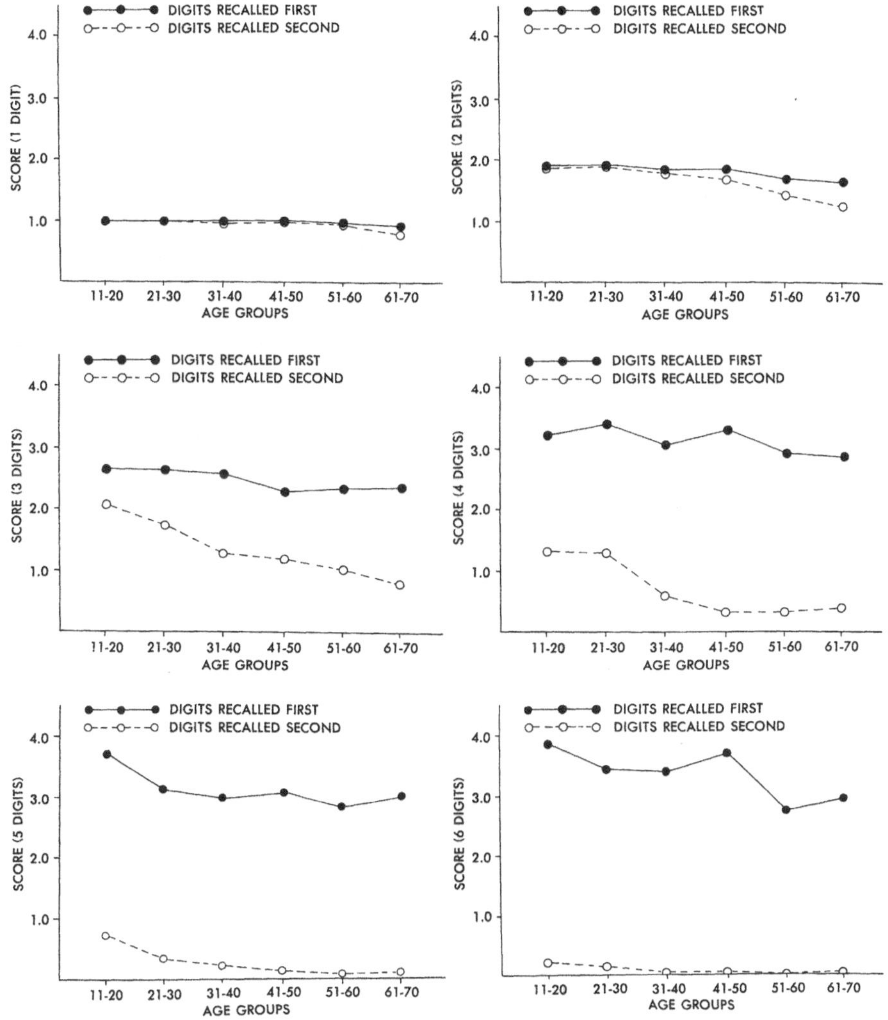

Fig. 3.8. Recall of dichotic digits with from one to six digits in each half-set (B – L condition). (After Inglis and Ankus, 1965)

second half-sets. From the graphical representation of these data in Figure 3.9, it can be seen that the order effect was still there and that the age-related decline was certainly more marked in the digits recalled second.

The results from the two conditions $B-L$ and $B-R$, considered together, refute the notion that, for example, any unilateral decrease in auditory acuity

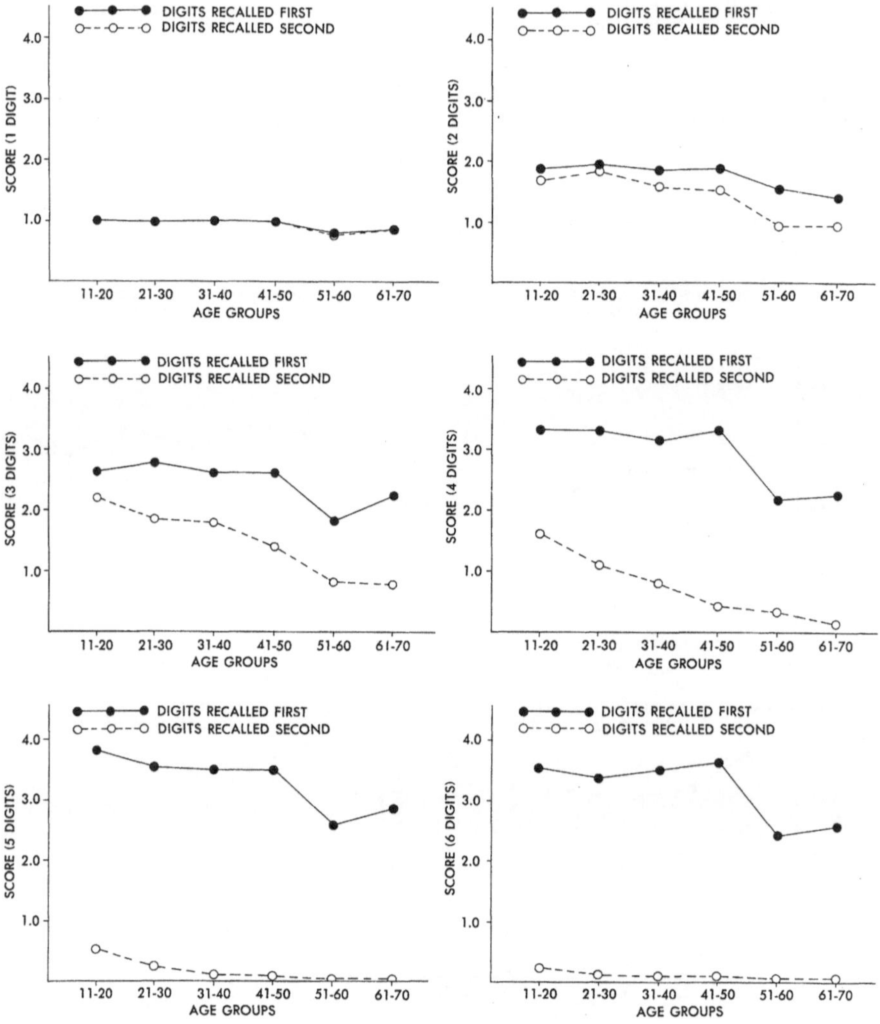

Fig. 3.9. Recall of dichotic digits with from one to six digits in each half-set (B – R condition). (After Inglis and Ankus, 1965)

could account for the appearance of the order effect noted under conditions of free recall. A marked age-related order effect appears independent of ear laterality.

In condition (*A*) the side to be recalled first was again specified by means of the light signals, in this case immediately after the dichotic digits were delivered. This procedure provided a control for the possible effects of differences in attention between the different age groups. It might be argued, for example, that previous findings were due to the fact that as people grow older they will—in the dichotic digit experiment—pay attention only to the material coming into one ear. If, however, the subjects know only after the digits have been delivered which side they have to report first, and further, if they attend only to one side, the ear order effect should vanish, or at least be greatly diminished, because they cannot know beforehand to which ear they should have paid more attention.

There were again eight sets of each length of span. The right and left signals also appeared an equal number of times in random order. There were, therefore, twenty-four spans requiring recall from the left ear first ($A-L$) and twenty-four spans requiring recall from the right ear first ($A-R$).

For the $A-L$ condition there was again a striking resemblance to the results secured under conditions of free recall, as can be seen from Figure 3.10. In the $A-R$ condition, although in five out of six cases performance on the second half-spans varied with age, so did performance on two of the six first half-spans. These latter data are portrayed in Figure 3.11, where the age-related order effect is clearly shown, the decline with age in the half-sets recalled second being more profound than in the half-sets recalled first.

When the results from conditions $A-L$ and $A-R$ are taken together, they suggest that the order effect *cannot* be entirely explained by the notion that older subjects attended only to the material presented to one ear. If selective attention could explain the results obtained under conditions of free recall, no increased order effect with age would be expected to appear in conditions $A-L$ or $A-R$ because the subjects could not, under these circumstances, anticipate which half-sets they would later be required to recall first.

It was concluded, therefore, that the results of this experiment once again confirmed that the responses made to dichotic stimulation under conditions of free recall are affected by age. Because it is the order effect that is exaggerated in older subjects, this finding lent support to the view that a short-term storage mechanism is affected by advancing years. The impairment of this system is related to, but probably not entirely responsible for, age-related defects in longer-term learning.

The results obtained in this experiment, when the order of recall was specified before delivery of dichotic digits, were similar to the results from free recall. Since the age-related order effect still appeared, regardless of which side was specified for recall first, this finding is quite incompatible with the notion that changes in responses to dichotic listening with increasing age might be due, for example, to a unilateral hearing loss that gets worse as people grow older.

The results obtained when order of report was specified after the delivery of the digits were also very similar to the results obtained under conditions of free recall. This outcome runs completely counter to the view that the changes

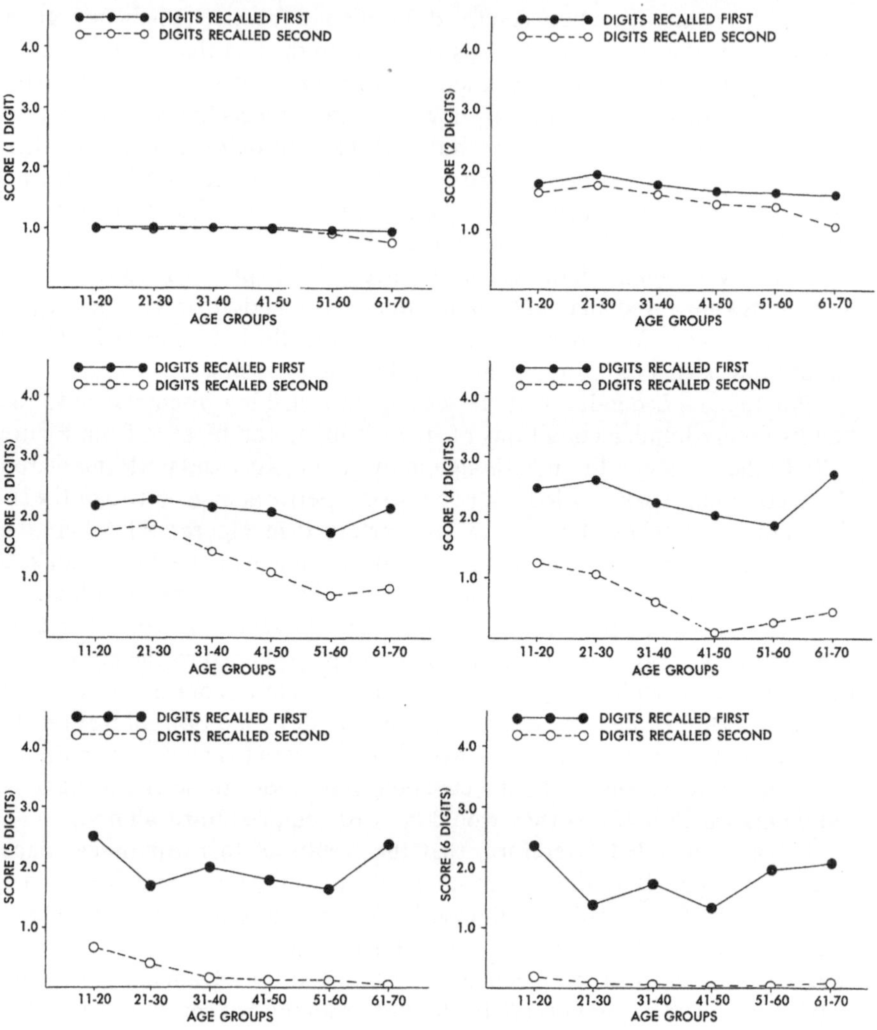

Fig. 3.10. Recall of dichotic digits with from one to six digits in each half-set (A – L condition). (After Inglis and Ankus, 1965)

observed with age might be due, for example, to the fact that older individuals attend to, or manage to perceive, the material from only a single channel under conditions of simultaneous stimulation.

All these findings, however, are compatible with the hypothesis that the age-related impairment shown in recall under the three experimental conditions is due to a decline in the efficiency of some short-term memory storage process. Further independent studies by Broadbent and Gregory (1965) and by Craik (1965) have produced similar findings.

The results confirm, in quite a striking fashion, Welford's (1956) suggestion that there may be some short-term storage process that deteriorates

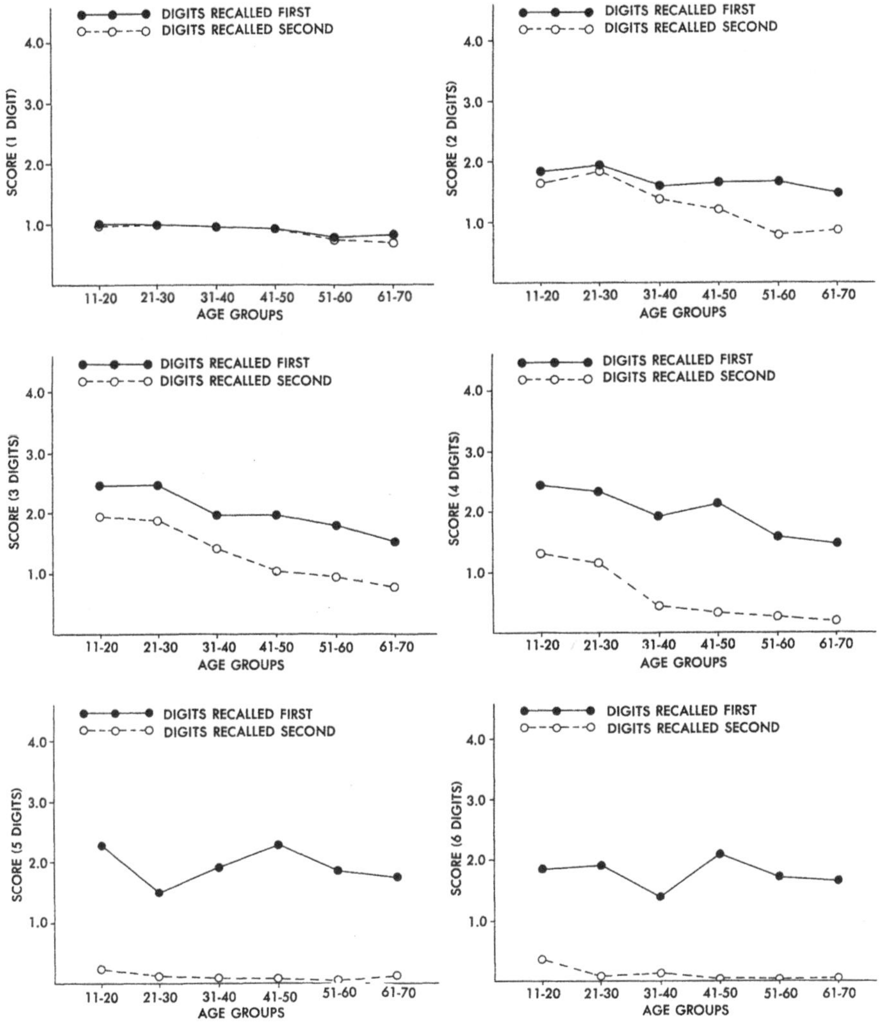

Fig. 3.11. Recall of dichotic digits with from one to six digits in each half-set (A – R condition). (After Inglis and Ankus, 1965)

with age. It should perhaps be reiterated that such findings do not, of course, exclude the possibility that other concurrent but independent functions may become progressively less efficient, or even break down altogether, as a result of age or disease. Nevertheless, the likely importance of changes in short-term storage can hardly be overrated. Both Hebb (1949) and Broadbent (1958), on the basis of rather different theoretical considerations, have proposed that all new material that the organism has to learn must first pass through the short-term store before being incorporated in the long-term store. This would make the former process quite fundamental to much ongoing adjustment. It is not difficult, then, to see how the diminished efficiency of this short-term store might produce intellectual impairment in the aged and how its complete breakdown might account for the severe memory disorder and disorientation seen in the psychoses of senility.

The main disadvantage of this kind of study, however—as in the case of the studies of thought disorder previously considered—is that we have not, as yet, discovered or devised any powerful procedures for *changing* the behavior in question. No matter how positive the outcome of such investigations may be at the descriptive level, it must be admitted that they leave a great deal to be desired. It seems likely that such dissatisfaction will remain until our procedures advance from measurement to manipulation.

A convenient bridge between observation and experiment is provided by the results of psychological investigations of the effects of temporal lobectomy for the relief of psychomotor epilepsy, which will constitute the first chapter in the second part of this book.

PART II

Experiment and the alteration of abnormality

4

THE EFFECTS OF *Neurosurgery*

THE EXPERIMENTAL METHOD requires that the investigator first alter the independent variables over which he has control and relate this manipulation to subsequent changes in the dependent variables that he then observes and measures.

If psychology is taken to stand in a "horizontal" relation to the other sciences, and so long as *behavior* is at some point involved in this scheme, the variables that are considered as either antecedents or consequences may be taken from a very wide range of events. Some studies, for example, may use behavioral stimuli as the independent variables and physiological responses as the dependent variables. This would be the case, for instance, in the investigation of the effects of pornographic films on autonomic arousal in human subjects. Other studies might reverse the relation between the two kinds of variable, as in the investigation of the effects of electroconvulsive shock upon psychomotor slowness in depressed patients.

The studies of the effects of temporal lobectomy, to be considered in the present chapter, are of the latter kind in that the most powerful source of variance is neurological—lying, in this case, in the hands of the neurosurgeon rather than in the hands of the psychologist. It is primarily the psychologist, however, who is trained and equipped to measure some of the crucial behavioral changes that result from these surgical procedures.

These investigations, then, form a convenient bridge from the first to the second Part of this text. Thus change is involved without, in this case, actually being produced by the psychologist, who has been mainly concerned with the measurement of behavior. The function that seems to be most affected by this kind of operation is once again "memory"; that is, it involves defects in some of those processes of learning that were considered in the preceding chapter. Also, the concern of these studies has still been mainly with the description of impairment rather than with its amelioration, although of course the object of the operation is the treatment of a serious disorder, temporal lobe epilepsy.

Although Gastaut (1953) has criticized those who would equate the notions of "temporal lobe" and "psychomotor" epilepsy, for the purposes of this present discussion these finer distinctions may be set aside. Temporal lobectomy in man has most often been carried out for the relief of so-called psychomotor epileptic attacks when these have been related to or triggered by abnormal functioning of the temporal lobes of the brain.

These attacks have been succinctly described by Gibbs, Gibbs, and Fuster (1948), who have noted that

> the chief clinical manifestations of psychomotor seizures may be described as follows. The patient becomes confused and as a rule amnesic but does not usually lose consciousness. His movements appear purposeful but are poorly coordinated and his manner is frequently negativistic. In general his behavior is that of a person acting out a bad dream. Often during the seizure there are manifestations of fear or rage with screaming and shouting. In most seizures the movements are simple, repetitive and more or less automatic. (1948, pp. 334–335)

Hill (1953) has pointed out that such patients may come to operation if there is both clinical and electroencephalographic evidence of a single focal abnormality in the anterior part of the temporal lobe, after it has been shown that the resulting seizures cannot be controlled by adequate anticonvulsant treatment.

The principal psychological findings on the effects of such neurosurgery have been made by Dr. Brenda Milner of the Montreal Neurological Institute and Dr. Victor Meyer, formerly of the Guys-Maudsley Neurosurgical Unit in London, England. The work of these investigators and their collaborators may best be considered in conjunction and in chronological order.

The actual surgical procedures used in London have been described by Falconer (1953); and the methods used in Montreal have been outlined by Penfield and Baldwin (1952) and by Penfield, Lende, and Rasmussen (1961). Examples of the brain areas removed are illustrated in Figure 4.1.*

*The author is most deeply indebted to Dr. Brenda Milner for her kindness in providing this illustration.

Fig. 4.1. Six examples of temporal lobectomy carried out at the Montreal Neurological Institute. Note the lack of significant differences between the size of left- and right-sided excisions. (Illustration supplied by Dr. Brenda Milner.)

Case C.K.

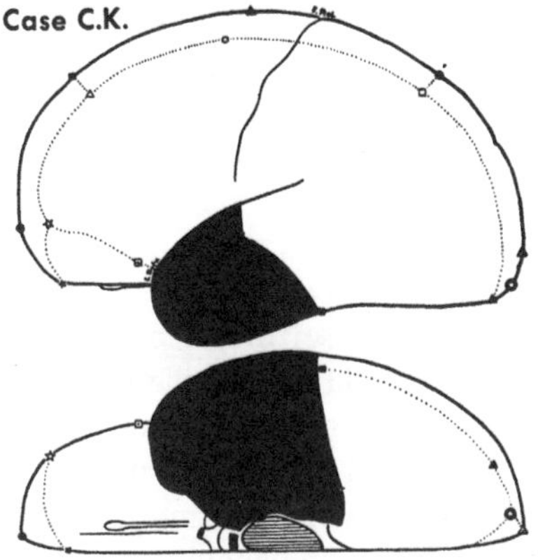

Case M.W.

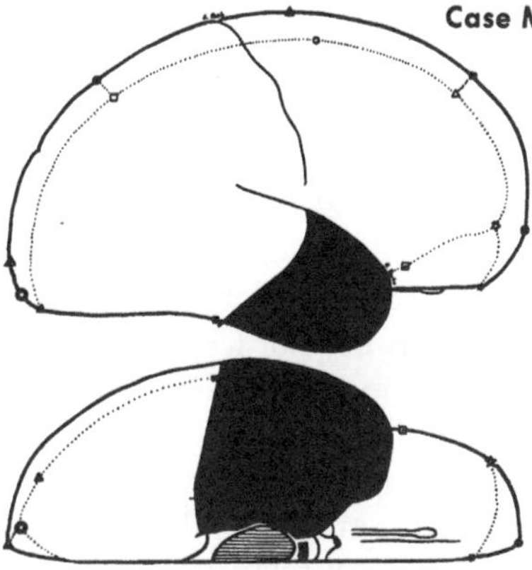

Case E.K.

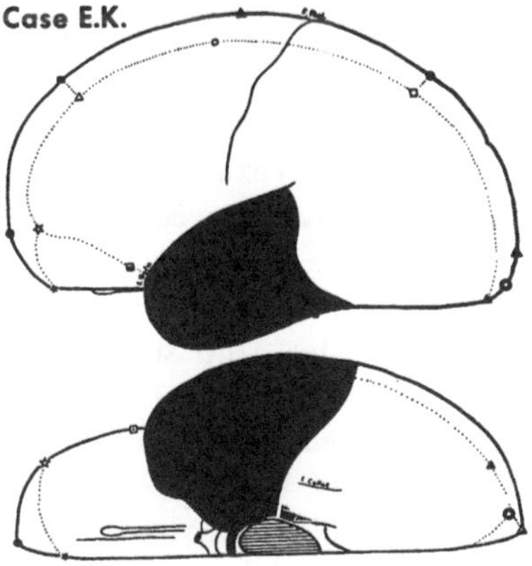

Case A.B.

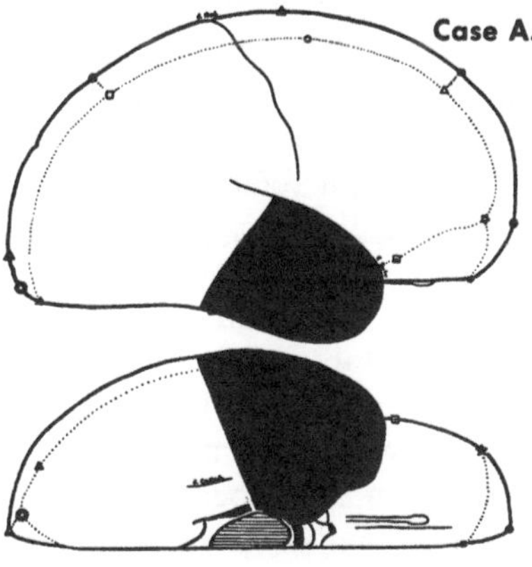

Case S.C

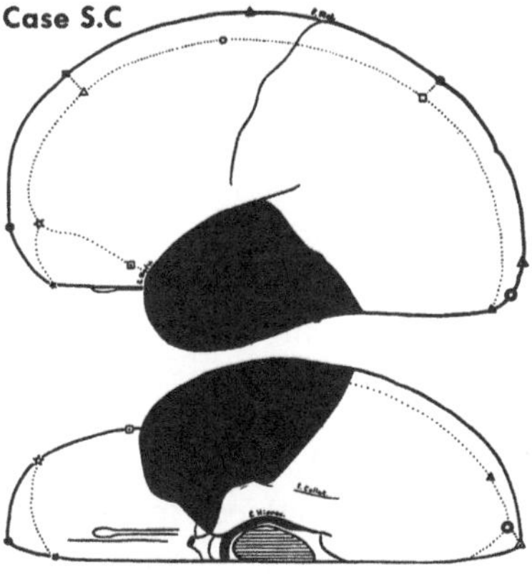

Case J.S.

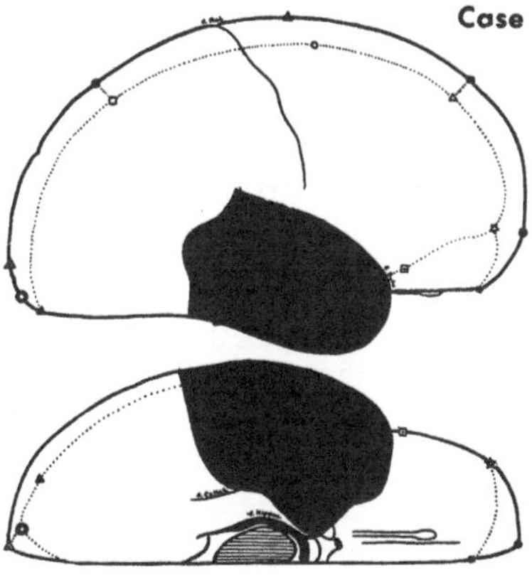

The therapeutic effects of these operations upon the actual epileptic symptoms have been reported upon by Falconer, Hill, Meyer, Mitchell, and Pond (1955), who found that in a series of thirty cases there was considerable relief from attack, after operation, for twenty-six of the patients. The same authors also reported improvement of associated personality disorders in these patients. A follow-up study of sixty-eight cases, by James (1960) similarly reported benefit from the operation in 57 per cent of those who had suffered from disorders of personality, as well as from seizures. Comparable kinds of improvement have been reported by Penfield and Flanigin (1950), and by Bailey, Green, Amador, and Gibbs (1953). The concern of the present chapter, however, is not with the therapeutic effects of this kind of surgery on seizures or personality disturbances but with the incidental information it has provided about relationships between brain function and behavior in human subjects.

The first systematic investigations of the psychological effects of temporal lobectomy for psychomotor epilepsy v.ere made by Dr. Brenda Milner (1952), working with Dr. Wilder Penfield at the Montreal Neurological Institute. After an extensive review of the literature on temporal lobe damage, with particular reference to animal studies, Milner (1954) examined the test performance of forty-five patients. Of these, twenty-five showed temporal lobe foci, as judged by EEG recordings (thirteen of these being right-sided and twelve left-sided); of the remaining patients, thirteen showed foci in either frontal or parietal areas of the cerebral cortex, and seven were "normal" controls. The last group was composed of convalescent hospital patients, who were matched with the brain damaged groups—as far as possible—in age, vocabulary, and occupational status, but who were not suffering from any psychiatric, neurological, or glandular disorders.

Because her review of temporal lobe dysfunction in animals seemed to show the principal effects of the operation to be upon visual capacities, Milner's original test battery consisted of sixteen tests, mainly, but not entirely, visuospatial in content. She also noted that a special search was made for any consistent differences between the effects of right- and left-sided temporal lobe lesions. The patients who came to operation were tested (from twelve hours to five days) before the operation and were retested (between sixteen and twenty-two days) after the operation.

Since the tests used in this investigation largely sampled performance in the visual modality, it is not too surprising that mainly visual defects were found, these appearing in both the right *and* the left temporal groups. Before the operation, it appeared that all the temporal lobe patients were inferior to members of the other groups on the McGill Picture Anomalies Test (Hebb and Morton, 1943), which requires the subject to spot incongruities in visually presented material, and on the Wechsler Picture

Arrangement subtest (Wechsler, 1944). The right temporal lobe group seemed markedly inferior to all the others (including the left temporals) on other tests of spatial patterning, both visual (the Triangular Blocks Test [unpublished] and the Wechsler Block Design subtest) and nonvisual (the Tactile Formboard Test; Halstead, 1947) in content. In view of Milner's (1958) later findings, for example that Picture Anomalies test performance is principally affected by *right* temporal lobe dysfunction, one might wonder (with all the acuity of hindsight) whether the expectation of visual defects based on the results of animal studies might not have biased these preliminary findings in human patients. The only impairment Milner found to be specific to the left temporal group was on verbal tests, and this was apparently caused by postoperative dysphasia, the inability spontaneously to recall words.

The clinical observation of two cases described by Milner and Penfield (1955) and Penfield and Milner (1958) showed, however, that unilateral temporal lobectomy, carried out on the side of the brain dominant for speech, could result in a striking defect in recent memory.

Before either of these latter reports had appeared, however, Dr. Victor Meyer, in association with Mr. Murray Falconer of the Guys-Maudsley Neurosurgical Unit in London, had begun to discover similar postoperative learning defects of a particular kind in some cases of temporal lobectomy.

It is perhaps significant that, in his own preliminary review of the literature, Meyer (1957a) paid most attention to the effects of temporal lobe dysfunction in man. This led him to the observation (Kolodny, 1928; Keschner, Bender, and Strauss, 1936) that "memory disorder" may result from tissue damage in this brain area.

In a preliminary report, Meyer and Yates (1955) described the effects of temporal lobectomy on eighteen cases, account being taken not only of the side of the lesion but also its relation to brain dominance for speech, at least insofar as this could be judged from handedness (right-handed patients being regarded as left-brain dominant). Of these eighteen cases, eleven had surgery in the dominant hemisphere, six in the nondominant hemisphere, and the remaining case was said to be of "doubtful" dominance. In this study, two kinds of test were given to these patients.

(1) Tests of Intelligence
  (*a*) Wechsler-Bellevue Intelligence Scale (Wechsler, 1944)
  (*b*) Progressive Matrices (Raven, 1958)
  (*c*) Mill Hill Vocabulary Scale (Raven, 1958)
  (*d*) Nufferno Speed and Level Tests (Furneaux, 1956)

(2) Tests of Learning and Retention
  (*a*) New Word Learning and Retention Test (Shapiro and Nelson, 1955b)
  (*b*) Paired-Associate Learning Test (Wechsler, 1945)

The patients were first tested about a week before the operation (range two to seven days) and retested again about one month after the operation (range twenty-one to twenty-eight days). Meyer and Yates (1955) have given a complete description of all their raw data, but not, unfortunately, of all their statistical analyses. Table 4.1 is a consolidated version of a number of their tables, the *N*'s reflecting the fact that not all the patients were given all the tests.

TABLE 4.1
Results on Intelligence Tests before and after Temporal Lobectomy[a]

	Dominant Group Means					Nondominant Group Means				
Tests	*N*	*Pre*	*Post*	*t*	*p*	*N*	*Pre*	*Post*	*t*	*p*
Wechsler IQ's	9					5				
Verbal		91.78	85.33	1.809	n.s.		98.80	98.60	0.0	n.s.
Performance		95.11	86.56	2.171	.05		104.00	102.00	0.0	n.s.
Full scale		92.67	84.44	2.218	.05		101.20	99.40	0.0	n.s.
Matrices	9	96.89	98.11	0.0	n.s.	3	105.67	106.67	0.0	n.s.
Mill Hill vocabulary	7	85.14	83.00	0.0	n.s.	2	89.00	89.00	0.0	n.s.
Nufferno Standard Scores										
Level	5	+0.10	−0.23	0.0	n.s.	2	+1.29	+1.44	0.0	n.s.
Unstressed speed	4	−0.15	−0.23	0.0	n.s.	2	+0.15	+0.09	0.0	n.s.
Stressed speed	2	+0.56	+0.43	0.0	n.s.	2	+0.93	+0.37	0.0	n.s.

[a] After Meyer and Yates, 1955.

From Table 4.1 it can be seen that the biggest intellectual changes take place in the Wechsler scores of the dominant group. This group has poorer scores on all the scales postoperatively, and the Verbal Scale difference falls just short of significance. The nondominant group did not show a significant change on any of the scales. The investigators then suggested that the Performance Scale difference in the dominant cases might be due to visual difficulties, such as hemianopia; expressive dysphasia might, in a few cases—on the other hand—account for the Verbal Scale change. The latter argument was supported by the lack of any significant difference in the Mill Hill Vocabulary Test scores, which partly involve the recognition and not the spontaneous reproduction of correct word definitions that is an embarrassment to dysphasic patients. As can be seen from the same table, neither the Matrices nor the Nufferno tests showed significant differences for either group.

The results on tests of learning and retention were much more striking and systematic, as can be seen from Table 4.2. This is again a consolidated version of a number of Meyer and Yates' (1955) separate tables. These data were interpreted to mean that the dominant cases alone showed a very marked impairment of learning one month after operation. These patients took more trials to learn up to a set criterion (hence the higher the learning score the poorer the performance), and they retained less of this learning after an interval. Four dominant cases were again retested, one year after the operation, and still showed the learning defect.

Like all good research, this investigation created more problems than it answered. In addition, the number of patients tested in each group was much too small for any secure inferences to be drawn. A more extensive investigation therefore had to be carried out (Meyer, 1957b).

First, it was evidently necessary to try to find out if the learning defect shown by the dominant temporal lobectomy cases was or was not specific to the single modality through which the material to be learned had been presented. Both of the learning tests used in the first study had involved only the auditory modality, the material being read aloud to the subject. It was therefore necessary to see if a similar defect would also be found if other kinds of learning tests (e.g., visual, and tactile) were used.

Second, it remained to be discovered if the learning difficulty was or was not specific to the single kind of material used. Both of the learning tests in the first study were verbal in content, involving words alone. It still remained to be seen if the same patients would fail to learn with, for example, pictorial material.

TABLE 4.2
Results on the Learning and Retention Tests before and after Temporal Lobectomy[a]

	DOMINANT GROUP MEANS					NONDOMINANT GROUP MEANS				
TESTS	*N*	*Pre*	*Post*	*t*	*p*	*N*	*Pre*	*Post*	*t*	*p*
New Word Test										
Learning scores	6	10.67	41.33	3.155	.01	2	6.5	5.5	0.0	n.s.
Retention scores (after 24 hours)		4.00	1.83	4.255	.001		5.0	5.0	0.0	n.s.
Wechsler Paired-Associates										
Easy pairs	6	5.67	4.17	2.680	< .05	2	6.00	6.00	0.0	n.s.
Hard pairs		3.00	0.17	5.896	.001		4.00	4.00	0.0	n.s.

[a] After Meyer and Yates, 1955.

Third, it was necessary to see if dysphasic difficulties alone could account for the apparent learning defect. Both of the learning tests that had been used required the patients to recollect or recall the responses. This mode of reproduction might be more difficult for a patient with expressive dysphasia than if he were simply asked to recognize the correct responses.

An attempt to elucidate these problems was reported by Meyer (1959) in a study that included a number of different kinds of learning tests, as follows.

(1) *Auditory-Verbal Recall (AVR).* This paired-associate learning test required the subject to learn pairs of words to a criterion, and it involved auditory presentation and the recall mode of response reproduction. Items involved such paired associates as the stimulus word "crush," which had to be associated with the response word "dark." In this subtest (for which a parallel form was available) there were eight such pairs in all, which, like all the subsequent tests to be described, had to be learned to a criterion of three consecutive correct responses for each pair. This test, of course, was almost identical to the Paired-Associate subtest of the Wechsler Memory Scale (Wechsler, 1945).

(2) *Auditory-Verbal Recognition (AVRg).* This subtest used material that was similar in content to the auditory verbal recall test, but it involved the recognition mode of response reproduction of eight stimulus-response pairs. Thus when the stimulus word "obey" was read out in the trial series, the subject would be required to recognize the correct response word "inch" from a number of other words, also read out to him in random order. The purpose of this subtest was to investigate the notion that expressive dysphasia might, by itself, produce poor results on the AVR test, since this disorder mainly impairs the capacity for the spontaneous recall of words.

(3) *Visual-Verbal Recognition (VVRg).* These items resembled the second test (AVRg), but stimulus and response words were printed in lowercase letters, about 1 cm. high, on separate cards that were shown to the subject. The correct response card had to be chosen from a series shown after exposure of the stimulus card. Again, there were eight pairs. This subtest was used to enable the effect of verbal material to be distinguished from the effect of auditory presentation.

(4) *Visual-Design Recognition (VDRg).* This test involved the association of five pairs of designs by the same means as for the VVRg subtest. The designs to be learned in this test are shown in Figure 4.2. It can be seen that this test involves the visual modality without involving words.

(5) *Visual-Design Recall (VDR).* These items, six pairs in all, required the subject to reproduce simple abstract designs as responses to stimuli provided by line drawings of common objects, as shown in Figure 4.3.

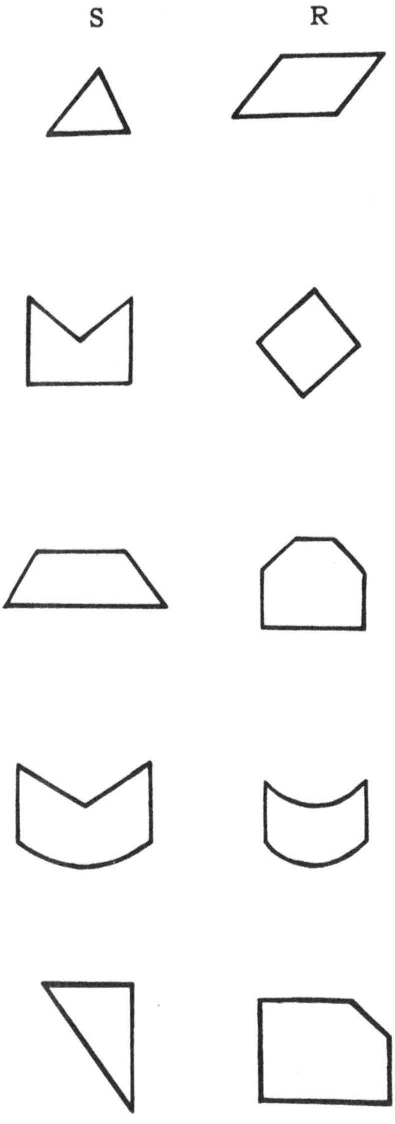

Fig. 4.2. Designs used in the Visual-Design Recognition Paired-associate Learning Test of Meyer (1957b).

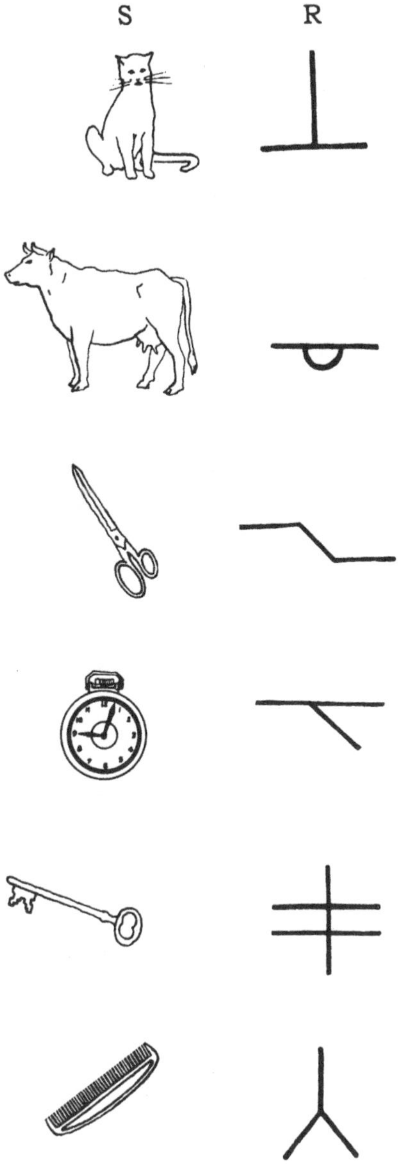

Fig. 4.3. Drawings and designs used in the Visual-Design Recall Paired-associate Learning Test of Meyer (1957b).

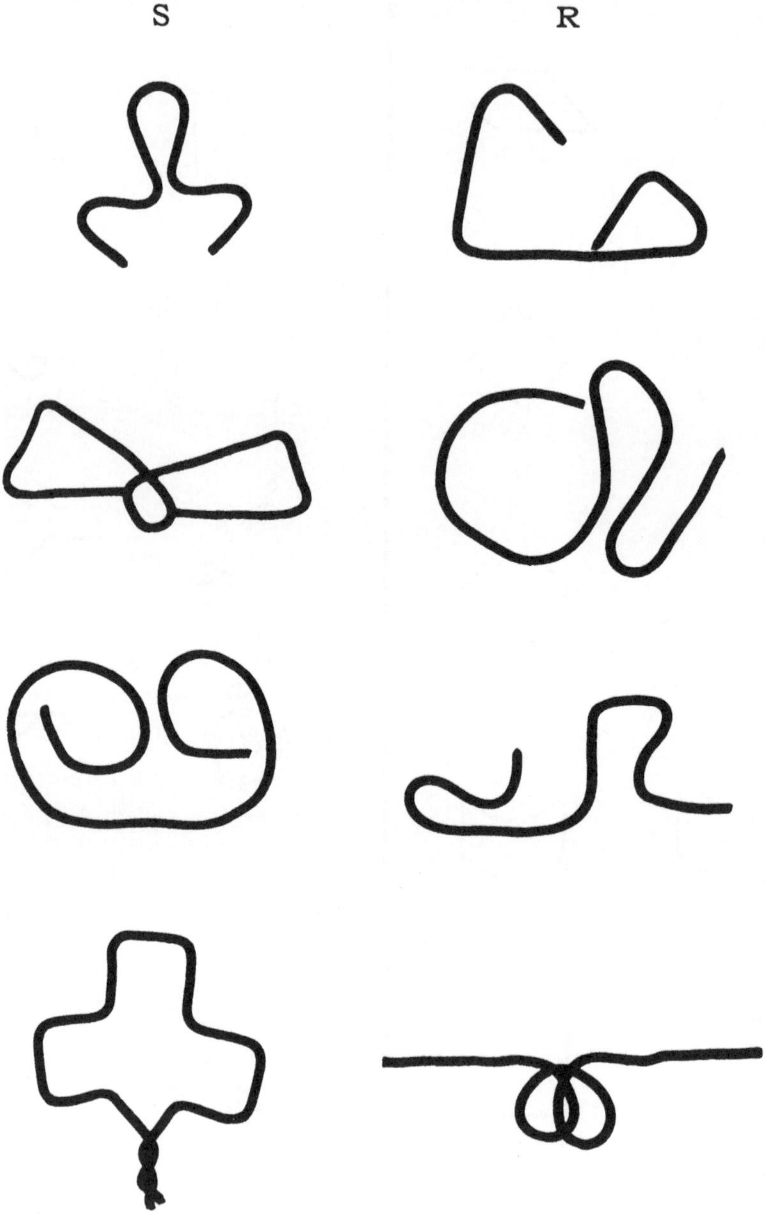

Fig. 4.4. Wire shapes used in the Tactile-Design Recognition Paired-associate Learning Test of Meyer (1957b).

(6) *Tactile-Design Recognition (TDRg).* This test required the subject, while blindfolded, to associate pairs of simple wire patterns and to recognize the correct response from the series of responses while holding the stimulus object in his preferred hand. The form of the wire shapes used, four in each series, are shown in Figure 4.4.

In addition to this series of tests designed to explore the three principal questions already outlined, Meyer also gave three of the intelligence tests used in the previous study (the Wechsler–Bellevue (Wechsler, 1944) Progressive Matrices and the Mill Hill Vocabulary Scale (Raven, 1958). The New Word Learning and Retention Test (Shapiro and Nelson, 1955b), on which the original deficit had been shown, was also administered.

In this study, twenty-five patients undergoing temporal lobectomy were tested. Of these, fourteen were "dominant" cases (i.e., right-handed, who were operated upon on the left side of the brain), and eleven were "nondominant" (i.e., right-handed with a right-sided operation). Of the latter, eight were clearly nondominant, and three were rather more doubtful. The preoperative testing took place from one to twenty-eight days before operation ($\overline{m} = 4.84$; $\sigma = 6.07$). The first postoperative assessment was carried out from twenty to thirty-five days after the operation ($\overline{m} = 27.84$; $\sigma = 3.01$). A second postoperative assessment of seventeen of the subjects (ten dominant, seven nondominant) took place eleven to fifteen months after the operation ($\overline{m} = 12.35$; $\sigma = 1.11$).

A preoperative comparison of the differences between the dominant and the nondominant cases on all the tests is shown in Table 4.3. It would appear from this table that the groups were indeed quite well matched before operation, being significantly different only on the Mill Hill Vocabulary (and nearly so on the Wechsler Verbal Scale) and on the VVRg test.

The next results to be considered, then, are those obtained one month after the operation. The *within*-group differences for the nondominant group may be inspected first in Table 4.4. In this case the mean differences were assessed by Sandler's A-test (Sandler, 1955). It is notable that the nondominant group showed little, if any, effect of the operation one month postoperatively. The two changes in the test scores, on the Matrices and the AVRg tests, both indicated a slight *improvement*, a decrease in the learning test score representing fewer trials taken to the criterion of learning.

Similar pre- and postoperative comparisons are afforded for the dominant group in Table 4.5. On the intelligence tests, on which the dominant group was poorer than the nondominant group before operation (with the exception of the Performance Scale of the Wechsler), the dominant group also did more poorly after the operation. Again Meyer (1959) has argued that the Verbal Scale changes were probably due to the dysphasic difficulties these patients suffered immediately after the operation, while the Performance Scale change

TABLE 4.3
Means, Standard Deviations, and the Significance of the Differences between the Means of the Dominant and Nondominant Groups on Preoperative Testing[a]

	DOMINANT GROUP (N = 14)		NONDOMINANT GROUP (N = 11)			
TESTS	$\overline{m}$	σ	$\overline{m}$	σ	t	p
Wechsler IQ's						
Verbal scale	95.36	13.05	108.54	21.93	1.875	.10 > .05
Performance scale	101.93	13.66	103.18	22.99	0.169	n.s.
Full scale	98.50	13.88	106.27	24.28	1.010	n.s.
Matrices' IQ.	102.64	15.71	106.36	19.88	0.524	n.s.
Mill Hill IQ.	88.07	7.64	105.00	18.87	2.801	.02 > .01
New word learning	9.46	2.92	8.36	6.67	0.593	n.s.
Paired-Associate Tests						
AVR	21.64	12.04	18.72	13.40	0.574	n.s.
AVRg	17.07	7.42	14.45	8.43	0.826	n.s.
VVRg	18.86	8.01	12.64	5.18	2.233	.05 > .02
VDRg	11.50	6.30	11.45	14.88	0.010	n.s.
VDR	25.33	24.16	20.62	21.02	0.514	n.s.
TDRg	26.64	14.82	22.91	20.01	0.536	n.s.

[a] From Meyer, 1957b.

might have been due to visual field defects, which also were a consequence of surgery. The results of this group on the paired-associate learning tests were indeed striking. The New Word Learning test, as before, showed gross postoperative impairment. The same type of impairment was reflected in both the AVR and the AVRg subtests. Again, the very greatly increased scores represent a greater number of trials to criterion and hence *poorer* acquisition.

These results immediately suggested that expressive dysphasia alone could not account for the apparent learning deficit, since recognition as well as recall was affected. The VVRg test moreover, was apparently unaffected by the operation in this group. In other words it did *not* appear that the verbal nature of the material could alone account for deficit after operation. The lack of impairment in any of the other subtests also suggested that the impairment was in fact restricted to learning in the auditory modality.

Meyer (1957b) also provided data on the one-year postoperative retest; attention may first be given to the comparisons he made between the preoperative and one-year postoperative test scores of the nondominant group, which are shown in Table 4.6. It can be seen from this table that the only significant differences found in the case of this nondominant group were in some of the cognitive tests, where these changes represented *improvement* in score.

Similar comparisons of before- and one-year-after-operation results are shown for the dominant group in Table 4.7. It can be seen from this table that some of the cognitive test scores are just about back to the level attained before operation. The large difference between the Wechsler Verbal Scale and Mill Hill Vocabulary Scale results was no longer found. Thus the claim that the one-month differences were caused by transient dysphasia was supported. Similarly, the previously found differences on the Performance Scale of the Wechsler vanished, presumably with a concomitant decrease in visual field defects. It should be borne in mind, however, that this group evidently did not make the large practice-effect gains that are shown in Table 4.6 for the nondominant group on the Wechsler Scale results, and this fact in itself may be of some significance.

TABLE 4.4
Means, Standard Deviations, and the Significance of the Differences between the Preoperative and One-month Postoperative Test Scores of the Non-dominant Group (N = 11)[a]

	PREOPERATIVE		ONE-MONTH POSTOPERATIVE			
TESTS	$\overline{m}$	σ	$\overline{m}$	σ	*A*	*p*
Wechsler IQ's						
Verbal scale	108.54	21.93	111.09	23.75	0.811	n.s.
Performance scale	103.18	22.99	102.82	22.22	3.275	n.s.
Full scale	106.27	24.28	107.82	23.99	1.817	n.s.
Matrices' raw scores	44.82	12.88	47.64	12.36	0.344	.10 > .05
Mill Hill raw scores	53.54	21.60	53.18	21.58	2.875	n.s.
New word learning	8.36	6.67	7.36	4.42	0.686	n.s.
Paired-Associate Tests						
AVR	18.72	13.40	16.45	10.04	0.626	n.s.
AVRg	14.45	8.43	12.45	7.70	0.215	.05 > .02
VVRg	12.64	5.18	11.64	4.61	2.785	n.s.
VDRg	11.45	14.88	10.63	13.31	1.148	n.s.
VDR	20.62	21.02	20.37	24.22	175.50	n.s.
TDRg	22.91	20.01	21.90	21.30	3.355	n.s.

[a]From Meyer, 1957b.

TABLE 4.5
Means, Standard Deviations, and the Significance of the Differences between the Preoperative and One-month Postoperative Test Scores of the Dominant Group (N = 14)[a]

	PREOPERATIVE		ONE-MONTH POSTOPERATIVE			
TESTS	$\overline{m}$	σ	$\overline{m}$	σ	A	p
Wechsler IQ's						
Verbal scale	95.36	13.05	84.57	16.70	0.118	< .001
Performance scale	101.93	13.66	95.93	14.85	0.258	.05 > .02
Full scale	98.50	13.88	89.43	16.38	0.135	.01 > .001
Matrices' raw scores	40.50	11.47	42.07	10.55	0.442	n.s.
Mill Hill raw scores	38.93	10.59	33.50	10.62	0.120	< .001
New word learning	9.46	2.92	41.78	23.[illegible]7	0.103	< .001
Paired-Associate Tests						
AVR	21.64	12.04	62.57	21.45	0.087	< .001
AVRg	17.07	7.42	39.14	22.54	0.129	.01 > .001
VVRg	18.86	8.01	22.26	9.72	0.405	n.s.
VDRg	11.50	6.30	12.78	7.06	1.358	n.s.
VDR	25.33	24.16	24.44	24.71	12.44	n.s.
TDRg	26.64	14.82	23.86	14.81	1.899	n.s.

[a] From Meyer, 1957b.

It should especially be remarked, however, that the performance of the dominant group was *still* significantly impaired on the learning tests that involved the auditory modality. This finding, like the failure to show differences between recall and recognition, was contrary to the notion that dysphasia could explain these results.

In an attempt further to elucidate the nature of the relationships between the defects shown by the dominant group, Meyer (1959) carried out a number of other analyses of his data. For example, he first intercorrelated the scores obtained on the auditory learning tests before and after the operation to make sure that they measured something in common, which could therefore reasonably be called (e.g.) "auditory learning ability." The mean correlation found was 0.63, which confirmed that the tests had a fair amount of common variance.

Second, to see if differences in intellectual level could account for the apparent learning defects, he correlated both the Wechsler Full Scale and Progressive Matrices test scores with the scores on the auditory learning tests. These correlations were found to be low and insignificant, with a mean of .18, which showed that intellectual level could not account for the learning test results.

Third, in order to find out to what extent dysphasia was responsible for the deficits found, the dominant cases were divided into a group with marked or moderate dysphasia and a group with mild or no dysphasia. The group with most dysphasia showed most decline on the verbal tests involving recall.

Fourth, in order to examine the influence of visual field defects on the Wechsler Performance Scale results, all the cases were divided into three groups: one with severe defect, one with quadrantic defect, and one with minimal defect. Analysis of variance showed that the larger the field defect the greater the deficit on the Wechsler Performance Scale ($F = 9.40$; $p < .001$).

Fifth, correlations were sought between the patients' age, degree of deficit, and the amount of recovery with time. Few of these attained significance.

TABLE 4.6
Means, Standard Deviations, and the Significance of the Differences between the Preoperative and One-year Postoperative Test Scores for the Nondominant Group (N = 7)[a]

TESTS	PREOPERATIVE $\overline{m}$	PREOPERATIVE σ	ONE-YEAR POSTOPERATIVE $\overline{m}$	ONE-YEAR POSTOPERATIVE σ	*A*	*p*
Wechsler IQ's						
Verbal scale	106.00	24.77	112.86	24.82	0.181	.01 > .001
Performance scale	101.00	26.01	111.43	21.89	0.243	.05 > .02
Full scale	103.43	27.29	113.14	24.07	0.190	.01 > .001
Matrices' raw scores	46.43	11.34	49.14	10.61	0.279	.05 > .02
Mill Hill raw scores	50.14	24.96	52.00	23.14	0.337	n.s.
New word learning	9.57	8.30	7.86	5.05	0.611	n.s.
Paired Associate Tests						
AVR	19.57	16.83	13.57	5.65	1.034	n.s.
AVRg	14.85	10.38	11.86	4.41	0.682	n.s.
VVRg	11.71	3.15	11.14	2.73	2.875	n.s.
VDRg	13.71	19.36	9.57	9.96	0.695	n.s.
VDR	26.50	24.81	18.25	18.62	0.557	n.s.
TDRg	26.28	24.49	23.14	15.33	1.421	n.s.

[a] From Meyer, 1957b.

TABLE 4.7
Means, Standard Deviations, and the Significance of the Differences between the Preoperative and One-year Postoperative Test Scores for the Dominant Group (N = 10)[a]

TESTS	PREOPERATIVE $\overline{m}$	PREOPERATIVE σ	ONE-YEAR POSTOPERATIVE $\overline{m}$	ONE-YEAR POSTOPERATIVE σ	A	p
Wechsler IQ's						
Verbal scale	94.80	13.29	89.20	16.03	0.347	n.s.
Performance scale	102.00	12.79	102.00	13.15	0.000	n.s.
Full scale	98.20	13.50	95.20	14.87	1.035	n.s.
Matrices' raw scores	40.20	11.40	42.00	10.71	0.457	n.s.
Mill Hill raw scores	39.70	11.67	37.60	10.51	0.709	n.s.
New word learning	9.40	3.34	31.00	21.97	0.199	.02 > .01
Paired-Associate Tests						
AVR	20.80	12.30	54.50	19.82	0.134	< .001
AVRg	17.00	6.68	35.90	19.25	0.171	.01 > .001
VVRg	18.40	8.38	19.90	10.17	3.960	n.s.
VDRg	11.10	6.08	13.80	8.53	0.374	n.s.
VDR	20.40	21.12	25.80	30.39	0.676	n.s.
TDRg	27.00	15.96	28.20	14.63	5.041	n.s.

[a] From Meyer, 1957b.

Sixth, it was shown that the extent of the operation, within the reported limits of 4.5 to 8 cm. of dissected tissue, was not correlated significantly with any of the test deficits found one month after operation.

Overall, then, Meyer's (1959) study showed that the main, striking, and significant effect of dominant temporal lobectomy in human patients is the production of a verbal learning defect specific to the auditory modality of communication. Right-handed patients operated upon in the temporal lobe on the left side of the brain have great difficulty in learning material to which they are required to listen. This disability, unlike the transient dysphasia and visual field defects, was shown to be present one year (and also, in one case, four years) after the operation. Because the dominant cases could learn to associate verbal material when it was presented visually, this suggested that the content of learning was not crucial.

While Meyer made these findings in London, parallel but independent investigations were continuing at the Montreal Neurological Institute. Milner (1958) has reported on the results from that center, which were obtained from testing thirty temporal lobe cases, all said to be left-brain speech dominant. Half of this group was operated upon in the left (i.e., dominant) temporal lobe, half in the right (nondominant) temporal lobe; and all were tested before, and about three weeks after, the operation. In addition, twenty-two patients with "atrophic epileptogenic lesions of frontal or parietal cortex" were also similarly studied before and after brain operation to determine to what extent any deficits found might be specific to temporal lobe damage. The inclusion of such control subjects, of course, represented an advance on the design of the studies reported by Meyer.

Milner (1958) also divided her results into two main categories.

(1) General Intelligence
(2) Specific Defects
  (a) Defects of verbal learning
  (b) Defects of pictorial comprehension

These will be discussed below in the same order.

(1) *General intelligence.* Unfortunately. Milner (1958) did not give a full account of all the data that she must have collected on all the patients tested, but some of the highlights have been collated in Table 4.8. The patients were tested on Form I of the Wechsler Adult Intelligence Scale (Wechsler, 1944) before operation and on Form II afterwards. Significant differences were found ($t = 2.57$; $p <$ 05) between the Verbal and Performance Scale means for the right (i.e., nondominant) temporal lobe group *before* the operation (VSIQ = 107.16; PSIQ = 97.6), with these patients doing relatively more poorly on nonverbal tasks. The dominant group, on the other hand, showed no significant difference between the scales before operation; but showed a significant drop on the Verbal Scale after operation. It would, however, probably be dangerous to regard all of

TABLE 4.8
Mean Results Obtained on Wechsler Scales before and after Brain Surgery[a]

	VERBAL SCALE IQ's				PERFORMANCE SCALE IQ's			
GROUPS	*Preoperative*	*Postoperative*	*t*	*p*	*Preoperative*	*Postoperative*	*t*	*p*
Dominant	107.2	90.6	?	.001	107.3	105.0	–	n.s.
Nondominant	107.1	104.6	–	n.s.	97.6	96.2	–	n.s.

[a] After Milner, 1958.

these results as absolutely definitive because they have not been entirely confirmed by a re-analysis of some of Meyer's data, reported by Meyer and Jones (1957). Their results have been compiled in Table 4.9 in a way that allows comparison with Milner's findings.

It can be seen that the two sets of data are in accord so far as the pre- and postoperative comparison of the mean Verbal Scale IQ's in the dominant group is concerned. In both cases there was a significant drop after surgery, presumably caused by transient dysphasia. The English patients in this group, however, also showed a significant fall in Performance Scale IQ, which was not shown by the Canadian group. Meyer and Jones did *not* find the significant difference reported by Milner in the preoperative Verbal–Performance scale difference in her nondominant group.

(2) *Specific defects.* Milner (1958) also found specific and different defects separately associated with dysfunction of the dominant and non-dominant lobes. In anticipation of her results, it may be remarked that these findings are not entirely congruent with her earlier claim (Milner 1952, 1954) that a common defect of visuospatial perception resulted from damage to either temporal lobe.

(*a*) *Defects of verbal learning.* After dominant temporal lobectomy, Milner (1958) reported—like Meyer and Yates (1955) and Meyer (1957b, 1959)—defects of learning. She held these to be defects specific to verbal material, however, and found them to exist before the operation and to be exacerbated afterward.

The learning defects she found were shown by results obtained on the Wechsler Memory Scale (1945). This, unfortunately, is a poor test for any analytic purposes since it is composed of such heterogeneous items; it tests old and new learning, verbal and nonverbal learning, and it also confounds verbal material and the auditory mode of presentation. Milner, however, chose to show the learning defect by comparing the mean scores of her various groups on the Wechsler Intelligence Scales with their mean scores on the Wechsler Memory Scales, as shown in Table 4.10.

TABLE 4.9

Mean Results Obtained on Wechsler Scales before and after Brain Surgery[a]

	VERBAL SCALE IQ's				PERFORMANCE SCALE IQ's			
GROUPS	*Preoperative*	*Postoperative*	*A*	*p*	*Preoperative*	*Postoperative*	*A*	*p*
Dominant	93.7	83.9	.102	< .001	98.9	90.7	.133	< .01
Nondominant	102.3	104.0	1.521	n.s.	99.9	98.7	4.040	n.s.

[a] After Meyer and Jones, 1957.

TABLE 4.10
Comparison of Mean Intelligence and Memory Quotients before and Three Weeks after Operation for Left Temporal, Right Temporal, and Frontal Lobe Cases[a]

		PREOPERATIVE MEANS			POSTOPERATIVE MEANS		
GROUPS	*N*	*IQ*	*MQ*	*IQ–MQ*	*IQ*	*MQ*	*IQ–MQ*
Left temporal	9	106.6	91.2	15.4	95.1	77.4	17.7
Right temporal	12	102.5	102.2	0.3	102.8	107.8	-5.0
Frontal	9	101.6	94.8	6.8	93.0	92.6	0.4

[a] From Milner, 1958.

Analysis of variance confirmed that the dominant temporal lobe group was significantly worse in IQ–MQ score than either of the other two groups. Milner (1958) of course realized that the overall Wechsler Memory Scale score could not be held convincingly to demonstrate a specific verbal defect. She noted, therefore, that the dominant group did not show impairment on such nonverbal items as the "Memory-for-designs" subtest. Furthermore, she found the greatest difference between the groups on the "Logical memory" subtest, in which subjects are required to recall as many elements as possible of a brief narrative after it has been read aloud to them. In addition to the usual immediate recall, she required delayed recall from her subjects about ninety minutes after they had heard the story, with the results shown in Table 4.11. Milner reported that this preoperative difference between the groups was significant at well beyond the .001 level. She also later (Milner, 1962) reported similar data, both before *and* after

TABLE 4.11
Delayed Recall of Logical Memory Items from the Wechsler Memory Scale: Preoperative Scores of Left Temporal Group compared with a Mixed Group of Right Temporal, Frontal, and Parietal Lobe Cases[a]

		PER CENT RECALL	
GROUPS	*N*	Mean	Range
Left temporal	15	13	6–21
Mixed controls	29	25	8–42

[a] From Milner, 1958.

operation, for fifteen dominant cases; these results are shown in Table 4.12. It can be seen that, for these few patients at least, learning ability was still impaired years after the operation.

Altogether, these results supply a substantial confirmation of Meyer's findings that dominant temporal lobectomy in man produces a defect of learning. Milner's conclusion that this is an impairment of *verbal* learning is not, however, as convincingly supported by the data as was Meyer's conclusion that the defect is one of verbal learning in the auditory modality, since the tests Milner used confounded material and modality. It is, however, of great interest that even so coarse a test as the Wechsler Memory Scale showed a defect to exist even before operation, a fact not ascertained by Meyer's more analytic paired-associate items.

TABLE 4.12
Immediate and Delayed Recall of Logical Memory Items from the Wechsler Memory Scale: Pre- and Post operative (1–4 Years) Mean Scores for 15 Cases of Partial Dominant Temporal Lobectomy[a]

	PREOPERATIVE	POSTOPERATIVE
Wechsler IQ	107.9	110.8
Immediate recall	21.0%	16.8%
Delayed recall	12.7%	11.0%

[a] From Milner, 1962.

(*b*) *Defects of pictorial comprehension.* In the same study, Milner (1958) noted that the patients with nondominant lobe dysfunction showed a clear, specific defect on a pictorial test, which significantly differentiated them from the dominant group. It will be seen that this conclusion is rather different from the one reached in her earlier work.

This differential impairment was shown on the McGill Picture Anomaly Series (Hebb and Morton, 1943), which involves the detection by the subject of some incongruity in the content of a fairly crude drawing or cartoon. Two kinds of score may be obtained from this test. First, the mean number of errors made by Milner's groups are shown in Figure 4.5. This figure shows that the right temporal lobe patients made significantly ($p < .01$) more errors, both before and after operation, than did any of the other brain-damaged subjects or normal controls. Second, the amount of time taken to complete this test differentiated between the groups, as can be seen from Figure 4.6. The right temporal lobe group also proved to be significantly slower on this test than either the left temporal or frontal lobe groups even before operation, and it became even slower after the operation.

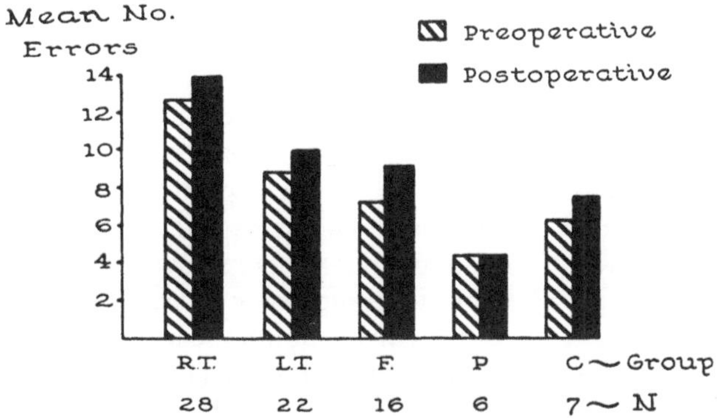

Fig. 4.5. Picture Anomalies Test mean error scores for right temporal (RT), left temporal (LT), frontal (F), and parietal (P) cases before and after operation, and for normal control subjects (C) tested twice. (From Milner, 1958)

These differences on the McGill Picture Anomaly Series between dominant and nondominant cases have not, however, been supported by th results of at least one independent study, reported by Shalman (1961). It has, however, been found by Kimura (1963) that right temporal lobe cases showed greater difficulty than left temporal lobe patients both in the immediate tachistoscopic perception and in the recognition of previously presented, unfamiliar visual designs.

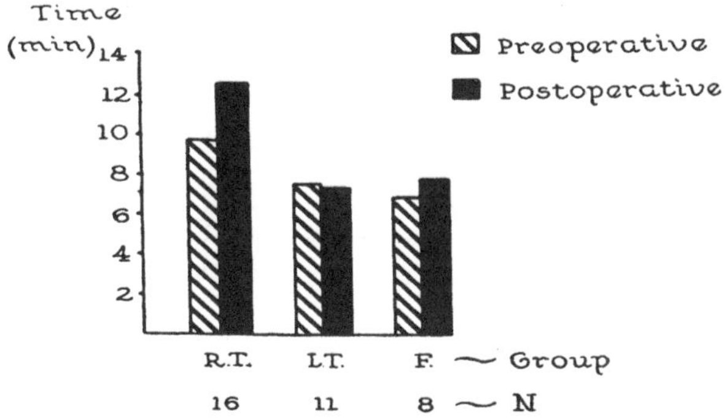

Fig. 4.6. Picture Anomalies Test time scores for right temporal (RT), left temporal (LT), and frontal (F) cases before and after operation, showing significant postoperative slowing for the right temporal group only. (From Milner, 1958)

The visuospatial effects of nondominant temporal lobectomy in man have not been secured as consistently as has the auditory learning defect after dominant temporal lobectomy. It seems, however, that very general, gross memory impairment is usually clinically evident after bilateral temporal resection in human patients. Such cases have been described by Scoville and Milner (1957) and by Milner (1959). The particularly deleterious effect of bilateral removal might, perhaps, be due to two factors.

In the first place, if the dominant lobe is removed, the minor lobe may still—to some extent—be able to compensate directly for the consequent defects by some process of transfer of auditory learning ability between the two lobes. In addition, it seems from Kimura's (1963) results that the nondominant lobe may subserve some visual learning function. It may be that patients who suffer from an auditory learning defect partly compensate for this by coming to rely more heavily, for example, on visual cues and aids to new learning. Removal of both the nondominant *and* the dominant lobe would rob the patient both of the possibility of transfer and of the possibility of substituting one kind of cue for another, thus resulting in the crippling, generalized memory disorder that has been reported in cases of bilateral temporal lobe removal.*

In a further analysis of the defects found after temporal lobectomy in man, Dr. Doreen Kimura, working at the Montreal Neurological Institute in association with Dr. Brenda Milner, has also used Broadbent's technique of dichotic stimulation (described in Chapter 3).

Kimura (1961) studied seventy-one patients whose chief presenting symptoms were the occurrence of epileptic seizures, usually due to atrophic

TABLE 4.13
Mean Age and Pre- and Postoperative IQ of Four Epileptic Groups[a]

GROUPS	N	MEAN AGE	MEAN IQ	
			Preoperative	*Postoperative*
Left temporal	33	30.0	109.5	103.6
Right temporal	18	33.7	109.4	104.4
Frontal	10	26.3	106.6	103.1
Subcortical	10	18.7	102.5	–

[a] From Kimura, 1961.

* Penfield (1959) has pointed out that bilateral interference with the hippocampal structures underlying the temporal cortex is a necessary condition for gross "memory" defect to appear after such surgery. This conclusion is supported by Brierley's (1961) review.

lesions dating from birth or infancy. The control data on the four groups into which these patients fell are presented in Table 4.13. Digits were read to these groups of subjects by a stereophonic tape-recorder under three different conditions.

(1) Two different numbers were presented simultaneously, one to the right ear, one to the left. Groups of six digits, each containing three such pairs, were required to be recalled. The pairs of digits were separated by about half a second. This was labeled the *simultaneous condition.*

(2) Six digits were presented alternately to the two ears with a half-second interval between numbers. This was labeled the *alternating condition.*

(3) All six numbers were presented to one ear with a half-second interval between the digits. This was labeled the *digit span condition.*

Kimura then chose initially to combine the scores made under conditions (1) and (2), which consisted of thirty-two groups of six digits each, making a total possible score of 192—or 96 for each ear. The mean totals of the four groups for this combined score on preoperative testing are shown in Table 4.14. Analysis of variance showed a significant difference between these mean scores ($F = 3.57$; $p < .02$), and subsequent t tests showed that the difference was due to a significant difference between the left and right temporal lobe groups, the left (i.e., dominant) temporal lobe group being significantly inferior.

TABLE 4.14
Mean Total Scores for Simultaneous and Alternating Digits for Four Epileptic Groups before Operation[a]

GROUPS	*N*	MEAN SCORE	RANGE
Left temporal	30	157.4	133 – 189
Right temporal	16	171.9	151 – 187
Frontal	9	165.3	139 – 186
Subcortical	10	161.8	134 – 186

[a] After Kimura, 1961.

The corresponding scores after operation for three of these groups are shown in Table 4.15. Analysis of variance of these scores produced an F ratio of 5.76 ($p < .01$); the difference between the temporal lobe groups was again significant ($p < .01$); and the difference between the left temporal and frontal group closely approached significance ($p < .06$). In fact, the operation produced a significant drop ($p < .02$) in the left temporal lobe group alone. It was also found that the impairment in all the temporal lobe cases was greater after operation in the contralateral than in the ipsilateral ear. Kimura has concluded, on the basis of these results, that temporal

TABLE 4.15
Mean Total Scores for Simultaneous and Alternating Digits for Three Epileptic Groups after Operation[a]

GROUPS	N	MEAN SCORE	RANGE
Left temporal	21	149.9	126–186
Right temporal	11	171.5	134–187
Frontal	8	164.8	136–191

[a] After Kimura, 1961..

lobectomy impairs the *perception* of auditory verbal stimuli. Her general conclusions were expressed as follows.

> Damage to the left (dominant) temporal lobe was found to impair overall performance on this task, irrespective of the ear to which stimuli were presented. In addition, unilateral temporal lobectomy on either side impaired the recognition of material arriving at the ear contralateral to the removal. This effect was independent of damage to the primary auditory receiving area, and it did not occur after frontal lobectomy. These results suggest that both temporal lobes take part in the elaboration of activity at the auditory receiving area of the same side, and that the left temporal lobe is particularly important in the perception of verbal material, at least in the auditory modality. (Kimura, 1961, pp. 164–165)

It has, however, been argued elsewhere (Inglis 1962b, 1965b) that the evidence provided by failure in output alone—of the kind cited by Kimura—cannot help us choose between possible alternative hypotheses. Thus output after dichotic listening might contain errors, as Kimura suggests, because the input had in fact failed to enter the system (i.e., because of a "perceptual" defect) *or* because the input had, for example, been subject to decay and/or interference while being held within the system (i.e., because of a "storage" defect), or both.

Kimura's interpretation, couched in terms of a "perceptual" defect, seems to neglect the importance of the storage processes that Broadbent (1958) has claimed enter into performance on this kind of task. His argument has been outlined and examined in Chapter 3 of this book, and need be only briefly reviewed here.

Broadbent (1958) suggested that the sequential recall of sets of digits. when they have been presented as simultaneous half-sets through different sensory channels (for example, both ears at once), requires the participation of some short-term store. Thus he showed that when digit-span stimuli were relayed to young normal subjects at a speed of two per second through headphones, half of the span to the left ear and—at the same time—the other half of the span to the right ear, these digits were in fact reproduced sequentially. One half-set was recalled first, and then the other, without much intrusion of the items from one half-span into the other. Under these conditions, the half-span recalled second usually contained more errors than the one recalled first; in other words, there was a kind of "serial-order" effect.

These facts led Broadbent to suggest that two kinds of mechanism may be involved in such performance. There is, first, a "*p* system" that can pass information only successively; second, there is an "*s* system" that can store such excess information as may arrive—for example, when the *p* stage is already fully occupied in dealing with information from another channel. The notion that there is a short-term storage process that deals with excess information may also be applied to the case where the two sensory channels lie within different sense modalities. In another experiment, Broadbent (1956) presented the half-spans simultaneously to eye and ear together, with similar results, showing that these phenomena are not peculiar to hearing but may be generalized to different senses.

In Chapter 3 it was suggested that it is this kind of storage system that deteriorates with age and breaks down in senility, producing the "poor memory for recent events" that is characteristic of some persons in the senium.

To see if Kimura's (1961) data reflect similar storage dysfunction—limited as this may be in temporal lobe patients to auditorily delivered material and to the half-spans recalled second in the contralateral ear—it would be necessary to analyze her data differently from the way she analyzed it. Account would have to be taken not only of total score, or simply of ipsilateral and contralateral recall, but also of which half-span is principally affected in each case. As she reported that the significant impairment shown by the contralateral ear was found only under conditions of simultaneous stimulation, and not under conditions of alternating stimulation, it is of crucial importance to know if the contralateral ear was usually employed by her subjects as the "storage" ear.

The storage hypothesis can be used not only to mediate predictions about the data already available, it can also produce expectations about data not yet collected.

So far as available data are concerned, it would be predicted that the significant difference found in response to dichotic stimulation by Kimura (1961) between left-sided and right-sided temporal lobe patients was due principally, if not entirely, to the poorer recall by the former group of the second half-span in each case, especially when this half-span was the one originally read into the contralateral ear.

So far as further predictions are concerned, advantage might be taken of Broadbent's (1956) demonstration that his model can also account for the effects of cross-modality simultaneous stimulation. Thus if there are modality-specific storage processes (and if, in the case of hearing, these are also side-specific), differences would be expected between patients perhaps before operation, and certainly after operation, in their responses to various kinds of simultaneous stimulation, depending on whether the operation had been in the dominant temporal lobe. Such dominance might of course best be established by the technique of injecting sodium amytal into the internal carotid artery (Wada & Rasmussen, 1960) rather than by the crude description of handedness used by Meyer (1957b).

In the case of left-brain speech dominant patients, it would be expected—if auditory storage alone were impaired—that if these patients were required to respond sequentially to simultaneous stimuli delivered auditorily and visually (a half-span to each sensory channel), the order of recall specified by the examiner would be crucial for the demonstration of deficit (Broadbent, 1957). If the instructions required the subject to recall the auditory stimuli before the visual, no impairment more marked than the serial-order effect described by Broadbent (1957) would be predicted.

In his terms, in this case, the auditory material would pass through the "perceptual system" related to that modality without involving storage. The visual material would be processed by a modality-specific "storage mechanism" unaffected by the dominant-side operation. If, however, the patient were now required to recall each auditory half-set after the visual half-set, the presumed damage to the storage mechanism in the auditory modality would result in a defect in the recall of these digits much more marked than the anticipated serial-order effect. The technique could be further refined by transmitting the auditory digits to one ear at a time. In this case it would be expected that the greatest deficit would appear in the dominant group when the material to be recalled second was transmitted to the contralateral ear.

It is, in any case, hard to see how the kind of disorder found by Meyer (1959) could be ascribed to changes in auditory perceptual functions alone. The patients in Meyer's studies could hear, understand, and repeat the words involved in the auditory paired-associate tests; they simply failed to connect them one with the other. Kimura (1961) admits that, under ordinary circumstances, it is difficult to show any effect of temporal lobe lesions on the efficiency of hearing with either ear. She suggests that under relatively abnormal circumstances (for example, accelerated speech, words accompanied by "white" noise, and so forth) slight defects in perception can be shown in the ear contralateral to the temporal lobe lesion. It is hardly conceivable, however, that these rather subtle changes could themselves produce the gross learning defects described by Meyer (1959) and by Milner (1958).

Kimura (1962) has disputed the relevance of the alternative hypothesis that relates her findings to a storage defect, but she has, as yet, not presented an analysis of her data in a form that would permit an evaluation of the order-accuracy of recall as compared to the side-accuracy of recall. She has pointed out that it is not incumbent on those who use Broadbent's technique also to employ his theoretical model. This argument would have more weight if a powerful alternative model were at the same time offered. It still seems, however, that Broadbent's original hypothesis can better comprehend the results of dichotic listening studies in cases of both generalized and specific learning defect, and can also generate more new and testable expectations, than any other hypothesis yet put forward to account for these phenomena.

In general, the investigations described in this chapter represent some of the most illuminating experimental evidence yet put forward concerning brain and behavior relationships in man. When one considers, for example, the large volume of work carried out and the small amount of return secured in the study of the effects of frontal lobectomy (Willett, 1960), it can be seen that, by comparison, these investigations have proved remarkably informative.

These results have suggested, perhaps for the first time, a rationale for the systematic detection of a specific kind of brain damage. Meyer and Falconer (1960) studied eight patients with space-occupying lesions or scarring of the temporal lobe. Five of these had dominant, and three had nondominant lesions. They were assessed on the same battery of tests as had been used in Meyer's (1957b) temporal lobectomy study. Each case was tested twice: from one to twenty-one days before operation, and from twenty-six to thirty-two days after operation (for removal of growth or scar).

No significant changes were seen in the intelligence tests. Changes in learning test performance are summarized in Table 4.16. The "*z* scores" in this table are derived from the formula

$$\frac{X_1 - \overline{X}}{\sigma x} = z;^*$$

in other words, they express each individual's score in terms of standard deviation units. It may be seen, then, that if an individual's score lay exactly *at* the mean, the corresponding *z* score would be zero. Scores above the mean are of course positive, they are negative below the mean and the larger they are the further they deviate from the mean.

---

*In this case, $\overline{X}$ was the mean preoperative score of a group of dominant temporal lobe epileptics, and σx was the standard deviation of their distribution of scores.

TABLE 4.16

Z-scores on Learning Tests as Compared with Norms Provided by Temporal Lobectomy Cases before and after Operation[a]

CASE NOS.	NWLT		AVR		AVRg		VVRg		VDRg		VDR		TDRg	
	Pre[b]	*Post*[c]	*Pre*	*Post*	*Pre*	*Post*	*Pre*	*Post*	*Pre*	*Post*	*Pre*	*Post*	*Pre*	*Post*
Dominant														
1	−7.03	+0.72	−3.27	+0.63	−2.01	+0.36	+0.48	+0.75	+0.71	+1.10	+0.39	+0.34	−0.49	+0.80
2	−2.58	+1.32	−1.94	+2.45	−0.12	+1.25	+0.35	+0.85	−0.008	+0.25			+0.72	+0.39
3			−4.51	−0.67	−2.15	+0.18	+0.86	+0.75	+0.24	+0.53	+0.30	+0.34	+0.18	−0.41
4	−3.61	+1.32	−4.09	+2.12	−1.47	+1.29	+0.36	+1.36	+0.55	+0.39	−0.28	+0.38	−0.83	−0.68
5			−0.03	+1.98	+0.28	+1.11	+1.23	+1.15	+0.71	+1.10	+0.55	+0.54	+1.12	+0.86
Non-dominant														
1	+0.05	+0.08	−0.02	−0.05	+0.53	+0.18	−0.65	−1.16	+0.38	−0.40			−0.25	+0.14
2	+0.20	−0.73	+0.20	−0.35	−0.05	+0.05	+0.89	+0.14	−0.44	−0.78	−0.06	+0.01	+0.24	+0.14
3	+0.35		+0.67		+0.41		+0.51		+0.37		−0.06		+0.29	

[a] From Meyer and Falconer, 1960.
[b] Preoperative scores related to scores of temporal lobe cases before operation.
[c] Postoperative scores related to scores of temporal lobe cases after operation.

Meyer and Falconer conclude from this evidence that

> Consistent with our expectations, most of the dominant cases before operation manifested a considerable impairment of auditory learning ability but not of visual or tactile learning, the scores for which remain comparable with our controls. In cases 1, 2, 3, and 4 the preoperative assessments with the three auditory verbal tests (NWLT, AVR, AVRg) mostly lie outside the preoperative distributions of the control group of dominant temporal-lobe epileptics. Only on AVRg do scores of cases 2 and 4 fall within the range of normal deviations, and even then their scores are high and in the expected direction of deficit. After operation there was no improvement in auditory learning in cases 1 and 3, which again was to be expected as the pathological nature of the lesions did not allow of recovery of the damaged portions of the temporal lobes. In cases 2 and 4, however, clinical recovery occurred as a result of operating, and in both cases considerable improvements on all the auditory learning tests were recorded so that their scores came to be within the preoperative distributions of the normative data. The two scores of these two patients, therefore, show striking improvements, and these improvements are probably due to restoration of normal temporal-lobe function consequent upon successful therapy without excision of any part of the temporal lobe. (1960, p. 476)

In other words, a naturally occurring disorder may have deleterious effects similar to, and be detectable by the same means, as neurosurgical excision of electrically abnormal tissue.

These studies, then, provide evidence of the usefulness of the psychological measurement of behavior as a dependent variable when the main, powerful independent variables lie substantially in the hands of the neurosurgeon. They constitute only one promising example of the collaborative, *experimental* study of abnormal behavior.

5

THE EFFECTS OF *Sensory Deprivation*

IT IS of course possible to manipulate the behavior of organisms, even to create abnormalities of behavior, without interfering directly with tissue structure. In this chapter, consideration will be given to experiments in which the powerful independent variables have been conceived and handled at the behavioral level.

This group of studies deals with what, at first sight, would seem to be a very simple kind of input; that is, little or no input at all. This work comprises conditions that have loosely been tied together by the label "sensory deprivation" (Solomon *et al.*, 1961).

These investigations began under the direction of D. O. Hebb of McGill University. Their ostensible concern was to see how human subjects would react to an excessively monotonous environment. Hebb (1961) has revealed, however, that another, covert purpose of these studies was to find out if a general reduction of stimulus variation would make these subjects more susceptible to the effects of propaganda, since elements of isolation and deprivation seemed to be part of the so-called "brainwashing" of political prisoners in Communist countries.

In the initial study, described by Bexton, Heron, and Scott (1954), the subjects were normal, male college students. They were paid to lie in bed twenty-four hours a day, in a lighted cubicle, and were allowed out only to eat or to go to the toilet. Their perceptual activities were restricted in a number of ways throughout the course of the experiment; for example, they wore translucent goggles that transmitted diffuse light but prevented pattern vision. Except when they were eating or were at the toilet, they wore gloves and long cardboard cuffs. The latter extended from below the elbow to beyond the fingertips, thus permitting free joint movement but limiting tactile sensation.

The subjects wore earphones, and communication between the subjects and the experimenters was maintained by a small speaker system, but—with exceptions that will be noted later—this communication was kept to a minimum. The earphones, in fact, helped to limit auditory stimulation, which was further reduced by the fact that the cubicle was partially sound-proofed; and each subject had a U-shaped foam-rubber pillow on which his head rested while he was in bed. A continuous hum from the air-conditioner, extraction fans, and the amplifier leading to the earphones in the pillow produced a continuous masking noise. A plan of the cubicle is shown in Figure 5.1. (The leads to the electroencephalograph were not used in the early experiments.)

The McGill group found that the principal effects of such treatment seemed to be upon (1) *cognitive* functioning and (2) *perceptual* functioning.

In addition to these effects, some very general observations were made. For example, the subjects tended to sleep quite a bit during the earlier sessions—but less as the experiment progressed. Bexton, Heron, and Scott noted:

> Later they slept less, became bored, and appeared eager for stimulation. They would sing, whistle, talk to themselves, tap the cuffs together, or explore the cubicle with them. This boredom seemed to be partly due to deterioration in the capacity to think systematically and productively. . . . The subjects also became very restless, displaying constant random movement, and they described the restlessness as unpleasant. Hence it was difficult to keep subjects for more than two or three days, despite the fact that the pay ($20.00 for a 24-hour day) was more than double what they could normally earn. Some subjects, in fact, left before testing could be completed. (1954, p. 71)

Consideration may first be given to the effects of this perceptual isolation on cognitive processes.

1. EFFECTS ON COGNITIVE PROCESSES.

Bexton, Heron, and Scott (1954) initially used twenty-two male college students as subjects in the situation described. In order to test the effects of isolation on general cognitive functioning, some intelligence test items were given before, during, and after the isolation experience. Obviously, if these were to be given *during* isolation, as well as before and after, they had to be items of the oral question-and-answer type. A second group of tests, requiring the manipulation of material, was given only before and after isolation.

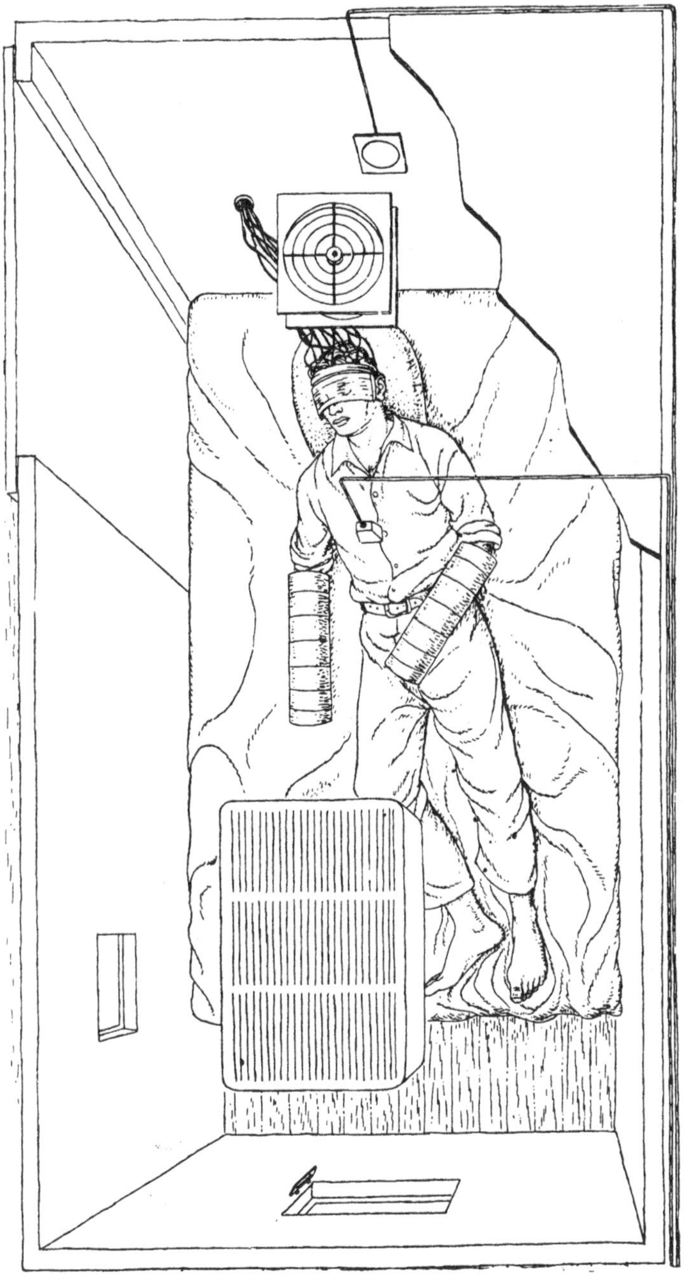

Fig. 5.1. The experimental cubicle with the ceiling cut away. The air-conditioner is above Ss feet and the exhaust fan is above his head. Also shown are a microphone and a receiver. (After Heron, 1957)

The first set, for which the results of twelve subjects are mentioned in the Bexton, Heron, and Scott (1954) paper, comprised the following.

- Multiplying two- and three-digit numbers
- Arithmetic "catch" problems
- Completing number series
- Making a word from jumbled letters
- Making as many words as possible from letters of a given word

Henceforth these tests will be referred to as subgroup I(A). Each subject was tested before going into the cubicle:

- 12 hours after going into the cubicle
- 24 hours after going into the cubicle
- 48 hours after going into the cubicle
- and on the third and fourth days after coming out of the cubicle

Twelve control subjects were given the same series of tasks at the same intervals. Bexton, Heron, and Scott (1954) noted that the experimental subjects were inferior to the controls on all these tasks, but that—perhaps because of the small number of subjects used—the differences were significant only for the "error" score on one of the word-making tasks above, as shown in Figure 5.2. In their discussion, however, they did not specify to which aspect of this graph the significance figure was attached. Neither did these authors cite a full list of the other tests given before and after experimental treatment: they stated only that the experimental subjects were significantly inferior ($p = < .01$) to the control subjects—on *leaving* the cubicle—on the Kohs Block Design Test and the Wechsler Digit Symbol Test. They were also significantly slower in copying a prose paragraph.

In a later paper, Scott, Bexton, Heron, and Doane (1959) reported further and in more detail on the cognitive effects of perceptual isolation; first, in relation to the same sort of intelligence test items described above, and second, on the susceptibility of subjects to "propaganda."

The intelligence test items again fell into two groups.

Group I: Intelligence test items

Subgroup I (A) included the five types of subtests already mentioned, and again they were given before, during, and after the isolation experience. Subgroup I (B) included (*a*) associative learning, (*b*) the Wechsler digit span test, and (*c*) an "analogies test."

These two sets were given twenty-four hours before the subject went into isolation and one hour before they came out of isolation. I (A) and I (B) together comprised what the authors called the "cubicle battery."

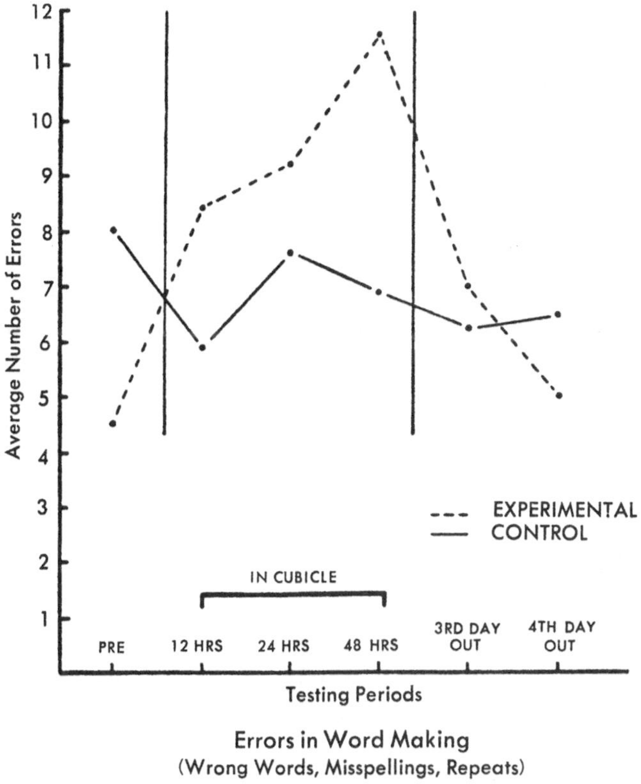

Fig. 5.2. Mean error scores for experimental and control subjects before, during, and after the isolation period on word-making test. (From Bexton, Heron, and Scott, 1954)

Group II: Items requiring the manipulation of test material

Although Scott *et al.* (1959) called this the "postcubicle" part of the battery, forms of it were also given twice, forty-eight hours before the isolation experience and immediately after the subjects came out of isolation.

This group was composed of the following items.

(*a*) Kohs blocks (Kohs, 1923)
(*b*) Wechsler digit symbol (Wechsler, 1944)
(*c*) Thurstone–Gottschaldt figures
(*d*) Copying a passage of unfamiliar material
(*e*) Delta Blocks Test (Hebb, 1945)
(*f*) McGill Picture Anomalies (Hebb and Morton, 1943)
(*g*) Mirror drawing

The "propaganda" material

This involved a ninety-minute recorded talk in favor of belief in all kinds of psychical phenomena, including telepathy, clairvoyance, ghosts, poltergeists, and psychical research.

The attitudes of the subjects to these phenomena were measured by questionnaire scales. There were fourteen such scales, and each scale consisted of five statements indicating different degrees of belief in the relevant phenomenon. Complete belief in any of the first four scales would be indicated by a score of 36, uncertainty by a score of 18, and complete disbelief by a score of zero. Each section of the questionnaire had a secondary set of scales that was concerned with the amount of interest that the subject felt in the topic and how important he felt it to be.

Scott *et al.* (1959) reported results on an experimental, perceptually isolated group, and on a control group. In the former group there were initially twenty-nine subjects, but only eighteen stayed in isolation long enough to complete part A of the cubicle battery; all were male college students with a mean age of about twenty-two years (age range 19–30). There was also a control group of twenty-seven male students, also with a mean age of about twenty-two (age range 19–32). Eight additional controls were tested on the "propaganda" part of the test. The schedule of testing was as shown in Table 5.1. The control subjects were of course given the same tests at the same intervals, without the isolation experience.

The propaganda records were first offered to the experimental subjects after they had been in isolation for eighteen hours. At that time each subject was told that there was a series of records that he could listen to if he wanted to. If he asked for a record, only one was played at that time, but he could ask for another whenever he wished. He was not told anything about the content of the records. The nine records were played through in series as the subject asked for them. When they were finished he was told "Those are all the records. You may have any of them you want played through again." On further requests, if no specific record was mentioned, the series was given in the original order, one record for each request. The control subjects were treated in a similar way. They were told about the records at approximately the same time in the testing schedule as the experimental subjects, and they were made to listen to the records at least once.

TABLE 5.1
Schedule of Testing[a]

PRE-ISOLATION

1–2 Weeks	*48 Hours*	*24 Hours*	*Immediately Pre-isolation*
1. Interview 2. 1st. administration of attitude questionnaire	1. 1st. form of the "post-cubicle" battery	1. Cubicle battery A 2. Cubicle battery B	1. Cubicle battery A 2. 2nd. administration of attitude questionnaire

ISOLATION

12 Hours	*24 Hours*	*48 Hours*	*1 Hour Pre-release*
1. Cubicle battery A	1. Cubicle battery A 2. "Propaganda" records	1. Cubicle battery A 2. "Propaganda" records	1. Cubicle battery B

POST-ISOLATION

Immediately	*3 Hours*	*3 Days*	*4 Days*
1. Post-cubicle battery	1. 3rd. administration of attitude questionnaire 2. Interview	1. Cubicle battery A 2. Interview	1. Cubicle battery A

[a] After Heron, 1961.

Group I

The results on subgroup I (A) of the "cubicle battery" may be portrayed as follows.

(*a*) *Multiplying two- and three-digit numbers.* The results for this test are shown in Figure 5.3. It would seem from the authors' comments that no statistically significant differences emerged on this particular item, either in or out of the isolation situation.

(*b*) *Arithmetic "Catch" problems.* The results for this subtest are shown in Figure 5.4. Again, there do not appear to be any significant differences between the groups.

(*c*) *Completion of number series.* These results are shown in Figure 5.5. The experimental group did significantly worse ($p = < .05$) than the controls on the first cubicle test trial.

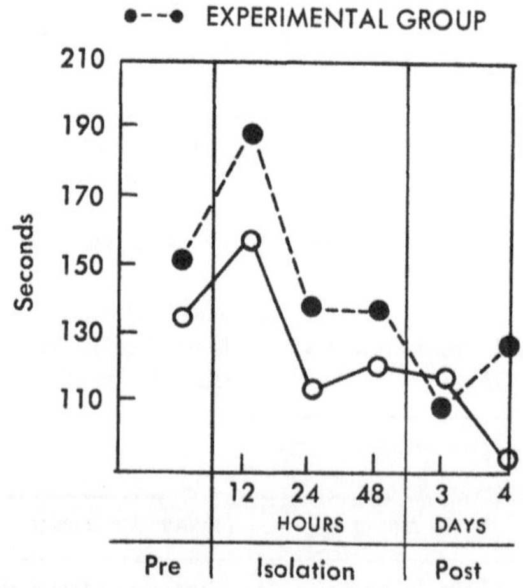

Fig. 5.3. Time taken on multiplication problems. (After Heron, 1961)

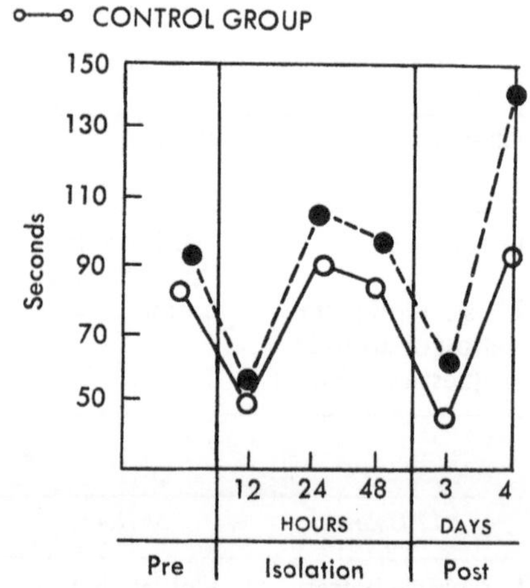

Fig. 5.4. Time taken on arithmetic "catch" problems. (After Heron, 1961)

(*d*) *Word making*. The results for this subtest were as shown in Figure 5.6. On this item *all* the isolation trials appear to be different, with the control group better than the experimental group; in fact, the latter group was significantly inferior ($p = < .02$) on all three test periods during isolation. Scott *et al.* also noted that on the word-making test the experimental

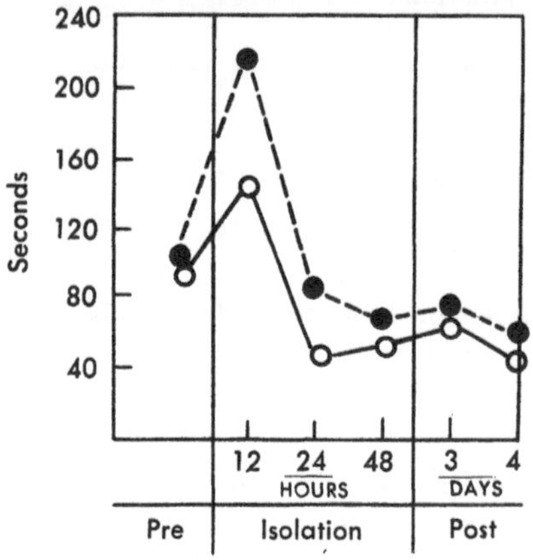

Fig. 5.5. Time taken on number series problems. (After Heron, 1961)

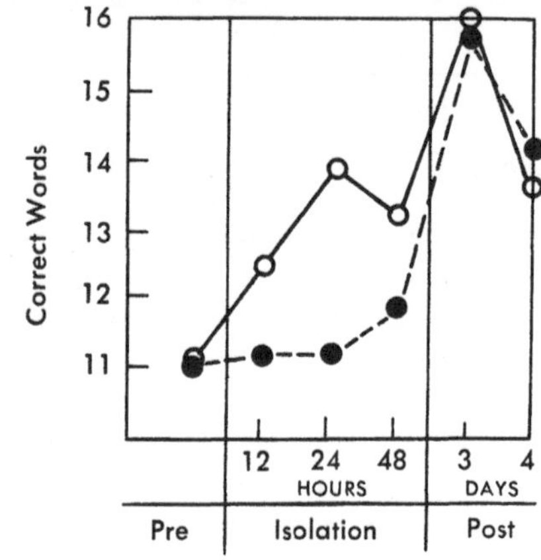

Fig. 5.6. Number of correct words produced on word-making problems. (After Heron, 1961)

subjects made significantly more errors at the first test period in the cubicle ($p = < .05$) and at the last ($p = < .02$). They also made fewer words altogether (correct plus incorrect words) than did the control subjects.

(*e*) *Anagrams.* Results for the two groups on this test are shown in Figure 5.7. The difference between the groups for the mean of all the isolation trials on this test approached significance ($p = < .10$). On the anagrams test the difference between the *error* scores of the two groups at the twenty-four hour test period was also significant ($p = < .05$).

No significant difference between the groups appeared on any of these tests when they were given outside the cubicle.

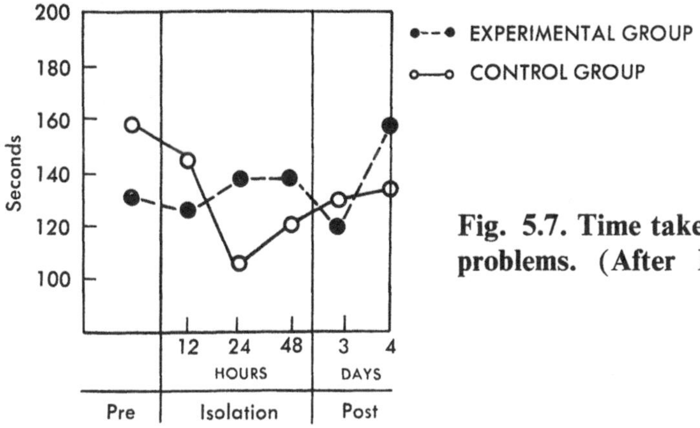

Fig. 5.7. Time taken on anagram problems. (After Heron, 1961)

So far as subgroup I (B) of the cubicle tests was concerned, there was no significant difference in performance between the two groups on associative learning, digit span, or the analogies test.

Group II

It may be recalled that the post-cubicle battery comprised seven items, forms of which were administered forty-eight hours before isolation and immediately after release from isolation. In six out of seven of these tests there were significant differences, in the "expected" direction, between the two groups, as shown in Table 5.2. The more apparent differences in this post-cubicle battery, as compared with the less significant differences shown by the cubicle battery, could conceivably have been due to the fact that the control subject's interest in the latter set flagged markedly with successive retestings—whereas they did not have so much chance to get bored with the post-cubicle battery. In any case, the latter results are strongly suggestive of some deterioration in performance on some cognitive tests after the perceptually deprived isolation experience.

TABLE 5.2
Mean Scores of the Experimental and Control Groups on the Post-cubicle Battery: p Values Based on Difference Scores[a]

TESTS	SCORE BASIS	EXPERIMENTAL GROUP			CONTROL GROUP				
		N	$\overline{m}$ *1st Testing*	$\overline{m}$ *2nd Testing*	*N*	$\overline{m}$ *1st Testing*	$\overline{m}$ *2nd Testing*	*t*	*p*
1. Kohs' blocks	Total time (secs.)	20	1088	931	25	1095	762	3.09	.01
2. Digit symbol	No. correct	19	52.9	68.2	24	52.0	74.5	3.34	.01
3. Thurstone–Gottschaldt	No. correct	12	5.5	5.4	18	5.2	8.1	3.29	.01
4. Copy passage	Time seconds	18	594	640	25	634	639	2.03	.05
5. Delta blocks	No. correct	12	9.4	13.2	19	11.4	19.9	3.31	.01
6. Picture anomalies	No. of errors	15	3.0	5.9	23	4.0	4.9	3.36	.01
7. Mirror drawing	Time seconds	12	219	108	19	223	103	0.45	.10

[a] From Scott, Bexton, Heron, and Doane, 1959; and Heron 1961.

The "propaganda" material

Attention may now be given to the effects of the "propaganda" material. These results may again best be summarized as in Table 5.3. They reflect the fact that, on the whole, *both* groups showed a significant change in attitude (toward greater belief) after listening to the records, but the changes shown by the control group tended to be smaller than those recorded by the experimental group. Scott *et al.* (1959) noted that only four out of thirty-five in the control group wanted to hear the records more than once, whereas sixteen out of twenty-four experimental subjects asked for repetitions.

The authors have commented that this might lead us to believe that the results obtained were due to the fact that the experimental subjects spent a longer time listening to the propaganda than the controls. They have also pointed out, however, that even if this were the case the results could still be attributed to isolation since it would mean that one of the effects of isolating the individual would be to make him willing to listen to material that he would normally avoid, and listen to it often. Presumably, this is because he becomes so bored that any form of stimulation is better than nothing at all. There did not, however, seem to be a y relationship between the number of times that the subject listened to the records and the degree to which his attitudes were changed.

Both during and some time after the isolation experience, the experimental subjects reported subjective difficulty in concentrating and in thinking.

The results so far may perhaps be best stated in the authors' own words, in which they concluded that

To sum up, the results indicate that the experimental conditions produced some deterioration in performance on some tests of cognitive ability while the subjects were in isolation and after they had emerged. Subjects reported that their minds wandered, and that they were no longer able to find anything to think about. It seems, too, that they became abnormally preoccupied with whatever patterned stimulation they did receive. These results may be attributed to some general disorganization of brain function which is also involved in the hallucinatory activity, disturbances of visual function and abnormal EEG's which occur under conditions of perceptual isolation. (Scott *et al.*, 1959, p. 208)

TABLE 5.3
Effects of Propaganda[a]

	EXPERIMENTAL GROUP			CONTROL GROUP			
ATTITUDE SCALES	*2nd Admin. (A) (Mean)*	*3rd Admin. (B) (Mean)*	*Significance of B–A*	*2nd Admin. (C) (Mean)*	*3rd Admin. (D) (Mean)*	*Significance of D–C*	SIGNIFICANCE OF (B–A)–(D–C)
1. Telepathy	20.21	26.92	< .001	18.30	24.50	< .001	> .10
2. Clairvoyance	16.08	25.10	< .001	16.26	22.09	< .001	< .07
3. Ghosts	8.00	17.46	< .001	11.80	16.31	< .001	< .03
4. Poltergeists	9.04	18.83	< .001	11.74	16.83	< .10	< .05
5. Psychical research	15.42	18.53	< .001	15.23	16.51	< .001	> .10
6. Total scale (1 to 5)	68.75	106.54	< .001	73.40	91.51	< .001	< .02
7. Interest	23.50	31.00	< .001	26.89	29.60	< .001	< .01
8. Importance	9.00	13.04	< .001	9.40	11.34	< .001	< .01

[a] From Heron, 1961.

2. EFFECTS ON PERCEPTUAL PROCESSES

Changes in perceptual functioning were commented upon by Bexton, Heron, and Scott (1954) in their preliminary report on the effects of sensory deprivation. Such effects were principally in the visual modality, and could be roughly divided into two types, depending on whether they occurred *during* or *after* isolation.

It will be recalled that in the McGill experiments the experimental subjects wore translucent goggles in the lighted cubicle, and that these transmitted diffuse light but prevented pattern vision. Under these conditions, some subjects reported visual experiences that resembled hallucinations.

The first kind of visual effects to appear were described by some subjects as like "having a dream while awake." When the experimenters then began specifically to ask subjects to report any visual imagery they experienced during isolation, *all* of the subjects so prompted reported more-or-less-complex hallucinatory-like experiences, varying from changes in "shading" in the visual field, through the appearance of lines and dots, to "wallpaper pattern," and right up to "a procession of squirrels with sacks over their shoulders marching purposefully across a snowfield and out of sight."

In addition to such visual effects there were also a few reports of hallucinatory kinds of phenomena involving other senses. One subject heard speech accompanying his visual hallucinations; another kept hearing the sounds of a musical box. Some subjects also described kinaesthetic and somaesthetic phenomena. One subject felt that he was two overlapping bodies at the same time, and he drew a diagram (Figure 5.8) to show how he felt.

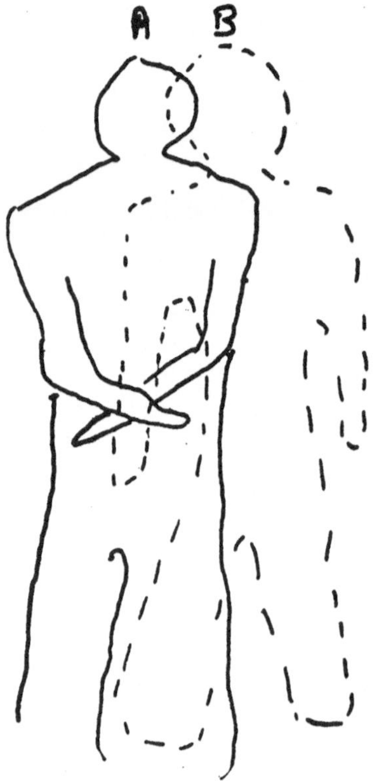

Fig. 5.8. Drawing made by subject who felt he was two people in cubicle, and was briefly undecided whether he was really A or B. (From Bexton, Heron, and Scott, 1954)

These changes were further reported upon by the investigators on the basis of their own experiences under the same conditions. Heron, Doane, and Scott (1956), themselves acting as experimental subjects, all reported hallucinatory activity after the first day of isolation. At first these were simple in form (dots, mosaics, etc.), and later became more complex (scenery, people, etc.).

There is some evidence, however, that reduced pattern vision alone may have produced such "hallucinations." Thus in the study by Doane, Mahatoo, Heron, and Scott (1959)—specifically aimed at investigating changes in perceptual function after isolation—seventeen experimental subjects were studied. Of these, thirteen went through the cubicle procedure, and of these two wore *opaque* (not translucent) masks. The four other subjects wore translucent masks only; and no gloves nor cuffs nor restraints in the cubicle were employed with them.

So far as hallucinations are concerned, Doane *et al.* (1959) reported that, among the "cubicle" subjects, of the eleven who wore the translucent goggles eight developed "hallucinations," of the two who wore opaque masks only one developed them. However, when in the latter cases translucent goggles were substituted for the opaque masks, *both* reported vivid hallucinations. Conversely, of those who wore the translucent blinders, five of the "worst" hallucinators—who were then put in complete darkness—at first reported an *increase* in the vividness of these visual phenomena, but later, within two hours, they reported a marked decrease; in three of these five cases they disappeared altogether. When these subjects were again presented with diffuse light stimulation, the hallucinations immediately reappeared. Of the four subjects who were masked with translucent goggles, but not otherwise constrained, two reported these hallucinatory phenomena.

Such results suggest that the principal element influencing the appearance of this kind of visual effect is unpatterned diffuse visual stimulation, not necessarily accompanied by any restriction of the other senses. Doane *et al.* (1959) have noted, however, that with multiple sensory restrictions the visual hallucinations seem to be more severe.

One difficulty with these hallucinatory phenomena is that, by their nature (as it is so far understood), they are available only to qualitative analysis. In addition to these within-cubicle effects, however, the original investigators reported curious effects after emergence from isolation, which have since been more systematically investigated. Thus Bexton, Heron, and Scott (1954) found that after release from isolation many subjects appeared to suffer a disturbance in visual perception, usually lasting no longer than one or two minutes. Their subjects reported difficulty in focusing, and they claimed that objects appeared fuzzy and did not stand out from their backgrounds. Some also said that there was a tendency for the environment to appear two-dimensional, and for colors to seem more saturated than usual.

These claims were examined, in terms of the investigators' own experience, by Heron, Doane, and Scott (1956). All three observers spent six days under conditions of perceptual isolation, and, on emergence, they reported visual effects that were "unexpectedly profound and prolonged." They were able to distinguish five kinds of effect, as follows.

(1) *Apparent movement independent of movement by the observer.* There was a pronounced unsteadiness and "drifting" of the visual field.

(2) *Apparent movement associated with head or eye movements of the observer.* They experienced an apparent "loss of position constancy."

(3) *Distortions of shape.* There was observed to be a tendency for straight edges and surfaces to seem curved, for fixated surfaces to bulge outward.

(4) *After-images.* Two out of three observers had pronounced negative after-images simply from looking at ordinary objects in a room.

(5) *Color and contrast effects.* Colors were seen as brighter, more highly saturated than normal. Some even looked luminescent.

Such effects were analyzed in a more systematic way in a later study, reported by Doane, Mahatoo, Heron, and Scott (1959). The experimental subjects in this study included seventeen male college students, thirteen of whom were confined in the cubicle (eleven wearing translucent and two wearing opaque masks); and four wore translucent masks but were not otherwise restricted. Twenty normal controls were also tested. As well as qualitative reports obtained both during and after isolation, the subjects in this experiment were given a variety of tests: of (1) visual perception, (2) somaesthesia, and (3) spatial orientation. The latter two kinds of tests were given before entering the cubicle and again after forty-eight and seventy-two hours of restriction. The visual tests were given only before and after incarceration.

(1) *Visual perception.* In addition to a series of standard tests, the subjects who were confined to the cubicle were asked to give a qualitative judgment of any changes they might have experienced on being released. Of the kinds of effect that Heron, Doane, and Scott (1956) reported from their own experience, the later subjects also reported qualitative changes in (1) spontaneous movements, (2) induced movement, (3) surface distortions, and (4) linear distortions—with the results shown in Table 5.4. Doane *et al.* (1959) were able to report on twenty subjects because they included the earlier observations of Heron, Doane, and Scott (1956).

The formal tests used for the estimation of changes in visual perception in the experimental group, as compared with the control group, are cited in Table 5.5. Doane *et al.* (1959) give only confidence levels for changes that *did* prove to be significant. Doane *et al.* concluded from these results that there are certain general areas of perception that seem to be affected

TABLE 5.4
Incidence of Various Disturbances of Visual Perception Immediately on Coming Out of Restriction: Qualitative Observations of 20 Subjects[a]

SPONTANEOUS MOVEMENTS	INDUCED MOVEMENTS	SURFACE DISTORTIONS	LINEAR DISTORTIONS
18	12	16	18

[a] From Doane *et al*, 1959.

by the isolation procedure. They argued that results from the visual tests indicated that the most prominent effects involved a decrease in the constancies and an increase in the after-effects of stimulation (figural after-effect, color adaptation, and the after-image of movement). From the table it can be seen that size constancy was markedly reduced, and shape constancy slightly reduced.

(2) *Somaesthesia.* Two tests of somaesthetic function were given. The first of these was a tactile form discrimination test that involved wire shapes

TABLE 5.5
Tests of Visual Perception and Changes in the Experimental Group as Compared to the Control Group[a]

TESTS	CHANGE IN EXPERIMENTAL GROUP	*p* VALUE
1. Critical flicker frequency	No change	
2. Figural after-effect	Increased FAE	.02
3. Size constancy	Decreased SC	.02
4. Visual acuity	Improved VA	.10
5. Phi-phenomenon	No change	
6. Brightness contrast	No change	
7. Autokinetic effect	Increased AE	.001
8. Color adaptation	Increased CA	.01
9. Shape constancy	Decreased SC	.10
10. Brightness constancy	No change	
11. Necker cube reversals	No change	
12. Archimedes spiral AF	Increased AE	.05
13. Tachistoscopic perception	No change	

[a] After Doane *et al.*, 1959.

glued to cards. On the first pre-isolation test the subject was shown the forms; he was then masked and required to recognize them by touch. The second and third tests were for tactile recognition after forty-eight and seventy-two hours of isolation, respectively. The results are shown in Table 5.6. Because of subject drop-out, only eight experimental subjects were available at forty-eight hours and only seven at seventy-two hours. It can be seen from this table that while the control subjects showed slight improvement, presumably due to practice (over the three test periods), the performance of the experimental subjects was significantly worse.

TABLE 5.6
Mean Error Scores on Form Discrimination at Three Test Periods[a]

	TEST PERIODS			*p*-VALUES	
GROUPS	*1. Pre-isolation*	*2. 48 Hours*	*3. 72 Hours*	*1–2*	*1–3*
Experimental	2.06	3.30	2.70	.001	.02
Control	2.63	2.08	2.03		

[a] From Doane *et al.*, 1959.

The second test of somaesthetic function was the two-point limen measured with the standard aesthesiometer. The two-point threshold was taken in four locations: (1) tip of left index finger, (2) volar surface of left forearm, (3) inner surface of right upper arm, and (4) forehead, just above the nose. The method of limits was used: one ascending and one descending series. The results of this testing are shown in Table 5.7. These results show a *decrease* (better performance or increased sensitivity) in the two-point limen for the experimental subjects in three of the four loci.

(3) *Spatial orientation.* This function was also tested in two ways. First came a paper-and-pencil test in which a pencil was held by the masked subject and placed at the starting point on a sheet of paper. He was instructed to move left 3 inches, make a right turn and go 2 inches, another right turn and 2 inches, a left turn and 3 inches, and so on, with a total of five turns. He was told that each turn was to be a right angle, and was warned that at the end he would be required to draw a straight line back to his starting point. The scoring system used was based on deviations of distances and angles from the correct ones.

Heron (1961) has provided an illustration of the kinds of change shown on the test by members of the experimental group, which is shown in Figure 5.9; the actual numerical results are shown in Table 5.8. It can be seen

TABLE 5.7
Mean Values for Two-point Thresholds[a]

		TEST PERIODS			p VALUES	
LOCI	GROUPS	*1. Pre-isolation*	*2. 48 Hours*	*3. 72 Hours*	*1–2*	*1–3*
Finger	Experimental	1.7	1.7	1.7	n.s.	n.s.
	Control	1.7	1.5	1.6		
Forearm	Experimental	29.6	26.7	24.0	.15	.15
	Control	23.4	23.3	23.7		
Upper arm	Experimental	29.1	21.9	23.8	.002	.05
	Control	32.8	32.8	32.4		
Forehead	Experimental	19.8	16.9	19.2	.02	.02
	Control	9.2	9.2	9.2		

[a] From Doane *et al.*, 1959.

TABLE 5.8
Mean Total Angular Deviations in Paper-and-pencil Spatial Orientation Test[a]

	TEST PERIODS			p VALUES	
GROUPS	*1. Pre-isolation*	*2. 48 Hours*	*3. 72 Hours*	*1–2*	*1–3*
Experimental	40.6	140.0	56.4	.05	.05
Control	58.8	57.0	53.3		

[a] From Doane *et al.*, 1959.

TABLE 5.9
Mean Total Angular Deviations in the Walking Spatial Orientation Test[a]

	TEST PERIODS			p VALUES	
GROUPS	*1. Pre-isolation*	*2. 48 Hours*	*3. 72 Hours*	*1–2*	*1–3*
Experimental	112.5	121.3	135.0	.10	.001
Control	146.5	115.8	102.8		

[a] From Doane *et al.*, 1959.

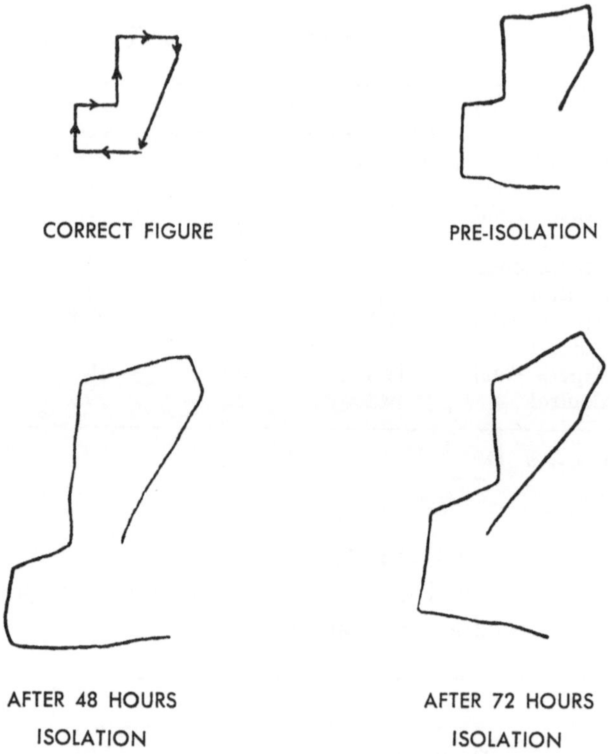

Fig. 5.9. Drawings of one experimental subject on paper-and-pencil orientation test. (From Heron, 1961)

from this table that there was much more deterioration in the performance of the experimental group than in the control group (especially after forty-eight hours).

Second, each subject's orientation was judged by his walking a similar course in an empty room. The comparative angular deviation scores for the groups on this test are shown in Table 5.9. Heron noted that their behavior on this test was congruent with what seemed to happen, so to speak, to their "real-life" orientation. Thus he remarked that a similar type of behavior was shown when the subjects were taken out to the toilet, in that sometimes, towards the end of the isolation period, they would become lost in the washroom and have to call to the experimenter to help them find the way out—in spite of the fact that on earlier visits they had been able to orient themselves adequately.

Doane *et al.* (1959) considered that these disturbances in spatial orientation might be a function of disorders of "spatial imagery" of a visual kind. These authors concluded that

> These results emphasize again the profound degree of disturbance that is produced by the isolation procedure as observed in this laboratory and elsewhere. Hallucinations of extreme vividness, impairment of thought processes, sensory and perceptual changes, together with significant changes in the EEG, all testify to the widespread effect on central neural functions that is induced simply by limiting the normal variation of sensory stimulation. (1959, p. 218)

The EEG changes mentioned in this statement have been briefly discussed by Heron (1961), who discovered that there was progressively slower EEG activity during the isolation period, while records taken when the subjects reported hallucinations showed alpha-blocking, and, in general, appeared similar to those that might be obtained from a subject in an alerted state.

These, then, were the principal accounts of the pioneering work in the field roughly subsumed by the title of sensory deprivation. The main question to be considered here is: What is the relevance of this material to abnormal psychology? Before any attempt can be made to tackle this problem, however, a number of other factors must at least be mentioned.

In the first place, since this work was done at McGill there has been an enormous development of interest in the topic. In their bibliography of the relevant literature up to 1962, Arnhoff and Leon were able to cite over 330 items. This burgeoning of interest has created both a diversification of techniques and a realization that differences in method may well produce differences in results. Very interesting analyses of the many variables that may be involved in "sensory deprivation" have been made, for example, by Ruff, Levy, and Thaler (1961), and by Brownfield (1964). They have distinguished several important elements.

(*a*) *The quantity, modality, and pattern of sensory input.* The original studies at McGill involved a reduction in the *patterning* of stimuli rather than any great reduction in absolute level of stimulation. On the other hand, some of the studies carried out at Princeton, by Vernon (1963) and his associates, have involved the use of a lightproof and soundproof enclosure.

(*b*) *The type of enclosure employed.* The way in which the subjects have been cut off from stimulation may be of considerable importance. This may, of course, range from the use of the eyeless leather mask, cited by Alcorn (1960), to the "hydrohypodynamic environment" used by Lilly (1956) and Shurley (1960), in which the subject is completely submerged in lukewarm water and breathes by means of an air-pump.

(*c*) *The amount of activity permitted.* In the original McGill studies, the subjects were instructed to move about as little as possible. As part of his extensive series of studies, Zubek (1964) has gone on to investigate the effects of immobilization imposed in the absence of other sensory constraints (Zubek, Aftanas, Kovach, Wilgosh, and Winocur, 1963; Zubek and Wilgosh, 1963).

It is therefore evident that a number of considerations can affect the outcome of this kind of experiment. Perhaps not the least influence is exercised by the kind of subject used. Even among the normal student subjects in the McGill studies, there were those who could tolerate the conditions at least until an experiment had completed its course. Others simply had to be released prematurely.

It is to be argued here that the different reactions of certain abnormal subjects is of importance for an understanding both of their disorders and of the mode of action of the deprivation condition itself.

In spite of the fact that striking changes are produced by grossly reduced stimulation, there seems to be a dearth of plausible hypotheses to account for the results obtained. This is, no doubt, partly due to the fact that—as we have seen—the term "sensory deprivation" has been used to label a multitude of fundamentally different conditions. These, in turn, have produced different findings, which are difficult to link together.

Among the attempts that have been made to integrate the various results within some framework, two broad classes of hypotheses may be discerned. These two classes derive from the two aspects of the "ghost-in-the-machine" analogy (Ryle, 1949) so often employed in the explanation of psychological phenomena, especially in the abnormal field.

First, there are explanations couched in terms of the neurological "machinery," whose function is held to underlie experience and behavior. Much attention has, for example, been paid to the arousal systems of the central nervous system, particularly to the ascending reticular activating system (or ARAS). The most detailed description of its likely role has been given by Lindsley (1961), who goes so far as to suggest that the action of the ARAS is the principal common factor at work in the kinds of disturbance that follow not only upon sensory deprivation but are also a consequence of sensory *distortion* (such as the effects of the delay of auditory feedback on speech processes) and sensory *overload.*

Since, however, the behavioral effects of these three conditions are so different, it is difficult to see why one should wish first to look for a *common* factor in their geneses. Deprivation and distortion, for example, appear to result in disorders of perception and cognition, and in stammering, respectively. It would therefore seem more profitable to try to construct hypotheses to account for the markedly different behaviors that are the consequence of these procedures.

At its simplest, the ARAS seems to be conceived as a kind of goad to the activity of the nervous system. Lindsley (1961) contends that the ARAS, together with the thalamocortical projection system, provides a general arousing and alerting mechanism. In this view, it is presumed to serve, for example, in adjusting the organism's level of attention or anticipation. Lindsley admits that active stimuli seem to be required to keep its functions going, and that—without such stimulation—boredom, inactivity, and ultimately sleep would be expected to prevail.

Here, however, the central difficulty of this hypothesis, in relation to the effects of sensory deprivation—at least in our present state of knowledge—seems to be exposed. Conceived of in this way, it would seem that, under conditions of sensory deprivation, there would be very little to keep such an arousal system ticking over. Somnolence and apathy would then be the likeliest outcome. Instead, there is evidence—such as that provided by Vernon *et al.* (1961)—that under conditions of deprivation the subjects certainly may go to sleep to begin with, but, with increasing time, they actually tend to become more awake and more alert individuals.

It is of course true that a more complex model might even explain this added complication, but unless we can spell out with a higher degree of precision the exact relationships between the mechanics of our model and our observations of behavior, there is a considerable danger of (at worst) substituting mystery for ignorance or (at best) replacing one kind of puzzle with another.

The second category of hypotheses comprises those that concern themselves with mental processes, or the functions of the "ghost" considered apart from the "machine." Quite a number of workers for example, have tried to deal with the effects of perceptual isolation in relation to abnormal psychology in terms of psychoanalytic theory. In Solomon's (1961) text, for example, these theorists are represented by Kubie (1961), by Azima *et al.* (1961), and by Goldberger and Holt (1961).

The last two authors conceive of the isolation effects somewhat as follows. They have claimed that the isolation situation is one in which there is crucial interference with "reality contact." This, they contend, results in a decrease in the efficiency of the so-called "secondary processes," that is, in rational, purposive, reality-attuned thinking, together with a facilitation of the "primary processes," or unrealistic, prelogical modes of thought and thought that involves inappropriate drive instrusions. Individual differences in susceptibility to the effects of isolation, Goldberger and Holt have said, can be explained in terms of the "ego strength" of the subjects involved. Thus the individual high on ego strength will be less dependent on reality contact for the maintenance of the stabilizing secondary processes than will the person who is low on ego strength. The former individual, it is claimed, will not be overwhelmed by his instinctual impulses and will show the least disturbance, whereas the latter will suffer more from restlessness, boredom, and other unpleasant forms of affect.

One major weakness of this kind of formulation has been pointed out by Kubie (1961), although he himself seems to favor a psychoanalytic hypothesis to explain behavior disturbances under isolation conditions. As he points out,

> It is obvious that some people go to pieces more easily than others. This has led to the use of such metaphorical terms as "ego integrity," or "ego strength" or "ego vulnerability." Unfortunately, these purely descriptive figures of speech are often mistaken for explanations of the phenomena. Actually, such terms are merely after-the-fact, allegorical descriptions of the end-results of what happens. (1961, pp. 214–215)

Azima *et al.* (1961) have suggested that the extreme dependency involved in the isolation experiments (e.g., demand feeding, demand evacuation, and the like) is conducive to a kind of "regression" that they say is one of the bases of the kinds of behavior disorganization that have been reported. It would seem difficult, however, to account convincingly for the effects observed by Hebb's group in these terms, other than by a series of *post hoc* rationalizations.

In fact, neither element of the traditional ghost-in-the-machine model seems particularly adequate for the description and/or explanation of the consequences of sensory deprivation. Even when aspects of this model account, to some extent, for what is already known, it is extremely difficult to see how they can enable the investigator to anticipate results that have not yet been obtained, or how they could cope with the curious variations that have been found in the experimental phenomena. It does seem possible, as the author has suggested elsewhere (Inglis, 1965c), to put forward a very simple behavioral (or "neuropsychological") model that may be superior to previous hypotheses, at least in these latter respects.

As Hebb (1958b) has reemphasized, all behavior—from the simplest motor activity to the most complex "thought process"—is to some degree dependent upon sensory control (and, it might be added, is to some degree dependent upon what may be called "sensory storage"). It is well known, for example, how the loss of sensory feedback from the limbs, as in tabo-paresis, can disrupt such an apparently simple motor activity as walking. Similarly, it is possible to imagine some such negative feedback cycle as the following being involved in more abstract perceptual and cognitive activities. The very simplest model must first require (for example, in problem solving) the initiation—by the elements of the problem presented—of the consideration of a number of solutions. This process may be conceived, in Hebb's (1949) terms, as the setting off of chains of cell assemblies and phase sequences.

Second, these solutions will be checked back against the elements of the problem in order to evaluate each of them for goodness of fit.

These processes may be looked upon as complementary and as functioning—at least in the normal individual—as a kind of negative feedback loop. It can be seen that this procedure resembles the Test – Operate – Test – Exit cycle described by Miller *et al.* (1960). Both the problems provided and the solutions attempted will, in addition, involve more or less "storage capacity," since, in many cases, all elements of the problem that has been set will not be immediately available—to be seen or heard—but will partly consist of instructions of a kind that require some input to be "stored," at least for the period during which solutions are being sought.

Similarly, the various solutions considered will not always have a concrete effect on the problem, although they *may* have. Often enough, however, it will be of importance also to "store" solution trials during the task period, and sometimes it may even be necessary to store impressions of goodness of fit between problems and answers.

This model suggests that *one* of the ways in which sensory deprivation may have deleterious effects upon cognitive functioning is by *depriving the acting, perceiving, problem-solving organism of the stimulus manifold against which his attempts at acting and problem solving may continually be checked.* Since, however, a certain amount of storage has been postulated as taking place in all phases of this adjustive cycle, again, in the *normal* organism, disturbances of perceptual and cognitive functioning would not be expected to appear immediately upon the elimination or reduction of the organism's sensory supports.

Initially, at least, both the nature of the problem and the probability of the solutions attempted might be kept within reasonable bounds by recent learning, or, in other words, by the storage of those relevant items related to the problem and its solution that were secured before deprivation. However, as these stored elements decay, the oscillations of solution-search might be expected to become wider and wider—and, for that matter, wilder and wilder—as the necessary constraining contacts with the problem elements diminish in availability in even their stored form.

It can be seen from this model that if a subject were denied both sensory support *and* storage capacity, the onset of the disruption of behavior would be expected to be much more rapid, and the disturbance itself would be likely to be more severe than in the normal person. Some of the earliest observations of sensory deprivation phenomena confirm this expectation. Thus Cameron (1941) some twenty-five years ago showed—in the case of elderly patients said to be suffering from nocturnal delirium—that their wandering and confusion could rapidly be induced by placing them in a darkened room during the day. This demonstrated that their disorientation was not brought about by the development of fatigue (as had formerly been supposed, since their symptoms were, characteristically, worse at night) but through cue-deprivation. Since these patients also showed severe learning disability, Cameron himself suggested that such delirium may be based on an inability to maintain a spatial image without the assistance of repeated visual stimulation. A number of these patients also showed a severe distortion of spatial imagery (e.g., in the displacement of the remembered positioning of environmental objects) within an hour of being blindfolded.

The results of this early experimental work are supported by clinical observations of the often extraordinary disruptive effects on behavior of operations for cataract in the elderly (Bartlet, 1951; Ziskind *et al.*, 1960). More evidence relevant to the effect of sensory constraints on the elderly has also been provided by Leiderman *et al.* (1958), who have described eight illustrative cases of transient psychiatric symptoms appearing in patients undergoing physical restraints as a sequel to such disorders as poliomyelitis, and after orthopedic surgery, and the like. It seems worthwhile to note that these authors state that

> Six of our eight cases were sixty years of age or older. It is possible that these elderly patients had varying degrees of organic brain disease. It is true that the acute and rapidly reversible mental changes seen in our elderly patients may be considered to be typical of early organic brain disease. It should be noted, however, that once the symptoms disappeared as the result of sensory stimulation, they did not recur. (1958, p. 394)

In terms of the present model, these symptoms could be conceived as being due to the disrupting effects of interference of the normal feedback cycle in individuals relatively handicapped in storage capacity, since it has been shown (Chapter 3) that short-term storage ability does seem to diminish with increasing age.

Here, then, as a consequence both of experimental and theoretical considerations, we may immediately derive an important implication for psychiatric practice itself. As Leiderman *et al.* have said:

> Having considered organic and emotional factors which may play a role in delirious states, we believe we have established that sensory deprivation is one other element that must be thought of. For example, if an elderly patient becomes disturbed and noisy, he may be given sedative drugs and be moved to an isolated room because of consideration for other patients. Such a maneuver, unfortunately, might enhance sensory deprivation and actually heighten the aberrant behavior. Thus, failure to consider the presence of sensory deprivation may lead to therapy which is diametrically opposed to that which is appropriate.
>
> The therapy of sensory deprivation is actually its prevention. It may be as simple a matter as the avoidance of darkness, silence and solitude. It may involve keeping on a night light, the provision of a radio or television set, or the presence of another

person. In more complex form it would include ward organization to enhance social contact, increased attention to more stimulating hospital decor, and music, occupational and recreational therapy.

At the same time, it becomes obvious that unduly prolonged bed rest, the use of "back wards" in psychiatric and general hospitals, and the excessive use of sedatives and restraints should be avoided. (1958, pp. 394–395)

Experimental studies in the geriatric field, also carried out at McGill University by Dr. V. A. Kral and his associates (Kral, Grad, Cramer-Azima, and Russell, 1964), have shown interesting differences in physiological indices of stress between young, old, and senile subjects in response to simple blindfolding.

It is difficult to see how other current hypotheses, couched either in terms of the ARAS or the ego, could lead one to expect these findings. It has also been suggested, however, that—for *some* psychiatric cases, at least—the effects of sensory deprivation seem to be beneficial. Harris (1959), for example, in studying a small group of patients, found that schizophrenics under conditions of sensory restriction may, initially at least, show some improvement. How, then, can the model advocated here cope with such findings?

In attempting to explain these results, further consideration must be given to aspects of the simplified perceptual-cognitive feedback cycle that has been described above.

Again taking the case of problem solving, it seems reasonable to suppose that in *normal* cognition those stimulus elements that are not relevant to the problem on hand are first "filtered out," thus limiting the *range* of possible problem solutions initially considered. The checking process, once initiated, then acts back, further to constrain the selection of possible answers as those solutions that were based on actual elements of the problem—but did not fit when they were checked—are discarded.

Now it is possible that the very first stage of these processes may be impaired in some kinds of thought disorder. It has been shown (Chapter 2) how an inadequate "filtering" of irrelevant elements in the first stage may even be the basis of the "overinclusive" kind of thought disorder that is believed to be characteristic of some schizophrenics. Such overinclusion has been shown in the performance of these patients on tests of concept formation. These patients will fail to preserve conceptual boundaries and will tend to include such a number and variety of categories that the problem becomes too generalized and too complicated for any solution to be reached.

By definition, however, neither phase of the simplified cyclical scheme of cognitive functioning put forward here can be affected without the other being, to some extent, impaired. In the overinclusive person, then, and under ordinary conditions of stimulation, the normal negative feedback process may from time to time be replaced by an increasingly disorganizing *positive* feedback cycle. Thus inefficiency of the filtering stage will cause the necessary checking procedures to be more complex and difficult; and impairment of the checking phase will result in a failure to reduce the ever wider consideration of even more irrelevant solutions. Clinically, the effect of such a positive feedback cycle may be a "blocking" of thought processes as too many impulses crowd and jam some parts of the efferent system— or even mania as all these impulses explosively emerge together.

It may in this way be suggested that patients already suffering from this kind of overinclusive thought disorder (i.e., some "schizophrenics") may show at least an initial *improvement* under conditions of restriction of the sensory environment because, for a time, the events that for them make up the *positive* feedback cycle are interrupted. The superabundance of stimulus elements that ordinarily bombard them are, so to speak, now filtered down for them by the new environmental constraints. It would be expected, however, that any improvement such patients show would last for only a very short time since the lack of sensory support for the checking phase would eventually outweigh any benefits they might at first derive from reduced input.

The data presently available on psychiatric patients fail, however, to provide an adequate test of this expectation. Studies reported by Gibby, Adams, and Carrera (1960), and by Cooper, Adams, and Gibby (1962), have found beneficial effects of sensory deprivation on some psychiatric patients including schizophrenics. Studies that have failed to show improvement, however, have also been reported—by Smith, Thakurdas, and Lawes (1961), and Cleveland, Reitman, and Bentinck (1963).

One possible reason for these incompatible findings may be that, as was noted in Chapter 2, the classification of schizophrenia comprises, a heterogeneous collection of disorders. The hypothesis advanced above is meant to refer not to this class in general but to overinclusive schizophrenics in particular.

Some additional evidence of the plausibility of the argument advanced comes from studies of the effects of the reduction of the sensory environment in the case of subjects receiving psychotomimetic drugs. It seems likely that some of these drugs act principally to decrease the efficiency of the first filtering stage of perception proposed above. Although it does not seem that any of the objective psychological research that has been devoted to such drugs (Rubin, 1957) has been directed specifically at this question; nevertheless, keen observers, such as Huxley (1956), have described their principal effect as the reduction of the efficiency of what Huxley calls the "cerebral reducing valve"—a conception that seems much like the "filter" proposed above.

One study of the combined effects of a psychotomimetic agent (Sernyl) and reduction in the sensory environment has been described by Cohen *et al.* (1960). The results of this investigation may best be summed up in the authors' words, as follows.

> Sernyl, without environmental sensory deprivation, produced the psychological changes in these (experimental) subjects which have previously been described as typical resultants of the drug. These include body image distortions, feelings of unreality and depersonalization, inability to maintain directed thinking, and hypnagogic phenomena. Also, instances of echolalia, echopraxia and catatonic-like posturing occurred. The usual statements of feeling "crazy" and "out of control" were readily expressed. Nausea and vertigo were prominent physiological symptoms.
>
> The most distinctive and interesting result of the combined condition was the fact that sensory isolation considerably damped the psychopathological and physiological effects of Sernyl. All subjects characteristically expressed the feeling of being more in control and less disturbed than with Sernyl alone. (1960, p. 346)

Since Cohen *et al.* (1959) had previously shown that some schizophrenic subjects also respond well to sensory deprivation, Cohen *et al.* (1960) have put forward an explanatory notion that is not unlike the hypothesis already detailed. They state:

> An interesting alternative possibility is that the psychotic-like state produced by Sernyl resembles schizophrenia to the extent that Sernyl-injected subjects tolerate sensory deprivation in the manner previously described as characteristic of schizophrenic subjects by Harris (1959) and by Cohen *et al.* (1959). These investigators found that schizophrenic patients responded to sensory isolation with much less anxiety and with more positive feelings than did control subjects.
>
> These observations may signify that the clinical psychosis of schizophrenia, like the model psychosis produced by Sernyl, engenders indiscriminate aversion to environmental sensory stimulation. Perhaps schizophrenic withdrawal is based upon the need to reduce or regulate normal levels of sensory influx which are too intense, too distorted, and hence too terrifying for the patient to tolerate. It may not be anxiety which produces perceptual dysfunction in schizophrenia, but quite the other way around. (1960, pp. 347–348)

The Sernyl-sensory deprivation interaction is somewhat complicated by the fact that Sernyl was originally described (Meyer, Greifenstein, and Devault, 1959) as a drug that *caused* sensory deprivation symptoms! In another study, which also suggested that reduced stimulation mitigated the effects of the drug, however, Lawes (1963) concluded that, while it might be regarded as schizophrenomimetic, its mode of action was *not* one of sensory deprivation.

While reduction in sensory inflow might, then, be expected to reduce overinclusive thought disorder, conversely, it might be expected that a modest degree of stimulation should be beneficial for some of even the most deteriorated of senile patients suffering from memory disorder. Emphasis here is on the adjective "modest," since any overload of stimulation is likely to call on other capacities that also are impaired. There is an analogue to this in physical medicine in that a modest amount of exercise may be good for wasted muscles where more strenuous activity would be bad.

The effect of social stimulation even on patients said to be suffering from persistent senile confusion, and hence ordinarily believed to have a doom-laden prognosis, has in fact been studied by Cosin *et al.* (1957, 1958). The behavior of such patients was rated before and after treatment, which involved organized social activity, craftwork, and the like. Such treatment was shown to have a significant, if transitory, effect. These authors concluded that

> So far as medical practice is concerned, any of the treatments used in this investigation will maintain persistently confused patients, who on account of a relatively long expectation of life may rightly be called "chronic," at a more dignified level of existence than is usually achieved in the geriatric wards of general and mental hospitals. (Cosin *et al.*, 1958, p. 42)

A neat demonstration of the simple variables that may control social stimulation and interaction in geriatric wards is provided by the work of Sommer and Ross (1958). In their study they were able to show that the mere redisposal of furniture could produce very significant changes in communication on a geriatric ward. If, for example, the chairs were grouped around small tables instead of being neatly ranged against the walls, this in itself nearly doubled the amount of verbal interaction between patients. In fact, these authors were able to show that the arrangement of furniture to secure social interaction may be as important a factor in stimulating patients as the more obvious amenities of ward decoration and the like.

In summary, then, it seems possible to put forward a much simplified model of perceptual and cognitive functioning, which is based on Hebb's (1949) original neuropsychological model, and which accounts for data on the effects of sensory deprivation at least as well as the perhaps more fashionable hypotheses about the ARAS or the ego. It is claimed that this hypothesis also generates further, testable expectations, and unites the experimental phenomena with some important problems in psychiatry and abnormal psychology.

The data reviewed also help show the possibility of an important interaction between the kind of studies described in the first part of this text and the complex kind of changes that may be brought about by reduced variation in the sensory environment.

6

THE EFFECTS OF *Reinforcement*

THE FINDINGS described in the last chapter illustrate the remarkable influence that the lack of environmental stimulation may have on behavior. Given the minimum necessary variation, however, human behavior—normal or abnormal—tends to be relatively independent of the effects of immediate external stimuli. Only in reflex reactions, such as blinking at a puff of air in the eye, do we find a more or less one-to-one relationship between stimulus and response.

A distinction between such simple reactions and more complex activities has been drawn by B. F. Skinner (1938), who has proposed the recognition of two classes of behavior. The first and lesser class is comprised of elicited responses, or such *respondent* behavior as the eye-blink. The second category, on the other hand, consists of emitted responses, or *operant* behavior. This class includes all those actions that are not necessarily evoked by particular, known stimuli. Although such operants cannot be elicited in the same way as respondents can, their emission, and in particular their *rate of emission*, can be brought under experimental control by the application of appropriate *schedules of reinforcement*. The central contention of Skinner's system might therefore be stated as follows. *If the occurrence of an operant is followed by the presentation of a reinforcing stimulus, the strength of the operant is increased.*

The typical experiment that Skinner and his students have carried out deals with learning behavior in which the organism performs some action, like lever-pressing, which is reinforced by the delivery, say, of a small quantity of food. In the case of the animal subjects often used (rats, pigeons, etc.), behavior is usually studied—for convenience—in some kind of restricted enclosure. This has become known as the "Skinner box," a term that Skinner (1959) himself does not approve.

The main aspect of this performance, with which Skinner and his associates have dealt, is *rate of responding* in terms of *cumulative response curves.* Thus a typical record obtained from a single organism over a brief period of time would resemble the curve in Figure 6.1.

Fig. 6.1 Section of a cumulative response curve. (From Skinner, 1959)

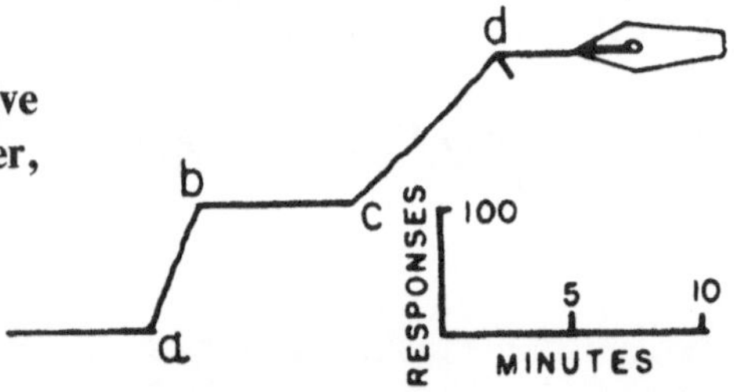

The figure shows a response curve in which the subject emitted about 100 responses between *a* and *b*, and then produced no responses—for about five minutes—between *b* and *c*. Between *c* and *d* a further 100 responses were completed, at a rather slower rate, since it can be seen that the slope of a–b is rather steeper than the slope of c–d. The southeast tick at *d* indicates that a reinforcement was delivered at that point. Typically in operant conditioning, not every response is reinforced, but some schedule of intermittent reinforcement is applied to the behavior of the subject. It is also worthwhile noting that, for this kind of curve, failure to respond (or "extinction") is represented by a horizontal line and not by a return to some zero baseline (as in ordinary learning curves).

A great deal of work has gone into the study of the effects of the various possible schedules of reinforcement on the behavior of lower organisms (Ferster and Skinner, 1957). These include such variants as the *fixed-ratio* schedule, in which a response is reinforced only after it has been emitted a certain number of times (e.g., one in five). In the *variable-ratio* schedule, the number of responses that must be emitted before a reinforcement is administered is allowed to vary around an average value. Other varieties of reinforcement schedule include the *fixed-interval* and the *variable-interval* schedule. All of these schedules have been extensively examined for their different effects on the emission and extinction of responses.

The promise of Skinner's scheme for the study of human behavior, both normal and abnormal, is considerable. For one thing, most human behavior is better characterized as operant than as respondent. Attempts to deal with human behavior in respondent terms have made it necessary to refer to many kinds of "internal" stimuli. Often enough, these are not only in practice but even in principle unobservable and uncontrollable—and therefore unsatisfactory for inclusion in any systematic theory. Since the understanding and control of operant behavior is not achieved through the manipulation of unknown or inaccessible eliciting stimuli but by specifiable reinforcing consequences, the whole range of human activity can at least be conceived in operant terms.

One of the first examples of the deliberate application of operant techniques to abnormal human behavior is to be found in a study by Fuller (1949), who undertook the operant conditioning of what he called a "vegetative human organism." This was an eighteen-year-old idiot, an inmate of an institution for the feeble-minded. Since this boy could make no organized movements of his body or limbs, but moved his arms occasionally, the response selected for reinforcement was a movement of his right arm to a vertical or near-vertical position. The usual technique of "successive approximations" was used; that is, any spontaneous movements similar to the desired movement were reinforced until the required behavior itself was evinced and recorded.

This subject was deprived of food for fifteen hours, then, when he moved his right arm at all, a small amount of sugar-milk solution was injected into his mouth through a tube. After two series of four sessions of reinforcement, Fuller reported that the rate of emission of the desired responses averaged about three per minute and were "well differentiated"—thus making an addition to this subject's repertoire of responses that was, at this particular level of functioning, quite appreciable.

Perhaps the earliest extensive and systematic attempt to apply operant principles to abnormal behavior has been made in the series of investigations conducted and supervised by Dr. O. R. Lindsley, formerly Director of Harvard Medical School's Behavior Research Laboratory at the Metropolitan State Hospital in Waltham, Massachusetts. His work has in fact ranged from the observational, descriptive use of operant methods (which might, in fact, be held to belong more properly in Part I of this volume) to their employment in the manipulation of disorder. For convenience' sake, the work of Lindsley, his associates, and a few others may be considered together here under three heads:

A. Descriptive Studies of Abnormal Behavior
B. Studies of the Effects of Various Treatments
C. Therapeutic Use of Operant Procedures

A. DESCRIPTIVE STUDIES OF ABNORMAL BEHAVIOR

One primary assumption made in the use of operant methods in the description of abnormality has been succinctly put by Lindsley, who has stated that

We must ... increase the precision of the measurement of ... behavior before we can determine the conditions under which the behavior occurs. Diagnostic and therapeutic studies are naturally facilitated by more objective and more sensitive measurement of psychotic behavior. Today there are many explanations of how patients become psychotic, many suggestions about how to cure them, but surprisingly few quantified descriptions of exactly how and under what conditions they are psychotic. (1956, p. 119)

If performance in the operant situation could be directly related to the crucial elements of psychiatric disorder, a number of advantages might be expected to accrue. It should be possible, for example, to make useful long-term studies with repeated measurements of the same performance in the same patients. Studies of this kind cannot, of course, easily be made with the usual rating scales or psychometric tests because repetition commonly blunts their validity. In the case of operant procedures, however, even practice-effect constitutes an important aspect of the main dependent variable; it is not merely an unwanted factor contributing to the error of assessment.

For his first studies, Lindsley (1956) created an expanded, man-sized version of the Skinner box. His schematic drawing of this enclosure is shown in Figure 6.2. The numbered details include the following elements.

(1) *Experimental enclosure.* These were 6 × 6 feet rooms, made of cinder blocks, noise-reduced, and designed so as to be easy to clean. All the items used had to be ruggedly constructed to survive the occasional violence of some patients.

(2) *Standard manipulandum.* The patient responded by operating a "bell-pull" handle, stoutly made of half-inch brass rod, which required a pull of 300 grams through 1 cm. to close the operating circuit.

(3) *Reinforcement magazine.* The reinforcements were dispensed through a kind of vending machine for the automatic, regular, or intermittent delivery of such objects as candies, coins, or cigarettes, which slid down an aluminum chute into a delivery tray near the subject's hand. Since it is desirable to have reinforcement take place as soon after the response as possible, a light went on by the tray immediately a reinforced response was made, acting as a *conditioned reinforcer* in anticipation of the slower delivery of the actual reward.

(4) *Stimulus panel.* This plexiglass panel allowed for the presentation of visual stimuli. Auditory stimuli could also be delivered—from loudspeakers concealed behind metal screens in the ceiling of the enclosures. When operant behavior is attached to prior stimulation, it is called a *discriminated operant*. This means that the stimulus becomes an occasion for the operant behavior but does not, itself, elicit the behavior in the same way as a stimulus does in a true respondent reflex.

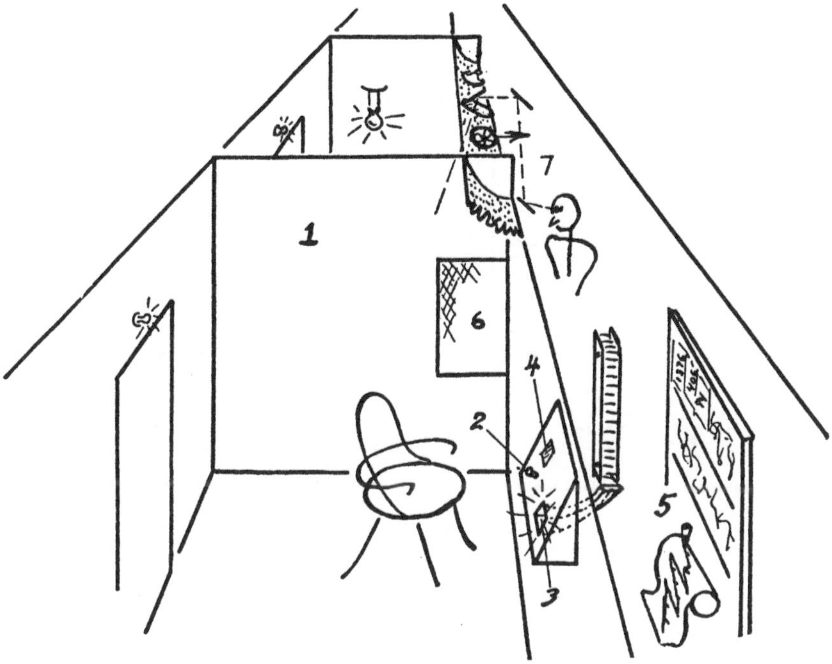

Fig. 6.2. Lindsley's version of the "Skinner box": (1) experimental enclosure; (2) standard manipulandum; (3) reinforcement magazine; (4) stimulus panel; (5) recording and controlling equipment; (6) communicating window; (7) periscope system. (From Lindsley, 1956)

(5) *Recording and controlling equipment.* All the responses were recorded on cumulative recorders and counters. All the reinforcers were delivered automatically on prearranged schedules.

An example of the system in operation is shown in Figure 6.3, and this situation has been described by Lindsley, as follows.

The patient is shown getting a reinforcement. A piece of candy has fallen into the chute below the manipulandum, and the chute is illuminated for five seconds while the room is darkened. This illumination and darkening is called a conditioned reinforcing stimulus and is designed to increase the effect of the reinforcement by shortening its delay. Experiments with lower organisms have shown that reinforcements have a greater effect in strengthening responses the more closely they follow the responses in time. A piece of candy cannot be delivered much quicker than one second after a response, but the flash of light (a conditioned reinforcement) can be delivered milliseconds after a response. Although we have not

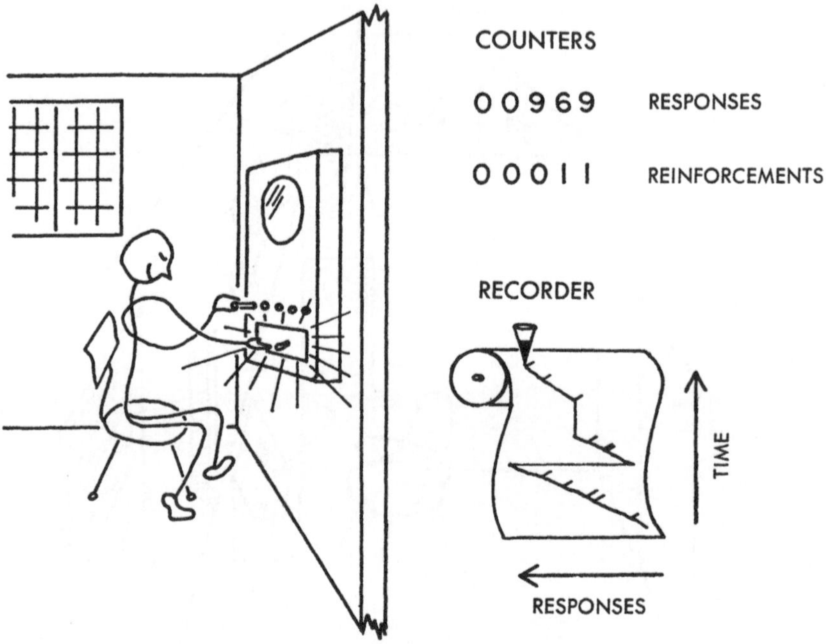

Fig. 6.3. The automatic reinforcement and recording of human operant behavior. (From Lindsley, 1956)

made direct experimental test, this immediate, conditioned reinforcement is probably also important in human operant conditioning. On the other side of the cinder-block wall, the counters have registered 969 responses and 11 reinforcements so far in this experimental session, and the cumulative response recorder has drawn an automatic graph of the responses plotted against time. The paper moves at a rate of 11 inches per hour (except when the magazine is operating, the eating time being subtracted from the record). The pen moves across the paper, one small step each time a response is made, and takes 500 responses to traverse the paper; then it is automatically reset. When a reinforcement is delivered, the pen makes a short diagonal "hatch" mark on the paper. In this manner an automatic, permanent, and continuous record of the patient's responding and the delivery of each reinforcement is obtained.

In the record shown, the patient may be seen to have responded at a fairly steady rate for approximately thirteen minutes, to have stopped responding for five minutes, and then to have continued responding at the previous rate for five minutes. (1956, pp. 129–130)

(6) *Communicating window.* These windows between the booths (Figure 6.2) could be obscured for experiments with single subjects, or they could permit visual, social communication between subjects in adjacent booths.

(7) *Periscope system.* A wide angle mirror-and-lens periscope system allowed the patients to be observed from the control corridor behind the

experimental rooms.

Standard electrical devices also controlled the presentation of the reinforcements. These included small objects: candies, coins, cigarettes, morsels of food, tokens, and the like. Lindsley has even contrived a kind of "sexual" reinforcement, in the form of the presentation of nude male and female slides, and an "altruistic" reinforcement in which the plunger-pulling provided nothing to the subject but the sight of milk being supplied to a hungry kitten (safely exposed behind a plexiglass screen).

The kind of results achieved in the description of the psychotic behavior of chronic long-term mental hospital patients may again be subdivided. Some of Lindsley's initial findings related to the behavior of individuals, and some to groups of patients.

Behavior of Individuals

In the long-term study of psychotic patients made possible by the operant method, distinctive peculiarities have appeared in the performance of individual patients.

(*a*) *Resistance to extinction.* One of the odd phenomena that Lindsley (1956) observed in a few chronic psychotic patients was an extraordinary resistance to the extinction of responses once they were established. The results from one such case may be illustrated, as in Figure 6.4. This graph (which is not of course a cumulative record) represents the case in which a patient made about 5,000 responses per hour when reinforced by female nude pictures in a given experimental room (No. 2). After fifty hours of intermittent reinforcement on a one-minute variable-interval schedule, he was put on extinction trials; that is, the pictures were no longer shown to him but the experiment was continued to see how long he would keep on responding without reinforcement. As can be seen from the graph, after the first fifty hours of extinction trials he was still responding at rates above 5,000 per hour. This is in contrast to normal subjects and to most other patients, who show a fairly sharp decline in rate of responding within the first ten hours of extinction after fifty hours of intermittent reinforcement. When, however, the same patient was placed in another room (No. 6), where he had never received any reinforcement, his median rate of response was never above 2,000 responses per hour.

The clinical import of this particular abnormality, Lindsley has admitted, remains obscure; but he has produced descriptions of other behavior in the operant setting of which the clinical implications are clear and important.

(*b*) *Psychotic episodes.* Lindsley (1960) has noted that there are patients who usually respond at a high, uniform (i.e, "normal") rate but who have periods of very low, erratic response rates, which may last from twenty or thirty minutes up to several hours. During these lowered response-rate

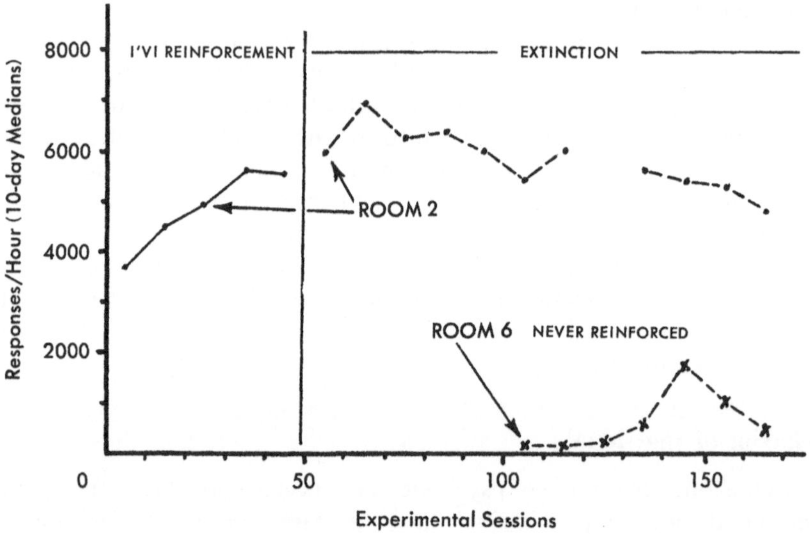

Fig. 6.4. Median responses per hour plotted against experimental sessions under conditions of intermittent reinforcement by projected-slide images of female nude figures. (From Lindsley, 1956)

periods they can often be seen to be displaying hallucinating, disturbed, destructive, or other psychotic symptoms, and it is one major advantage of Lindsley's method that it has enabled a precise, objective longitudinal measure of such behavior to be obtained.

In one case, for example, Lindsley recorded the psychotic vocal behavior of a patient on a voice-key at the same time as he recorded the plunger-pulls that constituted the reinforced responses. The results for the 747th experimental session may be seen in Figure 6.5. Lindsley has argued that this finding of such a functional incompatibility between the nonsymptomatic operant behavior and the symptomatic hallucinatory behavior may actually define an important characteristic of one kind of psychosis. Lindsley (1961, 1963a) has pointed out that this competition between the two kinds of response is not simply mechanical in nature; the vocal behavior of normal individuals, for example, does not necessarily interfere with their reinforced operant behavior in the same situation. Another important characteristic of this form of disturbance is that it can often be elicited by the delivery (from a concealed source) of auditory stimuli that approximate human speech. Normal subjects or nonhallucinatory psychotics, on the other hand, respond to such stimuli more skeptically, often asking "What are you trying to do, drive me crazy?"

Lindsley (1962a) has also studied another aspect of psychotic behavior in the experimental enclosure. In addition to the cumulative recording of vocal stress and plunger-pulling, he has similarly recorded the rate at which the subjects paced up and down by placing pressure-sensitive mats on the floor of the booth. He has reported the results for twenty-two male chronic schizophrenic patients. Each spent seven continuous hours per session in the experimental room. Whereas normal individuals, under these conditions, will operate so as to produce maximum reinforcement, none of the twenty-two schizophrenic patients did so. The most common pattern of behavior in these cases was the episodic but *independent*—and for them incompatible—emission of all three kinds of behavior.

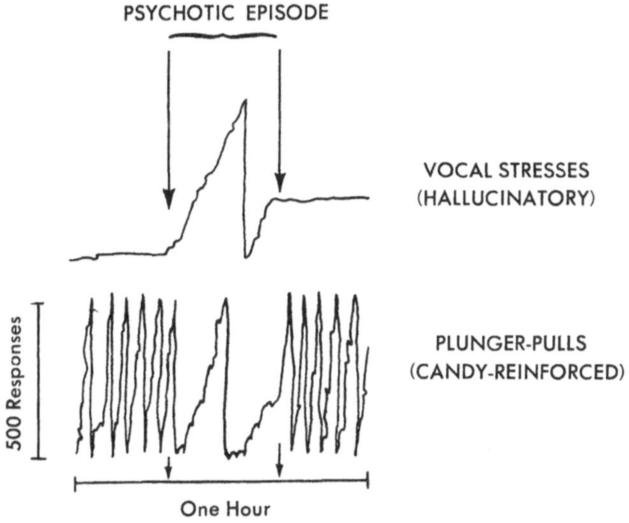

Fig. 6.5. A psychotic episode appearing in simultaneous cumulative response records of vocal stresses of psychotic (hallucinatory) origin and manual plunger-pulls, reinforced with candy, on an intermittent variable interval schedule. (After Lindsley, 1960)

These findings have led Lindsley to suggest that at least one kind of chronic schizophrenia may be defined by a disorder of reflex integration in which the symptomatic reflex has come functionally to dominate other systems of behavior. A further characteristic of such hallucinatory behavior has been examined and will be outlined when operant methods as treatment are considered (p. 150f.).

(c) *Psychotic phases.* Lindsley has similarly found that there may be long periods over which the psychotic symptoms interfere with the emission of operant behavior; and an example of these longer psychotic phases is shown in Figure 6.6. The possible importance of this kind of longitudinal observation is best summarized by quoting Lindsley as he points out that

In the intensive longitudinal studies several of the patients showed marked rhythms in their rate of response. These rhythms characteristically occur over relatively long periods of time. For a few weeks the rate of response will be consistently high. Then, for a few weeks or months, the rate will be consistently low. We have called these periods of low response "psychotic phases." They are not related to temperature, humidity, phases of the moon, home visits, or changes in ward assignments or hospital social environment. They are related to ratings of the patient's ward behavior until the behavior rating scales lose their sensitivity as a result of repeated administration. (1960, pp. 72–73)

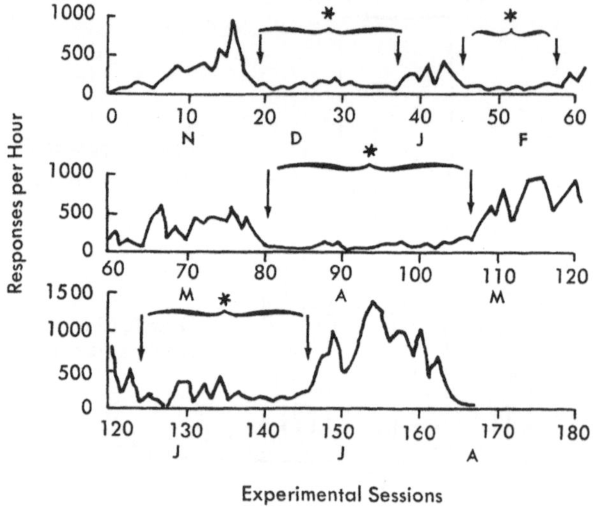

Fig. 6.6. Psychotic phases (*) in rate of response of a chronic psychotic responding on an intermittent schedule of candy reinforcement. Each experimental session lasted one hour and was conducted on successive weekdays. The initials of the months of the year (beginning with November) are printed below the experimental session closest to the first of each month to indicate calendar time. (After Lindsley, 1960)

This statement reemphasizes that a major advantage of the operant learning situation is that so-called practice-effects become part of what the investigator is interested in; they are no longer merely embarrassing, ineradicable sources of error, as in ordinary standardized psychometric tests or rating scales. Concerning the performance shown in Figure 6.6, Lindsley has stated:

> At the start of the experiment the patient was hospitalized for 20 years and was 52 years old. He was first hospitalized at the age of 18 and diagnosed as a manic-depressive. The diagnosis at admission for his current period of hospitalization was dementia praecox, hebephrenic type. His latest hospital diagnosis (in 1951) was schizophrenia, paranoid type. A current "blind" diagnosis was organic psychosis.
>
> It is easy to see how long-term hospitalization and the loss of social reinforcement could suppress the socially observable behavior of a patient to such a low level that such behavioral rhythms, which were originally easily observed without instrumentation and used to diagnose a manic-depressive psychosis, could later only be recorded by sensitive, and highly quantified behavioral recording devices.
>
> It is important to note the havoc that can be wrought by including such a patient in a drug evaluation study of the type that would run a 30-day placebo control while the patient happened to be in a psychotic phase, and a 30-day run when the patient was in his following more normal phase. The drug would be interpreted as therapeutic. It is also important to note that such patients could be of great value in attempts to show physiological or biochemical correlates of psychosis. For, here in a single physiological system, we have a naturally oscillating amount of psychosis, which could be correlated with samples of biochemical materials in order to determine correlations without confounding the data with interpatient differences in behavior or chemical quantity. (1960, p. 73)

Behavior of groups

In addition to the observation of individual psychotic patients, Lindsley and his associates have also examined group differences. For example, relationships between severity of illness or depth of psychosis and reinforced operant behavior in a group of chronic psychotics have been described by Mednick and Lindsley (1958). They examined the operant performance of twenty-two male chronic psychotic patients who had been hospitalized from three to forty-seven years, with a median of 16 years, and they compared their results with the performance of six male hospital attendants. The patients had had from ten to 448 hour-long experimental sessions, with a median of eighteen sessions. Each of the normal subjects was run for fifty hour long sessions, then put on extinction trials. All were reinforced with a mixture of candy and cigarettes on a one-minute variable-interval schedule of reinforcement.

Three operant response measures were used as indices of abnormality: R/Hr, or hourly rate of response; No. IRT $> 10''$, or number of interresponse times greater than ten seconds; and Σ IRT $> 10''$, or the sum of the interresponse times greater than ten seconds. This sum was obtained from a clock, which started ten seconds after each response and ran until the next response was made.

In addition to these measures, estimates for the patients were obtained on a number of clinical rating scales, including the Fergus Falls Behavior Sheet (LMBS)—a scale devised by Lucero and Meyer (1951) that deals with ward behavior. The Tulane Psychological Test Behavior Rating Scale (TBS), developed by King (1954), which attempts to quantify behavior shown during psychological testing, was also used. Among the standardized psychological tests given was a shortened version of the Wechsler–Bellevue (Wechsler, 1944), and, if the subject was untestable on the Wechsler, an attempt was made to give the Ammons Full Range Picture Vocabulary Test (APV) (Ammons *et al.*, 1950). The Rorschach test was also used. The psychotic group was further subdivided, into twelve "untestable" and ten "testable" patients, on the basis of their ability to perform on these tests. Mednick and Lindsley (1958) have presented data on the operant conditioning measures for the first ten hours of the study for each group, as shown in Table 6.1.

TABLE 6.1
Median Values on Operant Conditioning Response Measures for Untestable, Testable, and Normal Subjects[a]

SUBJECTS	R/hr.	No. IRT > 10 sec.	Σ IRT > 10 secs. (expressed in mins.)
Untestable	19	9	58
Testable	1,421	44	41
Normal	9,566	2	0

[a]From Mednick and Lindsley, 1958.

The authors reported that a statistical evaluation of the differences between the three groups on these measures was made by using Finney's 2 × 2 contingency tables (Finney, 1948). All the groups differed significantly ($p < .01$) on the median Σ IRT > 10″. The difference between testable and untestable patients on R/Hr was also significant, $p < .04$. The data on the ratings and tests are shown in Table 6.2.

A significant relationship ($p < .04$) was found between the characteristic of testability and the rate of response. The other main finding of interest was that there was a nonsignificant rank-difference correlation of the median rate of response for the first ten hours with LMBS ratings of only 0.23. The same correlation for the ten hours nearest the date of rating, however, was .81, significant at the .001 level.

Mednick and Lindsley therefore concluded that the operant conditioning performance of chronic psychotic patients and certain clinical variables were

TABLE 6.2
Median Values of Rating Scale and Test Data Describing Untestable, Testable, and Normal Subjects[a]

			RATINGS		TESTS				
		YEARS IN	*LMBS*	*TBS*	*IQ*[b]		*Rorschach*		
SUBJECTS	N	HOSPITAL				*R*	*M*	*W*	*F+*
Untestable	12	14	1.9	21	–	–	–	–	–
Testable	10	18	3.1	306	84	9	–	9	86
Normal	6	–	–	420	107	13	2	8	95

[a] After Mednick and Lindsley, 1958.
[b] IQ for testable patient *S*s was on basis of abbreviated Wechsler or APV.

related. It seems fair to comment, however, that the data on this group of patients are, curiously enough, in some ways not as satisfactory as the data on individual patients already described. This may indeed be a reflection of the fact that where a *functional* analysis of behavior is possible, *correlational* analyses seem much less satisfactory.

Skinner (1956) himself emphasized this fact when he pointed out that most of the experiments described in his *Behavior of Organisms* (Skinner, 1938) were done on only four rats. When some critics claimed that these groups were too small, he retorted that, on the contrary, they might be considered too *large*. He has argued, from his experience of trying to work with larger groups, that "any gain in rigor is more than matched by a loss in flexibility." In the larger-scale work, he noted.

> We were forced to confine ourselves to processes which could be studied with the baselines already developed in earlier work. We could not move on to the discovery of other processes or even to a more refined analysis of those we were working with. No matter how significant might be the relations we actually demonstrated, our statistical Leviathan had swum aground .... Another accident rescued me from mechanized statistics and brought me back to an even more intensive concentration on the single case. In essence, I suddenly found myself face to face with the engineering problem of the animal trainer ... (and) ... no one goes to the circus to see the average dog jump through a hoop significantly oftener than untrained dogs raised under the same circumstances. (1956, p. 228)

In other words, the refinement of the *quality of experimental cortrol* may reduce the need for a *quantity of experimental data.* For general psychology, the question of control versus quantity has been most extensively considered by Sidman (1960); and it is a topic that will again be considered, in relation to abnormal psychology, in Chapter 9. So far as the Mednick and Lindsley

(1958) study is concerned, while their findings might serve to persuade us of the relevance or validity of the operant techniques; they take us no further in the search for the means of changing abnormal behavior.

Operant methods have of course been used by Lindsley, both indirectly and directly, in the alteration of disorder. Examples of their indirect application may be considered under the next heading.

B. STUDIES OF THE EFFECTS OF VARIOUS TREATMENTS

The operant techniques developed by Lindsley have, in fact, themselves been used for the evaluation of various kinds of treatment. If we lack a rational, completely effective treatment, we may have to rely on empirical, partially effective nostrums. The more ineffective these are, however, the more precise our capacity for the description of the treated disorder must be. Thus a "complete cure" of any behavior disorder would commonly involve such a great alteration that even the coarsest instruments might serve to measure it; exodus from the mental hospital would serve as the criterion. The less effective the remedy, the more subtle the change may be, and, consequently, the more delicate must be the instruments for its detection.

Lindsley (1960, 1962b) has used his operant technique for the assessment of a number of different kinds of treatment, *physical* and *psychotherapeutic.*

Physical Treatment

Lindsley (1960) has cited an illustrative example in which an acute case of psychotic depression was treated with both electroshock therapy (EST) and insulin, and, at the same time, was tested by operant conditioning techniques that were reinforced—in one instance—by the delivery of candies and—in the other—by the "altruistic" reinforcement mentioned earlier (secured by feeding a kitten). The results of the two forms of treatment, in relation to the two kinds of conditioning, are shown in Figure 6.7.

It can be seen from this graph that the EST's were not at any time associated with any change in the very low rate of responding. After the 32nd session, insulin treatment began, and a larger increase in responding was associated with the first insulin coma. Lindsley (1960) has pointed out that the rate of response reinforced by feeding the kitten was increased much more than the rate reinforced with candy. This, he held, showed that the increase in the rate of responding was not simply caused by an increased need for sugar from consequent hypoglycemia. The major therapeutic effect was produced by the first coma. The rate was also increased after the next ten insulin comas, but it returned to the pretreatment level for the rest of the treatment time.

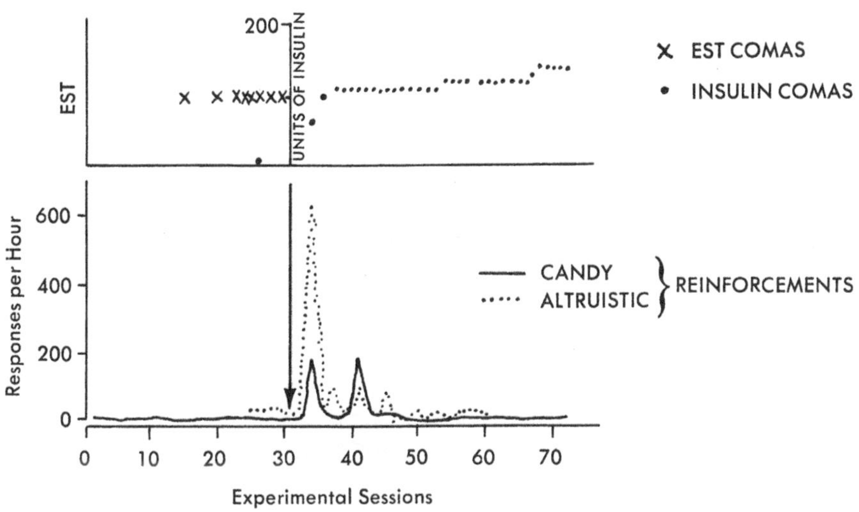

Fig. 6.7. Effects of EST and insulin on operant behavior reinforced by candy and by feeding a kitten. (After Lindsley, 1960)

In this kind of study, as in the more purely descriptive studies considered above, much rests upon the acceptance of an increase in the operant response as a valid index of improvement. This assumption is even more crucial in cases in which no change in operant rate accompanies or follows treatment. It is then difficult to be certain that the lack of change may not merely reflect test insensitivity. An example of a failure to respond is also given by Lindsley (1960) in the case in which the ataractic drug, iproniazid, was given to a regressed chronic psychotic patient, the effects being assessed by relating this treatment to responses on a one-minute variable-interval schedule. The results for 700 daily hour-long sessions with this patient are shown in groups of one hundred along the *x* axes of Figure 6.8.

As can be seen in the box on the second line from the top, 50 mg. of iproniazid were administered beginning on the 535th session—three times a day for four weeks—with no effect on the operant responses. At the 545th session, the drug dose was increased to 100 mg. three times a day. A slight temporary increase in rate of response was then noted. This increase was not, however, of any greater amplitude than some previously noted "spontaneous" increases, recorded as blips at various points along the *x* axes. Furthermore, this change was not maintained. For these reasons, Lindsley concluded that this amount of apparent recovery was not significantly related to drug administration.

In another study, Lindsley (1962b) examined both the immediate effects of a single 20 mg. dose of a new drug, benactyzine, and the effects of a placebo on manual (*MAN*) operant responses reinforced with candy (*CAN*) on a one-minute variable-interval schedule and on unreinforced (*EXT*)

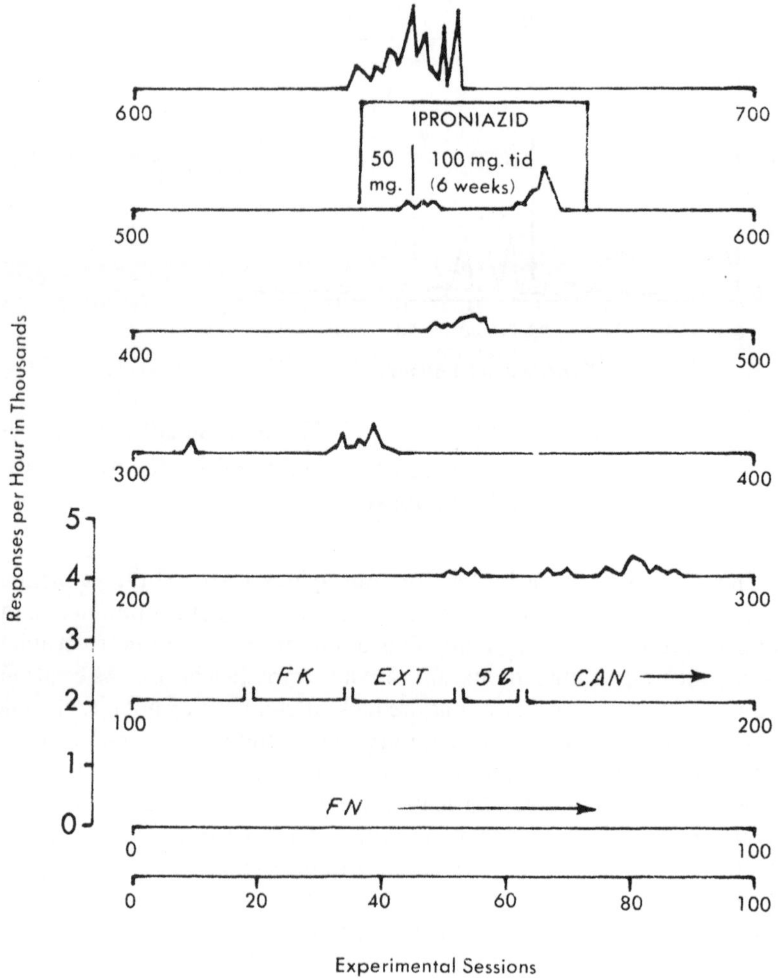

Fig. 6.8. Test results of daily sessions carried out over a period of 5 years and 7 months. Initials on the two bottom lines indicate the nature of reinforcers: thus FN female nude pictures; FK feeding kitten; EXT extinction; 5¢ five-cent pieces; CAN, candy. (After Lindsley, 1960)

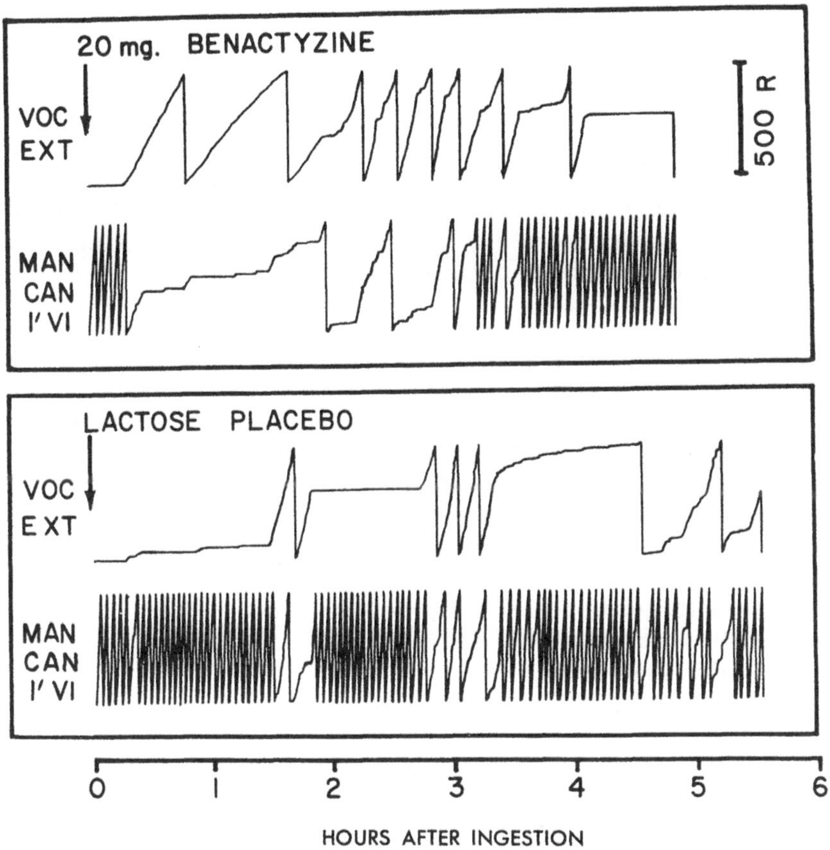

Fig. 6.9. Immediate effects of a single dosage of 20 mg. benactyzine on simultaneously unreinforced (EXT) vocal hallucinatory responses (VOC) and candy reinforced (CAN) manual operant performance (MAN), compared with the effects of lactose placebo, over two consecutive sessions. (From Lindsley, 1962b)

symptoms of vocal hallucination (*VOC*) in a hallucinated chronic psychotic adult. The simultaneous cumulative records of manual and vocal responses, under drug and placebo respectively, are shown in Figure 6.9.

It can be seen from the upper record that the patient showed much more vocal symptomatic behavior when he was on the drug, even though these responses were never reinforced. During the placebo trial, represented in the lower diagram, fewer hallucinatory symptoms appeared.

Lindsley (1962b) concluded, on the basis of these results, that this drug was more likely to be hallucinogenic than therapeutic. This opinion was confirmed by subsequent clinical field trials.

Lindsley has convincingly argued that a truly beneficial drug might be expected to reduce the symptomatic behavior without reducing the adjustive (operant) behavior. The simultaneous measurement of these different processes should therefore enable the investigator to distinguish drugs with a specific effect on the recorded symptoms from those that, for example, have merely an overall depressant effect on the total output of behavior, both adjustive and maladjustive.

Psychotherapeutic Treatment

Lindsley (1963b) has also illustrated the use of operant measures in relation to the effects of psychotherapy. He has described, for example, one case in which a striking correspondence between operant responding and "therapeutic" events occurred over a number of treatment sessions. Since, however, these sessions were conducted by a student nurse talking to an inactive chronic schizophrenic patient, it seems likely that "psychotherapy" is too grand a label for the social process in which the two were engaged. In any event, the operant response changes recorded by this patient are charted in Figure 6.10.

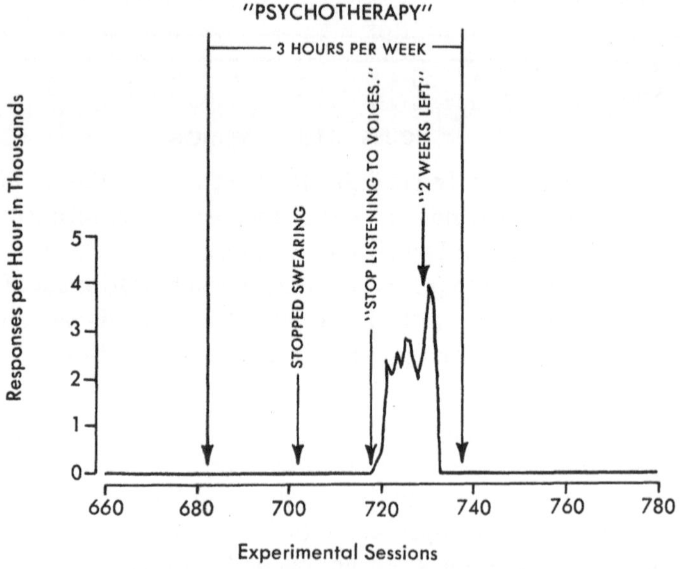

Fig. 6.10. Effect of "psychotherapy" sessions on operant rate of response in a chronic psychotic. (After Lindsley, 1963b)

The student nurse and the patient met for these so-called psychotherapy sessions for one hour a day, three days a week, beginning at the point indicated by the first arrow. At the time indicated by the second arrow, the patient stopped swearing during the treatment sessions. The nurse had become a little irritated because the patient seemed not to pay attention, and, at the same time, mumbled a lot to himself. At the third arrow, she bluntly told the patient to stop listening to his voices: "They are only part of your illness and you should not pay attention to them." On the third experimental session, immediately after this occasion, the rate of responding had gone up to over 2,000 responses per hour. This high rate of response was maintained even on the two days of each week that the nurse did not see the patient. During this time the patient did not seem to hallucinate in the ward or in the hospital grounds.

At the point shown by the fourth arrow, the nurse told the patient that she could see him only for another two weeks. His rate of response jumped about another 2,000 responses per hour immediately after he was given this information, then abruptly fell to zero responses per hour. At the fifth arrow, the nurse left the hospital and this treatment was stopped.

It can be seen from Figure 6.10 that the rate increase that occurred during this kind of treatment was abrupt in onset and termination. This fact, and the close association of operant recovery with apparently relevant therapeutic variables, Lindsley has claimed, left little doubt that such recovery was produced by the nurse's visits. This had been the highest rate of response emitted by the patient in over *four years* of daily experimental observation. Since, however, the patient was by no means "cured," and since his recovery was not maintained after termination of treatment, this form of psychotherapy seems to have had but a relatively weak and supportive effect.

Lindsley (1963b) then tried to extend the study of the effects of this kind of "psychotherapy" to the behavior of small groups of patients. After four student nurses had seen four chronic schizophrenic patients three times a week for ten weeks, a brief experiment was conducted. A one-hour session was divided into four fifteen-minute periods in the experimental room; that is, on this occasion the patient was again seated in front of the manipulandum, whose operation had been reinforced previously with candy rewards. In the first fifteen minute period the patient sat alone. In the second period the nurse merely sat in the room with the patient and told him she would keep him company. In the third period the subject was again left alone. In the fourth period the nurse came into the room again and asked the patient to get her some candy by operating the machine. The responses made by the patients under these different conditions are enumerated in Table 6.3.

These results were compared with responses made during four similarly arranged fifteen-minute periods, when a strange nurse participated instead

TABLE6.3
Effect of Nurse-therapist's Presence on Operant Performance of Chronic Schizophrenics[a]

	NUMBER OF RESPONSES			
Patients	*Period 1*	*Period 2*	*Period 3*	*Period 4*
1	0	4	0	14
2	1	0	0	15
3	0	0	0	11
4	0	0	0	714

[a] After Lindsley, 1963b.

of the patient's "nurse-therapist." These comparative results are shown in Table 6.4. Lindsley does not report on any statistical evaluation of differences, but, by inspection, it seems obvious that the "therapist's" requests were answered by the patient with much higher rates of responding than were the stranger's.

Even if one hesitates to accept the notion that the sympathetic nurse-patient relationship be regarded as a precise analogue of psychotherapy, nevertheless, a new means for the longitudinal assessment of a person-to-person relationship is at hand.

A more sophisticated technique for the functional analysis of therapist-patient interaction has also been devised by Lindsley (1962c) and his associates, and its use has been described by Nathan, Schneller, and Lindsley (1964). By means of reciprocal patient and therapist viewing and listening over closed-circuit television, matters can be so arranged that the patient can, for example, be made to "work" for the sight and sound of his doctor. The

TABLE 6.4
Effect of Stranger's Presence on Operant Performance of Chronic Schizophrenics[a]

	NUMBER OF RESPONSES			
Patient	*Period 1*	*Period 2*	*Period 3*	*Period 4*
1	0	10	0	8
2	0	0	0	4
3	0	0	0	0
4	0	0	0	0

[a] After Lindsley, 1963b.

apparatus can be set up in such a way that unless the patient continuously operates the appropriate manipulanda, the visual and/or auditory components of the televised therapist fade and disappear. An arrangement of this remote yoking is shown in Figure 6.11.

Lindsley has used the expression "conjugate reinforcement" to describe the way in which the intensity of the continuously available reinforcing stimuli may be made to vary directly and immediately with the rate of responding in this kind of situation. He distinguishes it from the "episodic reinforcement" found in the schedules previously described. He and his associates (Nathan *et al.*, 1964) have shown that this conjugate schedule

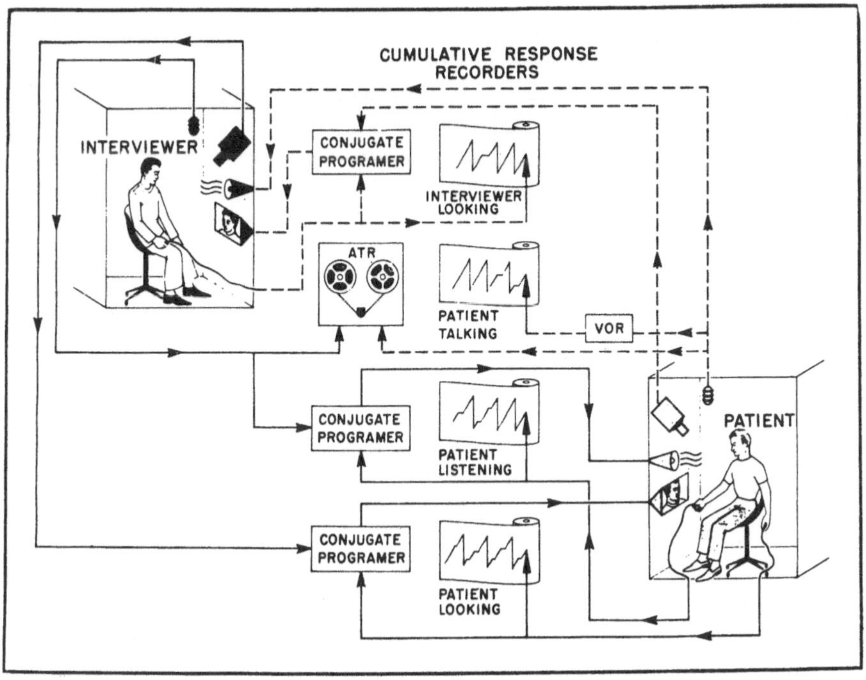

Fig. 6.11. Diagrammatic representation of connections between patient and therapist arranged for conjugate reinforcement analysis of their interaction. The looking, listening, and talking of the patient are shown recorded on three separate cumulative recorders. The looking responses of the interviewer are also recorded. VOR indicates a voice-operated relay and ATR a two-channel audio tape-recorder for recording interview content. (From Nathan, Schneller, and Lindsley, 1963)

can be used to permit a more continuous, and hence "finer grained," analysis of the moment-to-moment positive or negative changes in the value of the reinforcing stimulus. Thus, for example, the interviewer's questions about sensitive areas in the patient's life history may be shown to result in changes in the rate of the patient's responding for the sight or sound of the questioner.

More mundanely, Lindsley (1962c) has suggested that such a conjugate reinforcement hook-up might be used for copytesting television advertisements. The "value" of the commercial can be measured by how hard the consumer will work at the manipulanda in order to look and listen during critical periods.

Other uses of conjugate reinforcement more germane to clinical problems have also been suggested by Lindsley. For example, this kind of schedule can be used so that the subject's continuous activity serves instead to keep an aversive stimulus at bay. Lindsley (1957) has used this arrangement as a measure of depth of sleep. The operation of a microswitch taped to the subject's preferred hand was arranged so as to diminish the intensity of an unpleasantly loud pure tone. Rapid and continuous responding reduced this tone to zero intensity. Cumulative records then described changes in rate; a reduction in rate indicated the onset of sleep, cessation indicated deep sleep. Lindsley has also shown that the same technique can be usefully employed to measure onset of and recovery from anesthesia (Lindsley, Hobika, and Etsten, 1961) and the induction and emergence from coma of electroshock treatment (Lindsley and Conran, 1962).

C. THERAPEUTIC USE OF OPERANT PROCEDURES

In addition to their descriptive function and their use in the assessment of other forms of therapy, operant procedures can themselves be employed as a means for the direct treatment of disorders. One attempt at direct treatment by the use of operant techniques has been reported by Lindsley (1959), who tried to reduce vocal psychotic symptoms by differential positive reinforcement. In one case he examined the effect of reinforcing such vocal symptoms as compared with the reinforcement of lever-pulling. The vocal symptoms of an hallucinatory patient were recorded with the aid of a voice key, and the manual responses were recorded in the usual way.

Before any differential reinforcement of the vocal stresses took place, it was found that they were emitted at a rate of 500 per hour while the plunger was operated at a rate of 100 pulls per hour on a fixed-ratio schedule of 1 in 20. (Similar rates were recorded for over 130 daily one-hour sessions). Lindsley now changed the response-contingent reinforcements, rewarding the vocal hallucinatory responses and no longer reinforcing the lever-pulling behavior. The latter could therefore be regarded as subject to experimental extinction, and, in fact, decreased from 100 pulls to 10 pulls per hour over 170 hours. Although the vocal symptoms were then being reinforced, however, they did not—as might have been expected—increase in rate but actually *decreased* from 500 responses to 10 responses per hour after 170 hours of reinforcement. When the reinforcement was again changed to the manual responses, these increased from 10 to 50 pulls per hour over 110 hours. At the same time, the vocal symptoms (now under the extinction condition) actually *increased* from 10 to 600 stresses per hour.

Lindsley concluded that such vocal psychotic symptoms appear to be under some strong control that resists direct differential positive reinforcement. He has come to regard this resistance as a further crucial defining characteristic of hallucinatory behavior.

Lindsley and his associates have also suggested, or made therapeutic use of, operant techniques for disorders as diverse as mental defect (Lindsley, 1964a) and senility (Lindsley, 1964b). In these last two papers, Lindsley has made an interesting distinction between behavioral treatment (or behavior therapy) and behavioral prosthesis. Treatment, he has pointed out, aims to normalize the individual. It is probable, however, that in such conditions as amentia and dementia the behavior deficit itself is irreversible. For these conditions he has proposed that a range of aids be devised that would constitute "behavioral prosthetic environments." These could include the exaggeration and multiplication of discriminative stimuli for those whose defects are in part based on an incapacity to respond to stimuli when they are present at only average intensity or low redundancy. Thus, Lindsley has argued, an elderly person with generally weakened attention might, for example, respond more appropriately to a multiple-sense display than to ordinary unisensory notices designed to guide his behavior.

With characteristic ingenuity, Lindsley (1963c) and his associates have also turned their attention to the application of operant learning procedures to social behavior. Azrin and Lindsley (1956), for example, in one experiment showed how cooperation between children in a simple game could be increased by making the reinforcement of their performance contingent upon a kind of mutual aid. Cohen (1962) went on to show that the actual form of cooperation and competition may be a function not only of reinforcement schedules but of the extraexperimental relationships between subjects. Cohen and Lindsley (1964) have also gone on to see how cooperation, competition, and leadership may be examined by reinforcements made available through various forms of social interaction.

One interesting attempt at the treatment of abnormal subjects, and one which has used the principle of the reinforcement of cooperative behavior, has been reported not by Lindsley's group but by King, Armitage, and Tilton (1960). They have described what they have called an operant-interpersonal method as a therapeutic approach to the withdrawn behavior of schizophrenics of extreme pathology, their goal being to elicit more interest in the environment and to promote more appropriate social response patterns between chronic patients.

In their experiment, they chose four groups of twelve schizophrenic patients each, whose ages ranged from twenty-five to forty-two years. These patients had been in a hospital from more than four to over fourteen years. The diagnostic subclassifications included eighteen hebephrenic, eleven catatonic, five paranoid, and fourteen undifferentiated schizophrenics.

The authors also used a number of rating scales by means of which they hoped to assess the effects of their operant methods: Extreme Mental Illness Schedule (EMIS); Ward Observation Scale (WOS); Clinical Improvement Scale (CIS); and Amount of Verbalization Scale (AVS).

In their experiment, three of the four groups of twelve patients were used as controls, as follows. One group received "verbal therapy," involving the same amount of time as the experimental operant group (i.e., three sessions of twenty to thirty minutes a week). In these sessions, every effort was made to establish verbal communication by whatever means were possible. The kind of communication attempted ranged from talk about daily routine events to the subject's feelings and concerns.

A second control group received recreational therapy from three to five hours a week. The third group was called the "no therapy" group—but it in fact continued with usual ward activities, such as occupational therapy and so on.

Before we describe the procedure used with the remaining, experimental group, it is necessary to describe the so-called Multiple Operant Problem-Solving Apparatus (MOPSA), which is represented in Figure 6.12. The stimulus-response panel represented in Figure 6.12a measured 8 feet, by 8 feet, and included the following elements.

Operant levers. Projecting from the middle of the panel were three 6-inch-long wooden levers. To obtain the rewards, initially at least, it was only necessary for the subject to press the lever.

Reinforcement trays. Slots directly below the outer two levers opened on to trays that were used for dispensing reinforcements of candy and cigarettes.

Stimulus screen. A 14 × 14-inch screen for projecting slides was situated above the middle lever.

Complex response levers. At each side of the central levers are two 11 × 13-inch plates that could be concealed by covers. The authors noted, of this part of the apparatus:

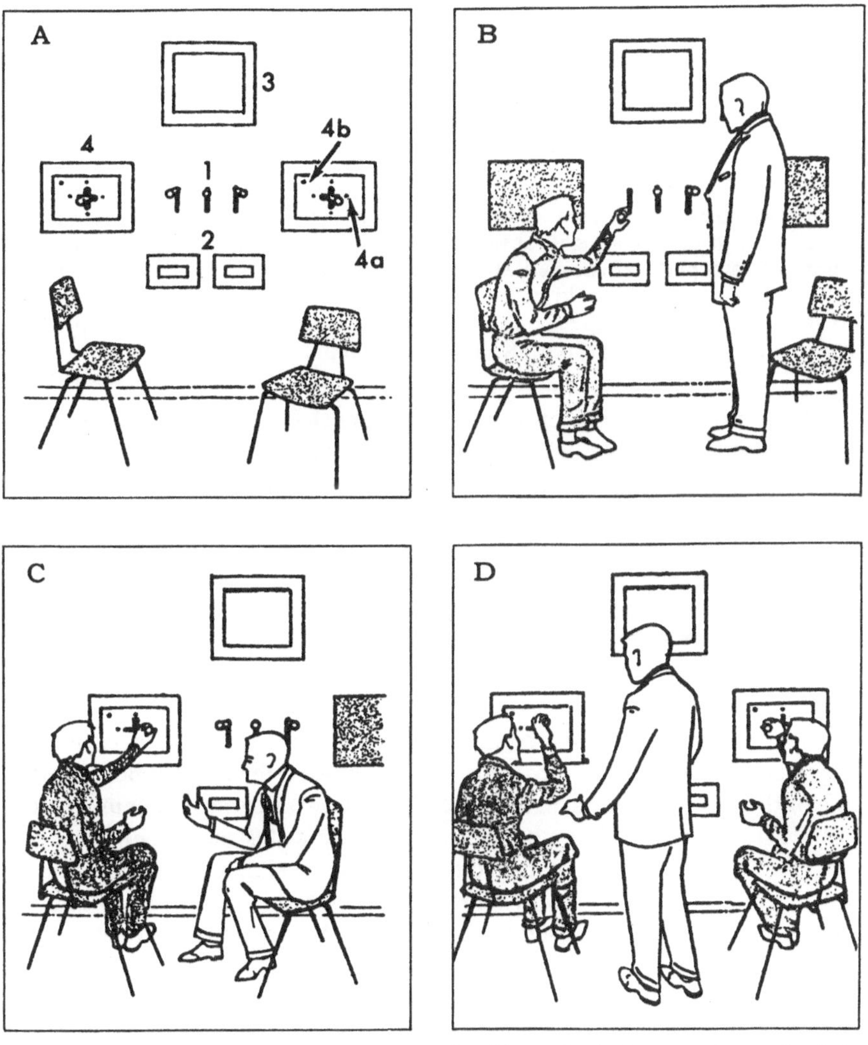

A. Multiple Operant Problem Solving Apparatus, MOPSA.
   (1) Operant levers;
   (2) Reinforcement trays;
   (3) Stimulus screen;
   (4) Complex response levers;
      (4a) Green lights;
      (4b) Amber light;

B. Phase 1 of the experimental trials: the subject learns the use of the operant lever.

C. Phase 2: the subject learns to operate the complex response lever.

D. Phase 3: the subjects learn to co-operate in problem solving.

Fig. 6.12. The operant-interpersonal method: apparatus and illustrations of the therapeutic phases. (From King, Armitage, and Tilton, 1960)

A cross, into which a lever could be inserted, had been cut in the center of each plate. Counterbalanced by just enough tension to return and maintain them at the cross intersections, the levers could be moved freely in the two planes of the crosses. If *S* [the subject] moved the lever of either cross from the position of rest to the end of the correct crossarm, a green light at the end of the arm (*4a*) became lit. Through a system of relays, problems could be introduced requiring from one to four movements (lights), along with various patterns of the "right-left–up-down" sequence. Movements had to be executed in a prescribed order so that an error canceled any previously correct responses, requiring that the entire sequence be started again. In addition to the green lights at the crossarms, an amber light located at an upper corner of each plate (*4b*) flashed when a problem was solved. By changing the relay system, new problems could be introduced, in a few seconds. As the two crosses could be operated independently or together, problems requiring cooperation between *S*s could be employed. (King *et al.*, 1960, pp. 278–279)

After solution of the problem, it appears that it was still necessary for the subject to press the operant lever in order to secure the reinforcement.

The twelve subjects were seen for from twenty to thirty minutes a session, three times a week for fifteen weeks, and the experimental procedure was phased as follows.

Phase 1. In this phase (Figure 6.12b) a subject was shown how to use the simple response levers, by example if necessary. When the subjects came to the point of responding to continuous reinforcement, they were put on intermittent reinforcement. This phase lasted about four weeks.

Phase 2. In this phase one of the aluminum plates of the complex response manipulandum was uncovered and a lever was inserted. The experimenter began with a "one-light" problem, which required the lever to be moved to one of the four crossarms, demonstrating that only this particular movement lit the green and then the amber light. This phase is illustrated in Figure 6.12c.

All of the 12 subjects managed to reach the level of a two-light problem, and five of these subjects consistently solved four-light problems. After three weeks, the experimenter used the situation to try to get the patients to talk more; for example, by asking after one movement had been made "Where do you go next?" This phase lasted about six weeks.

Phase 3. This phase was devoted to cooperative problem solving, which King *et al.* described as follows.

Seated in front of the second cross, the therapist informed *S*s that they would have to work as a team in order to obtain rewards. In a simple two-light problem, the therapist made the first movement and *S* the second, as well as vice versa. Quality of performance seemed to drop sharply in this interpersonal context, as most *S*s experienced difficulty in coordinating their efforts with another individual. As progress did occur, the therapist and *S* proceeded to three- and four-light problems in which all possible therapist-subject orders of responding were required. (1960, p. 279)

After this part of phase 3, two patients had to cooperate, as shown in Figure 6.12d. The problem-solving groups were then made even larger; for example, with two or more patients observing and sometimes correcting the performance of two others at the levers.

The results of these procedures, so far as they are reflected in the rating scale scores and other indices used, were promising, and in some cases unexpected—as can be seen below.

Extreme Mental Illness Schedule. The results for the EMIS improvement scores over the period of the experiment were compared for the various groups by analysis of variance. The outcome of this analysis is shown in Table 6.5. It can be seen from this table that there was a highly significant improvement in the EMIS scores related to differences between groups, and there was also a difference related to initial status (as measured by severity of illness and length of hospitalization). The between-therapeutic-group difference was in fact due to the greatest improvement being show by the operant group, this being followed—in descending order—by improvement in the control groups receiving recreational therapy, no treatment, and verbal therapy.

TABLE 6.5
Analysis of Variance of EMIS Improvement Scores[a]

SOURCES	df	MS	F	p
Therapeutic groups (T)	3	58.965	7.313	> .001
Verbalization Level (V)	2	22.312	1.057	n.s.
Initial status (I)	9	21.118	2.619	> .05
$T \times V$	6	3.924	0.487	n.s.
$T \times I$	27	8.063		
Total	47			

[a] From King, Armitage, and Tilton, 1960.

Ward Observation Scale. When the WOS score differences were examined by analysis of variance, the difference between the therapeutic groups was again significant ($p < .01$), the descending order of mean differences being found in the operant, recreational, verbal, and no therapy groups. Six months after the operant sessions were stopped, the experimental group was still significantly better on this scale ($p < .05$) than either the verbal or the no therapy group. A comparison could not be made with the recreational group because this form of treatment was being continued.

Clinical Improvement Scale. Group comparisons on this scale were made in a slightly different way, as is shown in Table 6.6. The experimental group was compared, by means of Fisher's exact test (Siegel, 1956), with the other groups by constructing fourfold tables that were based on two groups and on the two categories, improved and unimproved. The difference between the operant group and the verbal therapy group was greatest ($p = .009$); next came the no therapy group ($p = .019$). The difference between the experimental group and the group receiving recreational therapy was not significant on this measure ($p = .220$).

TABLE 6.6
Group Comparisons on the CIS Scores[a]

	GROUP TREATMENTS			
CIS RATINGS	*Operant*	*Verbal*	*Recreational*	*None*
Has become worse	0	1	0	0
Essentially no change	4	10	8	10
Minor improvement	3	1	2	2
Considerable improvement	5	0	2	0

[a] From King, Armitage, and Tilton, 1960.

Amount of Verbalization Scale. Changes in level of verbalization for the different therapeutic groups are represented in Table 6.7. When the experimental group was again judged against each of the others by Fisher's exact test in terms of "increase versus no-increase," this group was significantly more improved than the verbal therapy group ($p = .005$). Comparisons with the other two groups at least approached significance ($p = .089$). It is of interest to note that the amount of verbalization actually *decreased* in the case of some members of the verbal therapy group! This finding, to say the least, was quite unexpected.

TABLE 6.7
Group Comparisons on the AVS Scores[a]

	GROUP TREATMENTS			
AVS RATINGS	*Operant*	*Verbal*	*Recreational*	*None*
Decreased	0	6 (7)[b]	2	1
Unchanged	5 (5)[b]	6 (5)	8	9
Increased	7 (7)	0	2	2

[a] From King, Armitage, and Tilton, 1960.
[b] Numbers in parentheses represent assessments of change in verbal level as judged from therapists' notes.

Other indices of change included the answers to questions about a patient's desire to leave the ward, either to go to an open ward or out of the hospital. These questions were put to the patients by a psychologist who was not otherwise concerned with the project, and the results of this inquiry are shown in Table 6.8.

TABLE 6.8
Group Comparisons on Ratings of Desire to Leave the Ward[a]

	GROUP TREATMENTS		
RATINGS	*Operant*	*Verbal*	*None*
No interest	4	10	10
Some interest	5	1	2
Definite interest	3	1	0

[a] From King, Armitage, and Tilton, 1960.

When the experimental group was again separately compared with the others, in terms of an interest–no-interest dichotomy, both differences were found to be significant ($p = .019$). Members of the experimental group, compared with the others, were also found to have increased interest in occupational therapy; and the only one of a number of enuretics in each group who improved came from the operant group.

As for the concrete gains made by these methods, the authors have concluded:

> The judgments of the ward administrators led to only one patient of the operant-interpersonal group being transferred to an open ward, not an imposing gain. It is not [however] difficult to think of a reasonable defense for this finding. Since the patients were only seen for approximately 22 hours, there is the possibility of additional clinical improvement with a longer period of therapy. Further sessions could be devoted to extending the previous therapeutic pattern; i.e., increasing the complexity of the therapeutic environment. The therapeutic tasks would gradually require more complex discriminations and more conceptual solutions as the problems at the same time became more and more embedded in a verbal and interpersonal context. (1960, p. 285)

One difficulty, implicit in this kind of conclusion, lies principally in the admitted complexity of the kind of disorders commonly labeled "schizophrenic." It might again be questioned how homogeneous a group may be if it is composed of a number of individuals called "chronic schizophrenics." Even if they are further defined—as King *et al.* (1960) tried to define them—as withdrawn and anergic, it still is more than probable that even their most overt common symptoms would reveal marked differences on closer examination. There may, in fact, be a great deal to be said for treating each *individual* in terms of what is wrong with him; in other words, by taking the central aspect of behavior pathology and working on that by operant techniques. One may again recall Skinner's conclusion that a group of four organisms is "too large."

A number of workers have, indeed, begun successfully to apply operant procedures to the single case. Among Lindsley's own associates, for example, Barrett (1962) has reduced the emission of multiple tics by making musical reinforcement contingent upon their cessation.

One of the most ingenious and intriguing descriptive uses of this method, however, has been described by Brady and Lind (1961) in their treatment of a case of "hysterical blindness." They undertook the use of operant procedures to reinforce the awareness and use of visual cues in a man who had suffered from so-called total hysterical blindness for two years, and who had received ordinary general psychotherapeutic procedures without amelioration of his symptoms. Although this forty-year-old patient had once suffered from dendritic keratitis (about fifteen years before the onset of his "blindness") and had some slight corneal scarring, it was concluded from neurological and ophthalmological investigations that there was no organic foundation for his claim to complete blindness—a conclusion that was supported by his behavior. Although he claimed he could not see at all, he was able to avoid large obstacles in walking, to handle eating utensils, and could also reach accurately for small objects in ways that would be impossible for a person suffering from an organic blindness.

To begin to reestablish the effects of visual control on this patient's behavior, it was first necessary to devise a situation in which relatively simple, stable behavior could be generated. For this purpose Brady and Lind chose an operant conditioning situation in which the behavior to be reinforced was the spacing of responses (button-pressing) in a prescribed way; in fact, the patient was required to space his responses between eighteen and twenty-one seconds apart. In other words, a response that followed the preceding response by less than eighteen seconds or by more than twenty-one seconds was not reinforced, but served simply to reset the timing apparatus for the start of another period; a response that followed the preceding response within the specified eighteen to twenty-one second time interval was reinforced.

Technically, this kind of reinforcement schedule is called a Differential Reinforcement of Low Rate (DRL) of eighteen seconds, with a limited hold of three seconds. The immediate reinforcement for a correct response was the sound of a buzzer, but, in addition, social approval and ward privileges were increased when the patient made good scores—and were withdrawn when he performed poorly. The hope was that the patient might first come to respond to fairly gross visual stimuli and might later react to more subtle differences. It was also hoped that any control that came to be exercised by visual cues in the experiment would generalize to extraexperimental situations.

The number of responses in each three-second interval (taking a range from zero to twenty-four and over) was recorded automatically, and the number of responses falling in the correct interval was considered to be the patient's score for that session. After a stable distribution of interresponse times had been obtained in this way, visual stimuli were then introduced as cues for the correct spacing of responses. In other words, the patient could then acquire more reinforcements, and hence improve his score, by making use of visual cues. Thus the effects of these visual cues on his operant performance and general behavior could be studied systematically. During the entire experiment the patient was alone in the room; and all his responses were automatically recorded.

Brady and Lind (1961) described the progress of their experiment in terms of five phases, during which certain different behaviors were elicited from the patient—as illustrated in Figure 6.13. Each phase involved a number of sessions, and there were two half-hour sessions per day, five days a week.

Phase 1. This comprised sessions 1 through 6. During this phase of the experiment, the patient had to respond to the required time interval without any visual cues. The first histogram of the figure shows his results by session number 6; and it can be seen that the peak is already at the "correct" interval.

Phase 2. This included sessions 7 to 16, during which the indirect illumination of the room was increased by a barely perceptible amount during the correct eighteen- to twenty-one second period for response, although the patient was not informed of this added stimulus. Since the period of illumination corresponded with the correct period for response, the subject, if he were to pay attention to the light, could increase his accuracy of responding. The authors pointed out that

> Introducing this barely perceptible light had a profound influence on the patient's operant responding. Note [they say] the marked deterioration in the percentage of correct responses when the light was first introduced [session 7]. The introduction of this visual cue, then, was accompanied by deterioration rather than improvement in score. The greatest number of responses was made prematurely, in the 15- to 18-second interval. Premature responses reset the apparatus and hence postponed the appearance of the light. In other words, the approach of the crucial 18- to 21-second interval, now accompanied by a light, constituted a *preaversive situation*. By responding prematurely, the patient precluded the appearance of the light and thereby avoided an aversive experience. (1961, p. 336)

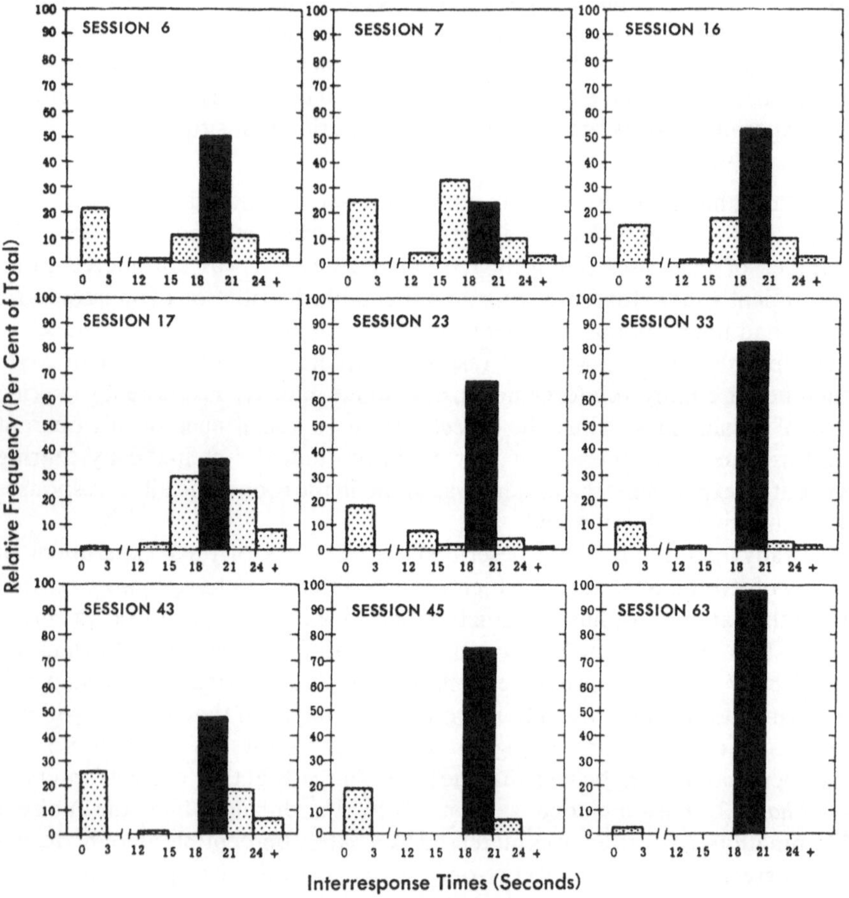

Fig. 6.13. Relative frequency distributions of interresponse times (IRT's) grouped into class intervals of three seconds each. Responses falling in the 18- to 21-second interval (black) are reinforced. IRT's between 3 and 12 seconds (occurring only rarely) have been omitted. (From Brady and Lind, 1961)

By trial 12, the patient's responses reached the level they had been at before the introduction of the light stimulus (see session 6), and a plateau of responding was maintained—at about 50 per cent correct—up to trial 16. For the first time, then, during trial 16, the patient was watched surreptitiously. It was found that he was sitting with his head resting on the table and was covering his eyes with his forearm. This was interpreted as indicating that he was now avoiding the presumably anxiety-provoking visual stimulus simply by covering his eyes. Since he had never been told about the light, the experimenters could hardly complain that he was breaking the rules, so for phase 3 they simply *changed* these rules.

Phase 3. This phase included sessions 17 through 23. In this series the light stimulus (a bulb of 100 watts) was placed in front of the patient; he was told that it was there and what its function was supposed to be. The results for session 17 are also shown in Figure 6.13. Again, the number of correct responses fell off—to about 30 per cent—but, by session 23, a level of 67 per cent was reached. The patient still, however, denied seeing the light; he claimed that he could feel the heat given off by the bulb when lit, and that this helped him, although such temperature changes were really too small to detect at the distance he was sitting from the bulb.

Phase 4. During this phase, from sessions 24 through 45, the light intensity was reduced by very small decrements; and by session 33 the patient made a score of 82 per cent correct responses. To make sure that improvement in time judgment alone could not account for this increase, the visual cue was attached to intervals *other* than the 18- to 21-second interval during two sessions of this phase (34 and 40), and the patient continued to make high scores in association with the visual cue. Brady and Lind go on to say that

> The patient's operant behavior changed abruptly in session 43 . . . . The percentage of responses during the correct interval dropped to half its previous value and the number of multiple responses (first-interval) rose sharply. At the end of the session, the patient came out of the room exclaiming that he could see the light. He appeared both anxious and exhilarated, and sought praise and approval for his accomplishment. He accounted for his poor score during this session despite his awareness of visual cues by stating that he felt almost paralyzed by the light. His score improved rapidly over the next two sessions, however, . . . and he became less anxious. (1961, p.337)

Phase 5. In sessions 46 through 63, the visual cue was replaced by more complex visual cues in which the patient had to discriminate patterns. With each new problem, the patient's performance tended to suffer some slight setback, from which it gradually recovered. By trial 63 (see Figure 6.13), in which a fairly difficult discriminative problem was used, nearly all the responses were correct.

The patient's clinical condition continued to improve during this phase of the study and he professed himself more and more aware of seeing, both in the ward and at home. At the time of their report, Brady and Lind (1961) found that the patient remained able to see thirteen months after his recovery.

A more detailed analysis of the same patient's behavior after relapse has, however, been published more recently by Zimmerman and Grosz

(1966). These authors have presented clinical and experimental evidence which has led them to conclude that the patient could perhaps always have been aware of visual cues.

Their use of better controlled operant procedures showed, for example, that on a visual discrimination task in which he was ostensibly "blind," the patient tended to perform at a level *worse* than chance. This could, perhaps, mean that he was "acting like a blind man" but actually over-estimating the number of errors the blind would make. This finding in combination with the observation that the patient was quite susceptible to social manipulation might suggest that he could have been feigning blindness and could have been consciously avoiding the emission of correct responses.

These authors have therefore concluded that the original study must be regarded as of methodological and descriptive rather than therapeutic importance.

These examples, drawn from the work of Lindsley and his associates, and supplemented by studies carried out by other workers, show the range and versatility of operant techniques in the investigation and the direct manipulation of abnormal behavior. Similar procedures have successfully been applied to other problems. Ayllon (1963) has applied these principles to increase the amount of self-help exercised by anergic chronic psychotic patients. Ellis, Barnett, and Pryer (1960), Orlando and Bijou (1960), and Spardlin (1962) have employed operant procedures to improve the performance of defective children, and Ferster (1961) has used them to influence the behavior of withdrawn, autistic children. Lovaas and his associates (Lovaas *et al.*, 1964; 1965) have made dramatic use of strong reinforcers in the case of children of extreme, so-called "schizophrenic" pathology. Mackay (1965) and Mackay and Inglis (1965) have reported on the application of operant procedures to the disorders of learning found in some elderly psychiatric patients.

To some extent, the functional relationships found between the application of operant techniques and outcome are so direct and immediate that, as already noted, they obviate the need for large groups and even for untreated controls. One kind of behavior that seems particularly sensitive to operant control, and which well illustrates this last contention, is verbal behavior. The operant control of verbal behavior in abnormal subjects will therefore be considered in the next chapter.

7

THE EFFECTS OF *Reinforcement on Verbal Behavior*

VERBAL BEHAVIOR, like other behavior, may be analyzed and manipulated in operant terms, Skinner (1957) has pointed out that for many years he has been concerned with the classification and manipulation of verbal responses. This interest first culminated in the William James Lectures, which he gave on this topic at Harvard University in 1947, and then in the book entitled *Verbal Behavior*, published in 1957. In his opinion, verbal behavior is a form of organismic activity that is worthy of study in its own right; it is not to be regarded merely as a right-of-way to an otherwise inaccessible "realm of the mind." This, of course, coincides with the general point of view that was expressed in our Chapter 1.

Even if we do not now believe that speech gives, directly or indirectly, any privileged access to mental events, nevertheless, it obviously is a very important form of behavior. The adult human being acts not only in relation to simple external and internal stimuli but also in relation to an immense, and immensely complex, range of self-produced and other-produced symbols. Berlyne (1954), for example, has discussed the usefulness of the notion of symbolic activity in the behavioral analysis of normal cognition. Inglis (1960b) has tried to show how different degrees of the avoidance of symbols related to anxiety might result in maladjusted behavior.

The most superficial inspection will show that verbal behavior is very often the vehicle, if not, indeed, the core, of abnormality. In some cases the main evidence of disturbance may be the patient's verbal complaints; in others, a disorder of verbal expression may itself constitute a crucial symptom of his pathology.

What Balint (1957) has called the "apostolic" function of the physician in the determination of the disorder from which a patient is eventually said to suffer may also be partly conceived in verbal operant terms. He has suggested that a patient usually offers a variety of complaints to his doctor, who selects some for his attention (and hence reinforcement) while rejecting or neglecting others (which may thus be extinguished). It is interesting to speculate that the very change in form and frequency of some of the disorders of behavior (e.g., "hysteria") that have taken place over the decades might be due to the degree of acceptance particular symptoms have been accorded by the psychiatrists to whom they were first tentatively offered.

Since verbalization is involved in the expression, evolution, and estimation of disorder, the control of such behavior might well be of major importance in the manipulation of abnormality. One of the most thorough and painstaking series of studies devoted to this end has been carried out by Dr. K. Salzinger and his associates of the Biometrics Research Laboratory of the New York State Department of Mental Hygiene. Salzinger (1959), in a comprehensive review of experiments devoted to the manipulation of verbal activity considered as operant behavior, has distinguished four categories of study, ranging from the more restricted laboratory situations to real-life settings.

(1) *Simple responses to restricted stimulus situations.* Under this heading Salzinger put those experiments typified by Greenspoon's studies (1951, 1955), which were, perhaps, mainly responsible for a powerful resurgence of interest in the application of reinforcement theory to verbal behavior. In Greenspoon's (1955) experiment, each of seventy-five subjects was asked to say all the words he could think of during a fifty-minute period. The experimenter produced one of two stimuli, which was made contingent upon the subject's responses. These were, so to speak, standardized grunts, "mmm-hm" and "huh-uh," one or the other being uttered just after the subject produced a word that fitted into a previously determined response class. One class comprised plural nouns, the other comprised all words that were not plural nouns. Greenspoon was able to show that the use of the stimulus "mmm-hm" could increase the frequency of emission of both kinds of response. The stimulus "huh-uh," on the other hand, increased nonplural nouns but decreased the production of plural nouns. Overall, the experiment confirmed that verbal activity could be manipulated by social reinforcement, and could therefore certainly be treated as a kind of operant behavior.

(2) *Complex responses to restricted stimulus situations.* In this category Salzinger included the work of Taffel (1952, 1955), who presented each of ninety subjects with eighty stimulus cards bearing a verb and six personal pronouns. The subject was required to respond with a sentence that used the verb and one of the pronouns. The subjects were divided into groups 1, 2, and 3. The experimenter did not react to any of the subjects' responses for

the first twenty trial cards. (This unreinforced, spontaneous emission rate is often called the "operant level.") Then the group treatments diverged.

For trials 21 to 80 in group 1, the experimenter said "Good" whenever any sentence was produced that began with the personal pronouns "I" or "we." Under these conditions, Taffel was able to show an increase in the rate of emission of such sentences. For group 2 the experimenter flashed a little light at the end of sentences that had used these personal pronouns, but this did not increase their use over the operant level baseline. For group 3, no reinforcement was given for any of the trials, and again no increased use of the selected pronouns was found. Taffel was therefore also able to conclude that verbal responses can be operantly conditioned, and that the social reinforcement provided by the word "good" is effective in a verbal situation.

(3) *Simple responses to nonrestricted stimulus situations.* In this group Salzinger included studies of the kind described by Verplanck (1956), in which the experimenter gained control of the appearance of particular words (e.g., "aunt," "uncle") in the ordinary course of conversation by giving appropriate verbal reinforcement for the emission of these selected elements.

(4) *Complex responses to nonrestricted stimulus situations.* This category of Salzinger's comprises the most life-like studies of the experimental manipulation of verbal behavior. An example is again available from the work of Verplanck (1955), who showed—with seventeen different experimenters—that the rate of "stating opinions" was increased in twenty-four subjects when their opinion-stating was reinforced by agreement or the paraphrasing of their statements by the experimenter. (The following studies, by Salzinger and his associates with abnormal subjects, fall within this last category.)

Salzinger (1960) concluded, from his review of material on the experimental analysis of the interview, that one profitable way of looking at this situation was in terms of the behavior of the interviewer as the independent variable and of the behavior of the person interviewed as the dependent variable.

The first study in a series that was devoted to the manipulation of the behavior of abnormal subjects was reported by Salzinger and Pisoni (1958), who were concerned with the problems of identification, elicitation, and modification of the rate of emission of verbal *affect* responses. In fact, they set out to reinforce "statements about feelings" made by schizophrenic patients during a brief interview. They chose this kind of response because, they argued, the estimation of one critical diagnostic sign, "flatness of affect," is often based upon a *lack* of such statements in the patient's verbal repertoire, as this is gauged by psychiatric interview impressions.

In this study, Salzinger and Pisoni (1958) studied the verbal behavior of thirty-six schizophrenic patients. Twenty of these were treated as experimental subjects and sixteen as controls. The patients in both groups were interviewed twice. The interview started with the usual inquiries about age and other personal information.

For members of the experimental group, the plan was as follows. During the first ten minutes, the rates of spontaneous production (i.e., the operant level) of affect responses was estimated. These responses were defined, for the purpose of this experiment, as any phrase produced by the patient describing or evaluating his own feeling state. These included all statements beginning with the personal pronoun "I" or "we," followed by an expression of affect, such as "I enjoyed it," "We like him," and so on. (Fifteen recorded interviews were scored independently for affect statements by two experimenters, and a high level of agreement was reached, showing that it was possible reliably to score the appearance of such statements in free speech.)

In the second ten minutes, the experimenter used an operant conditioning procedure, reinforcing each affect response by saying "mmm–hm," "I see," "Yeah," and the like. During the third ten-minute period, the experimenter withheld all reinforcement, thus constituting an extinction series. The control group had only one interview, of thirty minutes, and none of their statements were reinforced in any way; in other words, they were treated throughout as the experimental subjects were treated in the first ten-minute, operant-level phase.

The differences in the incidence of affective responses between the operant level, conditioning, and extinction trials for the first interviews of the members of the experimental group were tested by Wilcoxon's (1949) nonparametric analysis of variance, and were found to be statistically significant. Most affect statements were produced during the conditioning phase, the next greatest number during the operant level period, and the least number were produced under the extinction conditions. Typical response curves of patients who showed the conditioning effect to a marked degree are shown in Figure 7.1.

The differences in level between the three phases for the experimental group in the second interview were in the same order, but they did not on this occasion achieve statistical significance. No significant difference for the production of affect statements in different parts of the interview was found for the control group, who had never received reinforcement. When the experimental and control groups were compared phase by phase, there was, as expected, a significant difference between them in the conditioning phase.

As a further check on the lawfulness of their results, Salzinger and Pisoni plotted, for the experimental group, the number of affective responses

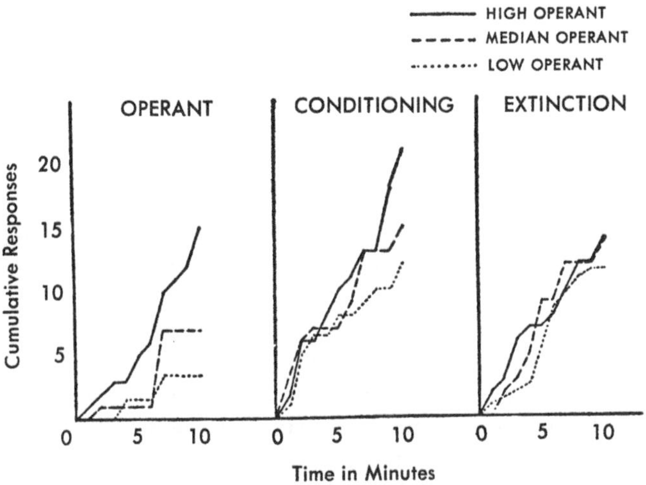

Fig. 7.1. Individual cumulative response curves for three patients who showed the conditioning effect. (From Salzinger and Pisoni, 1958)

made during the extinction phase of the interview against the number of reinforcements accorded during the conditioning phase, with the results shown in Figure 7.2. The authors noted that this relationship could best be expressed by a linear equation. They also pointed out that

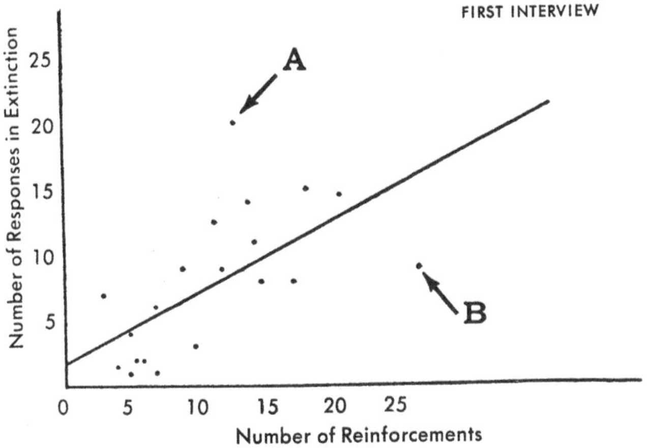

Fig. 7.2. Number of affect responses during extinction as a function of number of reinforcements in the first interview. (From Salzinger and Pisoni, 1958)

Two patients appear to deviate markedly from the rest of the sample. The diagnosis of one of these patients [*A* in Figure 7.2] was changed from schizo-affective to manic-depressive psychosis. She received 13 reinforcements and gave 20 extinction responses. The other deviate from the group [*B* in Fig. 7.2], who received 27 reinforcements and gave only nine extinction responses, was later found to be hard of hearing. (1958, p. 87)

A similar relationship between responses during extinction and number of reinforcements was shown for the second interview, as depicted in Figure 7.3. The differences in number of reinforcements were caused by individual differences in the rate of emission of affect statements. Salzinger and Pisoni (1958) were, however, able to show that only a small part of the correlation between the number of reinforcements and the number of responses to extinction could be accounted for by the correlation between operant level and number of reinforcements. Salzinger and Pisoni (1960) then extended their work on the reinforcement of affective statements to the study of normal subjects, so as to afford a comparison with the performance of these psychotic patients.

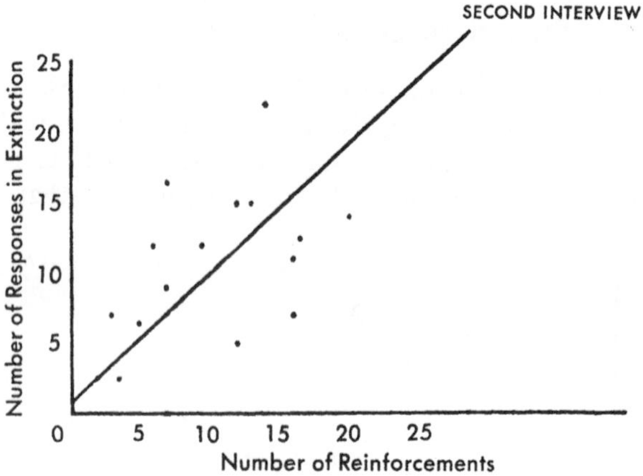

Fig. 7.3. Number of affect responses during extinction as a function of number of reinforcements in the second interview. (From Salzinger and Pisoni, 1958)

Twenty-six nonpsychiatric patients from the wards of a general hospital were used as subjects. All had a thirty-minute interview, divided into the same three ten-minute phases (i.e., involving operant level, reinforcement, and extinction). The same class of affect responses was reinforced as for the psychiatric group.

As in the case of the schizophrenics, there was a significant difference in the number of affective statements emitted during the three phases. The greatest number was again found under conditions of reinforcement, the next greatest during extinction, and the least during the pre-reinforcement or operant level phase.

When the schizophrenics and the normal groups were compared as a whole, there was no significant difference between them in any of the three phases. This result seems rather curious. If it is indeed the case that "flatness of affect" is judged by a lower emission of affective statements, and if it is right to expect to find this flatness in schizophrenics, then one might, for example, have anticipated that the psychotic group would be significantly different from the normal subjects during the operant level phase, which provides an index of the rate of spontaneous emission of such responses.

Salzinger and Pisoni, however, did not stop their analysis of the data at this point. They went on to *match* twelve pairs of schizophrenic and normal subjects on sex, operant level, and number of reinforcements received. This permitted a more valid comparison of the groups on the extinction phase. This comparison, in fact, showed that the normals were significantly more resistant to extinction than the schizophrenics. Figure 7.4 illustrates this effect for two matched pairs (one of high, one of low operant

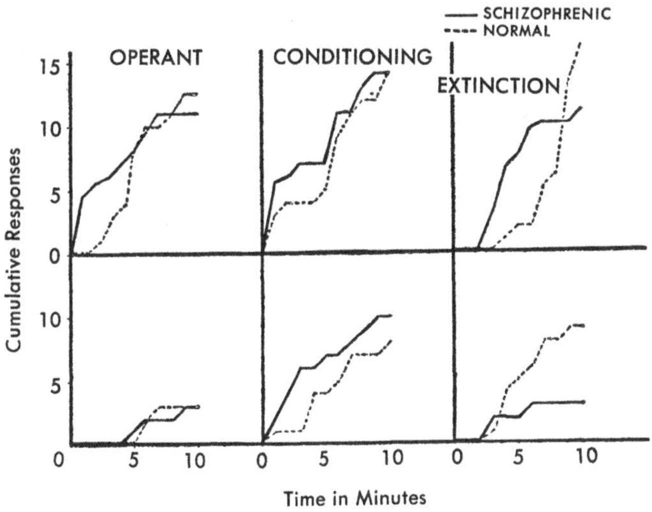

Fig. 7.4. Individual cumulative affect response curves for two pairs of matched schizophrenics and normals. The top pair shows two subjects with high operant levels, while the bottom pair shows two subjects with low operant levels. (From Salzinger and Pisoni, 1960)

level). This finding led Salzinger and Pisoni to conclude that the clinical impression of flatness of affect in schizophrenics may be due to the fact that they extinguish more readily in their production of affective references when such statements are no longer reinforced.

It would seem at least equally plausible to argue, however, that since—as suggested in Chapter 2—the label "schizophrenia" by no means describes a homogeneous group of disorders, it would have been more profitable to select patients for the experiment on the basis of flattened affect rather than in terms of diagnosis. In other words, affective flattening may be a sufficient but not a necessary characteristic of some part of this group of disorders. It would certainly be of interest to carry out a further series of experiments in which the subjects were chosen on the basis of this descriptive characteristic, rather than on the basis of diagnosis, in order to see what results would emerge from a similar experimental treatment.

Some questions remained to be explored, however, even in the case of subjects chosen by diagnosis. Salzinger and Pisoni (1961) therefore carried out further studies to discover (*a*) if the effectiveness of the verbal reinforcement depended upon whether it was given at the beginning of the interview period, or, as formerly, in the middle; and (*b*) if various arbitrarily assigned numbers of reinforcements made a difference to the number of trials to extinction (i.e., as a measure of conditioning strength).

To answer the first question, they used fourteen schizophrenic subjects, and each was interviewed for thirty minutes. During the *first* ten-minute period, in this case, self-referred affect statements were reinforced in the usual way. This was followed by twenty minutes (considered here as two ten-minute intervals) without reinforcement.

It was then possible for them to compare the results of this group with those of the experimental and control groups of their 1958 study. These results are shown in Table 7.1. On examination of the within-group differences by a nonparametric analysis of variance test (Siegel, 1956), it was found that the only significant change was in the second ten minutes for group A (whose treatment sequence, it will be recalled, was operant level-conditioning-extinction). On further examination, however, it proved that the members of group B had, on average, received fewer reinforcements during the conditioning period of their treatment. When the results of individuals who had received six or fewer reinforcements were removed from this group, a significant conditioning effect appeared. On these grounds, Salzinger and Pisoni (1961) felt able to conclude that the number of reinforcements awarded is more important than their placement in the interview sequence.

This conclusion also led to the second investigation, mentioned above, to see what difference in strength of conditioning might be produced by systematically altering the number of reinforcements given. The subjects were

TABLE 7.1
Sum of Ranks of Affect Statements for Each of the 10-minute Periods for the Three Groups of Patients Compared[a]

	SUCCESSIVE 10-MINUTE PERIODS					
GROUPS	*1st*	*2nd*	*3rd*	X^2r	*p*	*N*
A. Experimental group (1958 study)	41.5	50.5	28.0	12.82	.002	20
B. Experimental group (1961 study)	31.5	25.5	27.0	1.39	.50	14
C. Control group (1958 study)	30.0	37.0	29.0	2.37	.30	16

[a] After Salzinger and Pisoni, 1961.

thirty-two schizophrenics and the experimental procedure was divided as for group A (above); but in the second, conditioning phase, selected subjects were given a predetermined number of reinforcements for self-referred affect statements (four, six, eight, ten, fifteen, or twenty). Analysis of the results showed that the conditioning effect was obtained only in subjects who got ten or more reinforcements; there proved, in fact, to be a minimum total of reinforcements below which conditioning did not take place. It was also shown that subjects with faster rates of acquisition showed greater resistance to extinction.

In addition to this exploration of some of the parameters of verbal conditioning in schizophrenics, Salzinger and his coworkers have further examined the nature of the response units. Salzinger (1962), for example, has considered some of the problems raised by the fact that no two responses are ever precisely the same, so that care must be taken when any attempt is made to group a number of responses into a single class (e.g., "self-referred affect"). In the studies already cited, part of the evidence that "self-referred affect" does indeed represent a distinct class comes from the fact that appropriate reinforcement increased the incidence of this class—without, for example, increasing the amount of self-reference statements in general. In addition, Portnoy* and Salzinger (1964) distinguished between positive-, negative-, and neutral-affect verbs through the use of Osgood's

* Née Pisoni

Semantic Differential (Osgood, Suci, and Tannenbaum, 1957). They then separately conditioned the use of each of these classes in different groups of normal subjects in a modified Taffel-type verbal conditioning situation. Their results showed that verbs indicative of positive and negative affect did indeed constitute natural response classes.

In a further study of verbal conditioning in schizophrenic subjects, Salzinger and Portnoy (1964) first looked into the performance of chronic patients. Sixteen male chronic schizophrenic patients were each given the standard thirty-minute interview, divided into ten-minute operant level, conditioning, and extinction periods. No change in the reinforced self-referred affect statements was observed. These patients, in fact, behaved quite differently from the acute schizophrenic patients previously studied (Salzinger and Pisoni, 1958). The lack of change in the chronic patients proved to be due to their low operant level for *speech in general*; these patients spoke much less than acute patients or normal persons.

In the same paper, Salzinger and Portnoy (1964) were able to show that responses to the conditioning procedures had a certain amount of prognostic relevance. A group of fifty-eight patients diagnosed as schizophrenic were submitted to the self-referred affect-conditioning procedure. Of these, twenty-five received reinforcement for each of these statements they uttered during the conditioning phase, while thirty-three had previously been assigned an arbitrary number of reinforcements, ranging from four to twenty. After one-hundred-and-eighty days, the patients were characterized as still being in the hospital ("ins") or as having been released ("outs"). Analysis then showed that the patients who had left the hospital also tended to be those who had conditioned successfully, whereas those who remained in the hospital had not.

On a further subdivision of the groups, in order to select those for whom the most accurate prediction could be made, it was found that if first-admission females—with a high school education or better—were chosen, the congruence of conditioning effect and outcome was very high, as shown in Table 7.2.

The relationship between the prognostic criterion and the conditioning effect was significant ($p = 0.03$) by Fisher's Exact Probability Test (Siegel, 1956). That is to say, when only this restricted group of patients was considered, those who had both conditioned and extinguished were out of the hospital after 180 days, and those who did not condition, or who conditioned but did not extinguish, remained in the hospital. Since Lindsley (1956, see p. 135, above) has also observed a case in which there was a pathological failure to extinguish after conditioning had taken place, it may be that this kind of disorder specifies a kind of perseveration that would be interesting to investigate in its own right.

TABLE 7.2
Relationship between Outcome Status at the End of Six Months and Reactivity to Reinforcement[a]

REACTIVITY TO REINFORCEMENT	OUTCOME STATUS *In's*	*Out's*	*Total*
Conditioned & extinguished	1	6	7
Others[b]	6	1	7
Total	7	7	14

[a]From Salzinger and Portnoy, 1964.
[b]Includes subjects who did not condition and subjects who conditioned but did not extinguish.

In a further study, Salzinger, Portnoy, and Feldman (1964) tried to see (*a*) if the reduction of personal contact between experimenter and patient would reduce or eliminate the conditioning effect, and (*b*) if the reinforcement of one class of verbal response (either self-referred affect or speech in general) would increase the rate of emission of another class.

In this study, eighty-eight schizophrenic patients were divided into three groups. Group A ($N = 33$) was rewarded, by a flashing light, for any self-referred affect that was emitted during the whole thirty-minute interview. Group S ($N = 21$) was similarly rewarded, but on a thirty-second fixed-interval schedule, for the production of any speech during the interview. For group C ($N = 31$), the experimenters did not give any reinforcement during the thirty minutes of the interview.

It was found that, in absolute terms, group A emitted a significantly larger number of self-referred affect terms than group C, the largest difference occurring in the last ten minutes of the interview. Group A also emitted proportionately more self-referred affect than group S when the total number of words produced by each group was taken into account. The performance of a typical representative of each group is shown in Figure 7.5.

Also, as expected, group S emitted a significantly greater number of words than group C for all three ten-minute periods of the interview, and a significantly greater number than group A for the second and third ten-minute periods. This trend was illustrated by the records of three typical subjects, shown in Figure 7.6.

As the investigators conclude, the impersonal reinforcement used in this study proved effective; it was also shown to be specific to the response

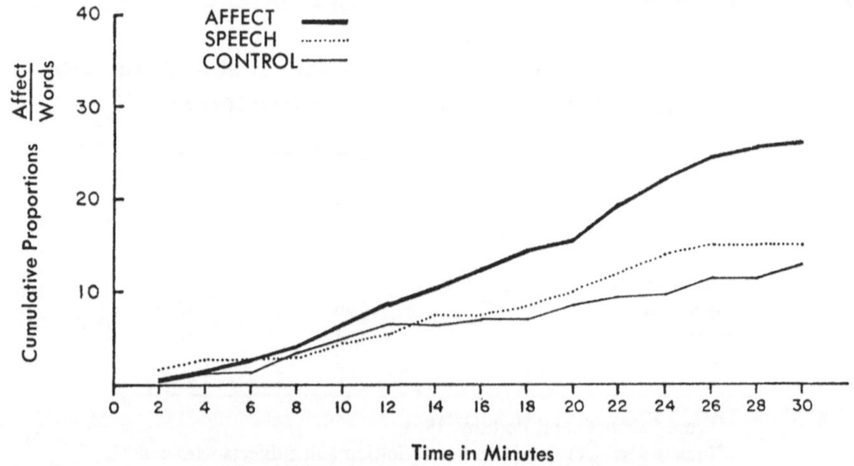

Fig. 7.5. Individual cumulative response curves of the proportion of affect to words for three subjects, selected at the median of each of the three groups. (From Salzinger, Portnoy, and Feldman, 1964)

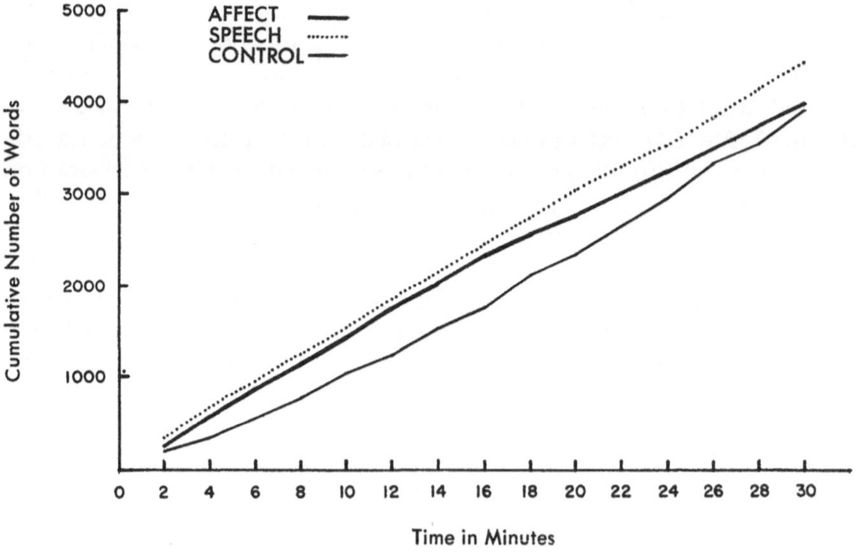

Fig. 7.6. Individual cumulative response curves of the total number of words for three subjects selected, at the median of each of the three groups. (From Salzinger, Portnoy, and Feldman, 1964)

class reinforced, whether narrow (self-referred affect) or broad (total speech output).

Because verbal behavior can purposely be manipulated, even by nonverbal reinforcement, the possibility exists that particular classes of response may be unwittingly reinforced by some therapists. As these authors cogently remark,

> . . . an observed frequency of a particular response class must always be interpreted in conjunction with the reinforcement contingencies between the occurrence of such responses and the behavior of the person obtaining that sample of verbal behavior. Thus when a therapist of one school claims that his patients talk a great deal about sex, and another denies this while claiming that his patients talk far more of interpersonal relationship problems, they may both be honest and accurate. The difference between them probably lies in the extent to which their theoretical outlook determines what type of speech they are interested in and consequently what speech they are likely to reinforce. (Salzinger, Portnoy, and Feldman, 1964, p. 514)

These studies by Salzinger and his associates undoubtedly rank as major contributions to the experimental control of abnormal behavior. Two related critical points should, however, be reemphasized. These derive from the fact that this work has perhaps been too much influenced by notions of psychiatric diagnosis. This has, in the first place, focused attention upon such labels as "schizophrenia" rather than upon the disordered behavior itself. This, in turn, has led to the use of manipulation for static rather than dynamic purposes, as in the creation of prognostic indicators rather than the further development of methods of control.

Salzinger and his colleagues have, however, used verbal operant techniques for the alteration of specific deficits in children. Salzinger *et al.* (1962) had previously studied the effects of reinforcement on the spontaneous continuous speech of normal children between five and seven years of age, and had shown that their speech rate increased with impersonal reinforcement (i.e., lighting up a toy clown's nose) and that it stabilized or decreased when reinforcement was withheld. Reinforcement procedures were thereafter applied by Salzinger, Feldman, Cowan, and Salzinger (1965) to the speech-deficient behavior of two young boys, three years and seven months and three years and ten months of age.

The first of these children, when admitted to the hospital, was hyperactive and could produce no recognizable words—only a wide selection of whines, screams, and grunts. He was not toilet trained. The principal treatment given this child was spread over 195 forty-to fifty-minute sessions, in which a variety of edible reinforcements (candy, peanuts, etc.) was given on different schedules—first for word-like sounds, later for words or close approximations to words. Salzinger *et al.* note that, overall, the rate of actual word emission remained low; it was, however, higher than it had been before the experimental approach was tried. Furthermore, the animal-like sounds the child had formerly made were extinguished. His previous destructive hyperactivity was also brought under some degree of control by making the reinforcements available in only one restricted part of the experimental room. Also his toilet habits were improved by being selectively reinforced when the appropriate behavior was evinced.

The second child also was initially almost speechless, except for the word "no," and very afraid of strangers. He was not toilet trained and was slightly hyperactive. The first steps in his treatment involved "shaping" his behavior toward the experimental room. He was given candy for movements that, by a series of successive approximations, finally brought him into the room where eventually he would stay with the experimenter over the hour-long operant session. In this case, a considerable amount of intelligible speech behavior, including simple requests and color-naming, was eventually established—after 56 sessions.

Whereas the first child secured only about twenty-five words, and was able to employ them only in the form used in the conditioning situation, the second child began to employ simple grammatical constructions that had never themselves been specifically reinforced. The second child also improved in his social behavior, and was less fearful of strangers.

This brief account does scant justice to the extended and painstaking work carried out on these two children, but it may illustrate that the kind of manipulation attempted is best applied if it is designed to fit the disorder of the individual case and if it is conducted and continued according to the progress made by that case. It also reinforces the contention that satisfactory progress can best be made and maintained when that progress can be measured. Thus the instatement of verbal behavior from a zero or near-zero baseline requires no indirect external validation. The disordered behavior has in fact been assessed and altered directly. A somewhat similar procedure had previously been used for the reinstatement of verbal behavior in mute adult psychotic patients by Isaacs, Thomas, and Goldiamond (1960).

As Krasner and Ullmann (1965) have noted, a major issue brought out by Salzinger's work is the importance of the human reinforcer. Unlike Lindsley's studies (see Chapter 6), which have principally used mechanically controlled, impersonal reinforcement conditions, the work considered in the present chapter has mainly involved social and personal reinforcement. One possible relevance of this latter kind of reinforcement in the person-to-person relationships subsumed under the general term "psychotherapy" has already been noted by Salzinger, Portnoy, and Feldman (1964). As they have pointed out, it may well be the case that exponents of different therapeutic schools inadvertently reinforce the kind of admissions and insights they believe they should produce. It might also be true that they reinforce *useful* verbal habits that generalize into other adjustive behavior. It would certainly be of interest to see if this is the case, and, if it is, to see what reinforcers and what behavior are effective.

Krasner (1955) has very clearly made this point, as follows.

> Put in terms which would permit a behavioral analysis, the problem is to isolate the dimensions of the therapeutic situation and to determine what the lawful relationships are between the therapist's behavior as the independent variable and the patient's behavior as the dependent variable. Seen in this light, the problem of analyzing the therapeutic situation becomes one of analyzing the relationship of two people in terms of their specific behavior. No matter how psychotherapy is defined or just what approach is used, there is general agreement that something called a "relationship" between two people is involved. What we are suggesting is that future experimenters interested in the problems of psychotherapy focus their efforts at understanding this "relationship" by studying the effects of certain behavior of the therapist which might reinforce certain responses of the patient. (1955, p. 20)

The same author has noted—in his review of studies of the conditioning of verbal behavior (Krasner, 1958)—that the nondirective form of psychotherapy developed by Rogers (1951) and his associates has much in common with the verbal conditioning paradigm. It also appears to be the case that this therapeutic school has done most to emphasize the importance of research into the processes of psychotherapy. It is this work, in the main, that will be considered in the next chapter.

8

THE EFFECTS OF *Psychotherapy*

THE PREVIOUS CHAPTER was principally concerned with the experimental manipulation of verbal behavior; attention may now be turned to the verbal manipulation of other behavior.

It seems likely that, when in distress, man has always sought solace by talking about his troubles to another. In the recent past, however, systems have been evolved that try to specify the particular form or content of discourse that may be the most effective in the relief of anguish and abnormality. Many forms of the "talking cure" tend to be comprised by the general label "psychotherapy." In their attempt to distinguish the prime features of this kind of treatment, Ford and Urban (1963) cite four characteristics that are common to the main varieties of psychotherapeutic procedure.

First, they say, psychotherapy usually involves two people in confidential personal interaction. Emphasis here is on the confidential quality of the interchange because the person who seeks relief is commonly required frankly to reveal his thoughts and feelings to the other in a way that is seldom demanded—or even allowed—in ordinary social intercourse. Second, these transactions are almost exclusively verbal in nature. Although other nonverbal behavior is sometimes observed and evaluated (Scheflen, 1964), most of the exchange between therapist and patient is carried out through talk. Third, this arrangement usually extends over a fairly long span of time. Fourth, the aim is to produce a change in one of the participants. Thus Ford and Urban conclude:

We emerge with a characterization of individual verbal psychotherapy as a procedure wherein two persons engage in a prolonged series of emotion-arousing interactions, mediated primarily by verbal exchanges, the purpose of which is to produce changes in the behavior of one of the pair. (1963, p. 17)

It must be evident, of course, that these features include only some of the homologues that may be derived from a very wide range of different theories and techniques of psychotherapy.

The fourth defining characteristic (cited above) refers to *change*. Although most psychotherapists believe that they often do produce improvement, their belief has not always been founded upon good evidence. Like any other remedy, the effectiveness of psychotherapy can be judged only in comparative terms and not just by the enthusiasm of its salesmen. Perhaps the most polemical statements on this theme have been made by Eysenck (1952a, 1960) in his evaluation of the *outcome* of psychotherapy. He has argued that, because most disorders eventually get better by themselves, the value of any specific treatment must be judged by its rate of cure in excess of the rate of spontaneous remission. Eysenck has reviewed much of the relevant evidence and has been unable to find any advantage for the effects of psychotherapy of the neuroses over—for example—the effects of simple custodial care.

It would be impossible for the author to summarize Eysenck's contentions more succinctly than Eysenck does himself, in the following passage.

It appears that eight major conclusions can be derived from the literature:

1. When untreated neurotic control groups are compared with experimental groups of neurotic patients treated by means of psychotherapy, both groups recover to approximately the same extent.

2. When soldiers who have suffered a neurotic breakdown and have not received psychotherapy are compared with soldiers who have received psychotherapy, the chances of the two groups returning to duty are approximately equal.

3. When neurotic soldiers are separated from the Service, their chances of recovery are not affected by their receiving or not receiving psychotherapy.

4. Civilian neurotics who are treated by psychotherapy recover or improve to approximately the same extent as similar neurotics receiving no psychotherapy.

5. Children suffering from emotional disorders and treated by psychotherapy recover or improve to approximately the same extent as similar children not receiving psychotherapy.

6. Neurotic patients treated by means of psychotherapeutic procedures based on learning theory improve significantly more quickly than do patients treated by means of psychoanalytic or eclectic psychotherapy, or not treated by psychotherapy at all.

7. Neurotic patients treated by psychoanalytic psychotherapy do not improve more quickly than patients treated by means of eclectic psychotherapy, and may improve less quickly when account is taken of the large proportion of patients breaking off treatment.

8. With the single exception of the psychotherapeutic methods based on learning theory, results of published research with military and civilian neurotics, and with both adults and children, suggest that the therapeutic effects of psychotherapy are small or nonexistent, and do not in any demonstrable way add to the nonspecific

effects of routine medical treatment or to such events as occur in the patients' everyday experience. (1960, pp. 719–720)

It need hardly be said that these conclusions, although carefully documented, have not gone undisputed (e.g., Rosenzweig, 1954). Even if we ignore the many angry responses that convey mainly the rage and pain of those psychotherapists who have felt, so to speak, their couches being ripped from under them, many feel that much remains to be accounted for. Eysenck himself has recognized this.

Clearly, the matter cannot be left there. It will be necessary in the first place to account for the fact that so many therapists and so many patients believe quite firmly in the efficacy of psychotherapy; this is an undoubted fact, which appears to be in contradiction to our conclusions, and requires explanation. In the second place, it will be necessary to examine the consequences of our conclusions, in so far as they are relevant to psychological theories of neurotic disorder and breakdown; quite clearly the failure of a commonly held belief to be supported by the facts must have some repercussions on widely held theories which have given rise to such beliefs. (1960, p. 720)

One way around the problem set by critics such as Eysenck has been taken by those psychotherapists who choose to emphasize *process* rather than outcome. Instead of asking what comes *out* of psychotherapy, they ask what goes on *in* psychotherapy. If the outcome is truly negative, however, this effort would seem to be but an empty exercise.

There is, however, one group or school of psychotherapists that has for some time been interested in both process *and* outcome, and in the relations between the two. This is the client-centered group that owes its main allegiance to the work and writings of Carl Rogers (1942, 1951, 1961). Rogers refers to the beneficial outcome of psychotherapy as "constructive personality change" (which we will sometimes refer to as CPC) and he has (Rogers, 1957) defined a number of process characteristics that he believes must obtain in psychotherapy if such change is to be secured. In summary, he has said:

For constructive personality change to occur, it is necessary that these [following] conditions exist and continue over a period of time:

1. Two persons are in psychological contact.
2. The first, whom we shall term the client, is in a state of incongruence, being vulnerable or anxious.
3. The second person, whom we shall term the therapist, is congruent or integrated in the relationship.
4. The therapist experiences unconditional positive regard for the client.
5. The therapist experiences an empathic understanding of the client's internal frame of reference and endeavors to communicate this experience to the client.

6. The communication to the client of the therapist's empathic understanding and unconditional positive regard is to a minimal degree achieved. (1957, p. 96)

Rogers and his associates have pointed out that this kind of description of the elements essential to both therapeutic process and outcome is relatively neutral so far as specific theory about their mode of action is concerned. These conditions, it is claimed, can be discerned in the activities of therapists of many schools. These conditions, however, are regarded as *necessary* for change to take place. It is conceivable, then, that those studies of psychotherapy that have examined only outcome have been vitiated by their failure to establish whether these essential elements were present, or absent, in the treatments whose effects alone were examined. Studies of process, however, which have ignored outcome, could not be expected to determine whether or not these elements were essential since this can be done only by relating them to their effects.

Extensive and systematic studies concerned with both process and outcome together have been initiated in conjunction with Carl Rogers and have been reported principally by Dr. Charles B. Truax and his co-workers. These studies perhaps provide one of the best available models for the objective and nonpartisan study of the effects of psychotherapy. Truax and his colleague, Carkhuff, (1964a) have phrased their central argument as follows.

The essential question, "What are the effective elements in psychotherapy that produce constructive behavioral and personality change?" leads quite naturally to the theory of the general linear equation, as the most simple and useful available model. Using this model, we may set the task for clinical theory and research as that of specifying the variables in psychotherapy which successfully predict observed constructive behavioral or personality change in patients. Once the variables are successfully discovered and measured, the problem becomes the empirical one of establishing, by the usual statistical procedures, the relative importance (or weights) of the known variables that most successfully predict personality or behavioral change.

The proposed model can be stated as:

$$\mathrm{CPC} = K + TV_1 + \ldots TV_n + PV_1 + \ldots PV_n + SV_1 + \ldots SV_n + IV_1 + \ldots IV_n + e,$$

where: CPC = Index of Constructive Personality Change
K = Constant
TV_{1-n} = Therapist Variables 1 to n
PV_{1-n} = Patient Variables 1 to n
SV_{1-n} = Situational or Contextual Variables 1 to n
IV_{1-n} = Interaction or Process Variables 1 to n
e = Error.

The general linear equation will yield the fewest elements of psychotherapy possible: the criterion measure of constructive change in the patient can be expressed as a linear function of the psychotherapy variables, and each psychotherapy variable can then be tested for the significance or importance of its effect in the resulting equation. This formulation simply asks the basic question of whether or not a given variable has a significant effect, and whether that variable continues to have an effect when other variables are included in the same linear equation. This is indeed a major question in the field of psychotherapy, especially in view of the present proliferation of concepts, if, for example, the activity level of the therapist were found to be a significant predictor of personality change in psychotherapy, would it still make a difference in outcome if high levels of therapist authenticity and accurate empathic understanding were also present?

It could be argued that the real world is not so simply constructed that linear relationships will always be found. Curvilinear relationships seem inevitable. However, the model is still appropriately useful: we might, for example, transform some of the quantitative measures of the effective therapy variables so that one would be expressed, as say, the log value, a second as an exponential value, and the third as an arc sine value.

Such an all-encompassing, but basically simple, model has the advantage of making no assumptions about the nature of psychotherapy, the nature of personality, or the nature of personality change. It has the advantage of excluding no past or future explanations of the "dynamics" of therapeutic personality change. Indeed, future research will inevitably draw heavily upon current theory and clinical practice. Thus, the model is simply an empirical one that can be used equally well by psychoanalytic, client-centered, behavioristic, or eclectic researchers and practitioners who aim for more effective treatment.

The linear model also provides a convenient way of organizing the state of our present findings from psychotherapy research. (1964a, pp. 127–128)

The variables to which the most consideration has so far been given by Truax and his colleagues fall into two of the groups specified in the above model: therapist and patient variables. These comprise, in the former case—and in the order specified by Rogers (1957)—the therapist's self-congruence (TSC), unconditional positive regard (UPR), and accurate empathy (AE); and, in the latter case, depth of self-exploration (DSE). Before each of these characteristics is separately defined, it would seem necessary first to describe how, in general terms, Truax and his group have designed their experiments. Their procedures are probably best conceived in terms of the kind of flowchart illustrated in Figure 8.1. It represents the following scheme, which has, in its essentials, been common to many of Truax's studies.

(1) The therapeutic interviews with the patients or clients are tape-recorded and then coded—to preserve anonymity and to prevent the contamination of later analyses by any knowledge of patient or therapist characteristics other than what may be secured by the means permitted in the experimental design.

(2) Short extracts are then taken from intermittent therapeutic sessions.

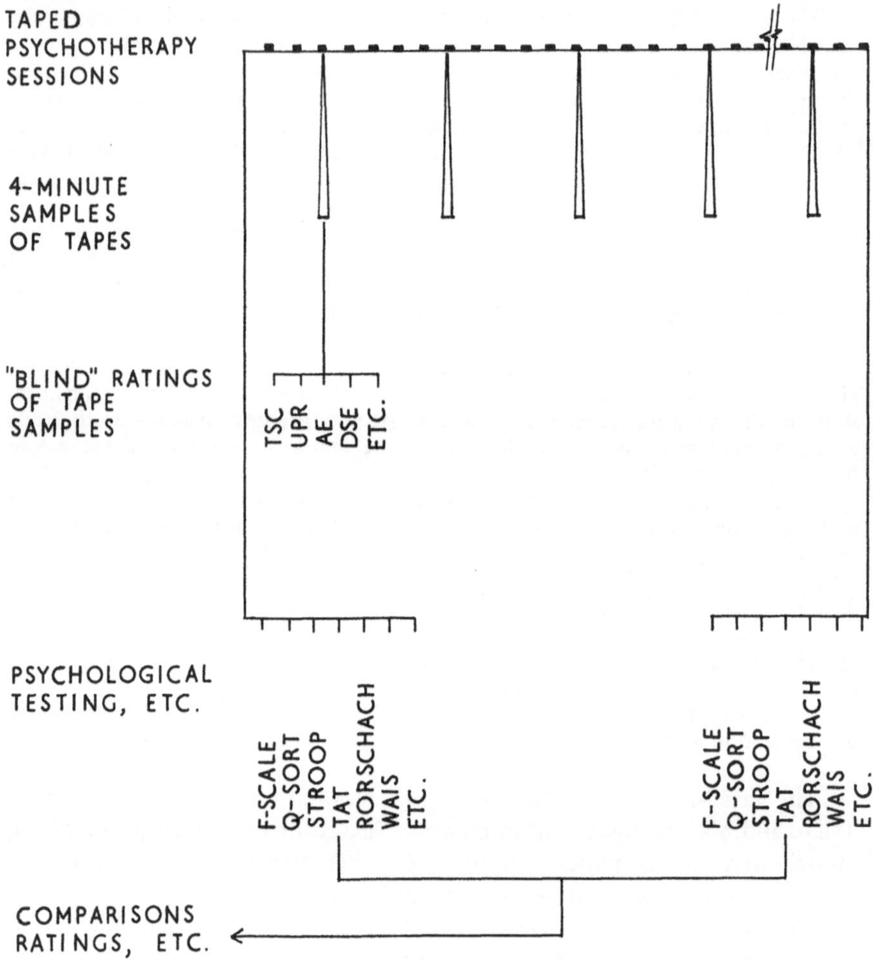

Fig. 8.1. Flowchart diagram of the general experimental scheme of research with tape-recorded therapeutic sessions. (After Graham, Hunter, and Inglis, 1964)

Fig. 8.1 shows four minute samples of interviews taken every fifth session. Evidently, the length of samples might be varied, as could their position or frequency in the sequence of interviews from which they were taken, and the total number of interviews might be longer or shorter. These extracts are coded and then used in such a fashion that their actual position in the series of therapeutic sessions is not known when they are rated.

(3) Commonly, Truax and his associates have had these extracts evaluated on a number of characteristics by raters who have been trained in

the use of certain scales but who have otherwise known very little about abnormal psychology or theories of psychotherapy. They have mainly been bright college undergraduates. More than one person has usually been used to rate the samples in terms of any given scale, which means that the reliability of rating can be determined by correlations between raters. Obviously, if the raters were to disagree about any quality, it could not then be regarded as one with good reliability, and this would be reflected in a low correlation between their opinions. These raters have been trained in a practical way, for instance, by being required to listen to samples of sessions already graded on the attributes in question. The principal attributes rated have, in fact, been the following.

(*a*) *Therapist's self-congruence (TSC).* This characteristic, which is one of the therapist variables held to be of importance in the production of beneficial change in the patient, defines the quality of "genuiness" or "transparency" (Truax and Carkhuff, 1963). To display this quality, the therapist must, in fact, present his real self in the encounter. Truax (1962a) has developed a five-point scale for the assessment of this characteristic. At the "low" end of the scale, or stage 1, Truax and Carkhuff (1964b) have said

> . . . the therapist is clearly defensive in the interaction and there is explicit evidence of a very considerable discrepancy between his experiencing and his current verbalization. Thus, the therapist makes striking contradictions in his statements . . . or, the therapist may contradict the content . . . with the voice qualities. (1964b, p. 132)

At the "high" end, or stage 5, these authors have stated

> . . . the therapist is freely and deeply himself in the relationship. There is an openness to experiences and feelings by the therapist of all types . . . both pleasant and hurtful . . . without traces of defensiveness or retreat into professionalism. (1964b, p. 133)

A positive correlation would of course be expected between this therapist variable and good therapeutic outcome.

(*b*) *Unconditional positive regard (UPR).* This characteristic has also been calibrated on a five-point scale designed by Truax (1962b), who tried to define five stages along a hypothetical continuum related to the nonpossessive warmth of the therapist. At the "low" end of the scale, stage 1, Truax and Carkhuff (1964b) have noted that the therapist

> . . . may be telling the patient what would be "best" for him, or may be in other ways actively either approving or disapproving of his behavior. The therapist acts in such a way as to make himself the locus of evaluation and the therapist sees himself as responsible *for* the patient. (1964b, p. 130)

At the "high" end of the scale, stage 5, the therapist

> . . . communicates unconditional positive regard without restriction. At this stage, the patient is free to be himself even if this means that he is regressing, being defensive, or even disliking or rejecting the therapist himself. The only channeling by the therapist may be the demand that the patient communicate personally relevant material. (1964b, p. 131)

The prediction would of course again be that therapists who were rated high on this scale would produce more constructive personality change in their patients than therapists who were rated low on this quality.

(*c*) *Accurate empathy (AE).* An attempt has been made to measure this quality on a nine-point scale to detect both the therapist's sensitivity to current feelings and his ability to communicate this understanding to the patient verbally (Truax, 1962c). The "low" end point of this scale, stage 1, has been described by Truax and Carkhuff in these terms:

> The therapist seems completely unaware of even the most conspicuous of the client's feelings. His responses are not appropriate to the mood and content of the client's statement and there is no determinable quality of empathy, hence no accuracy whatsoever. (1964b, p. 126)

At the "high" end, or stage 9, the therapist

> . . . unerringly responds to the client's full range of feelings in their exact intensity. He expands the client's hint into a full-blown but tentative elaboration of feeling or experience with unerring sensitivity or accuracy. He is completely attuned to the client's shifting emotional content; he senses each of the client's feelings and reflects them in his word and voice. (1964b, p. 127)

Allied to this characteristic, but apparently not identical with it, is "concreteness" (Truax and Carkhuff, 1964c). The therapist is least concrete when he responds to his patient at an abstract, intellectual level. He is most concrete when quite definite feelings and experience are specified. Both accurate empathy and concreteness would be expected to correlate directly with good outcome, or positive personality change.

The next characteristic that has been assessed is a patient variable.

(*d*) *Depth of self-exploration (DSE).* Measurements of this quality seem to have a rather uncertain status in Truax's scheme. Sometimes it functions as one of the independent variables predictive of personality change, at other times it seems to be regarded as one of the indices of personality change itself.

To estimate the extent to which the patient demonstrates this quality in the psychotherapeutic setting, Truax (1962d) has devised a ten-point scale. At the "low" end of the scale, or stage 1, Truax and Carkhuff have stated that the patient actively evades personally relevant material *even* when the therapist speaks of it.

Near the other end of the scale, at stage 8, the patient

is actively exploring his feelings, his values, his perceptions of others, his relationships, his fears, his turmoil, and his life choices (1964b, pp. 138–139).

The expectation is that this quality, too, will be positively correlated with constructive personality change.

(4) The assessment of positive change itself (or CPC) as the dependent criterion variable has been less adequately considered by Truax and his associates, who seem to have settled for variety in their measures, perhaps even at the expense of validity.

The indices of CPC they have used have included the following tests (but not necessarily in the same order).

- Authoritarian F Scale (Adorno *et al.* 1950)
- Minnesota Multiphasic Personality Inventory (Hathaway and McKinley, 1951)
- Q-sort tests (Stephenson, 1953)
- Rorschach Test (Klopfer and Kelley, 1946)
- Stroop tests (Thurstone, 1944)
- Thematic Apperception Test (Murray, 1943)
- Wechsler Adult Intelligence Scale (Wechsler, 1955)
- Wittenborn Rating Scales (Wittenborn, 1951)

While, on the face of it, it might seem reasonable to expect that positive personality change should be reflected in improved performance on such tests, especially in those that purport to be tests of personality, the actual validity of many of these measures has not been demonstrated beyond cavil. It seems a pity, in fact, that Truax and his associates have not yet devoted the analytic care to their main dependent or outcome variable that they have accorded the dissection of their independent or process variables.

Given this general scheme, however, attention may now be turned to the results of some of the specific studies reported by Truax and his colleagues. Truax (1963) has briefly described an investigation in which the subjects studied included fourteen schizophrenic patients who were receiving what seems to have been (from a less detailed description than one might wish to see) individual psychotherapy of an unspecified brand. These patients had been in treatment for a period of up to three and a half years. One four-minute tape-recorded sample of therapist-patient interaction was taken from every fifth interview for each of the fourteen patients, giving a total of 358 samples in all. In line with the procedure described above, each sample was coded so that the raters could not know whether it came from an early or late interview, or from an improved or deteriorated case.

Although it is not absolutely clear from this paper how the measure of CPC was assessed, it would appear from Truax and Carkhuff's (1964b) description that multiple criteria were used. These included psychological test-change data (comprising pre- and posttherapy scores on some or all of the tests cited above), diagnostic evaluations of personality change made "blind" by two psychodiagnosticians unconnected with the research, and an unspecified measure of the hospitalization experience after the beginning of therapy. Unfortunately, in neither of these papers is the actual procedure for the analysis of data cited in full. It is not certain whether the relation between, for example, therapist self-congruence and CPC in this study was assessed by correlating the whole range of scores on both variables or by a chi-square form of analysis in which a group high on the CPC criterion was compared with a group low on CPC in terms of the TSC scores. Truax states only that

> Analysis of the data showed a significant tendency for the therapist in improved cases to be rated higher in self-congruence during the therapeutic sessions than therapists in nonimproved or failure cases ($p < .05$) (1963, p. 259).

So far as unconditional positive regard is concerned, the analysis of the relation between it and the dependent variable CPC seems to have been of the chi-square type mentioned above. Thus Truax has noted that

> samples from improved cases were consistently higher in unconditional positive regard than samples from unimproved or failure cases ($p < .05$) (1963, p. 259).

Analysis of the association between accurate empathy and CPC may have been carried out in the same way for Truax concluded that,

> as predicted, . . . the therapists of the more improved patients were judged to have offered significantly higher levels of accurate empathy throughout the course of therapy than were received by the unimproved patients ($p < .05$) (1963, p. 258).

The beneficial effect of accurate empathy was confirmed for (presumably neurotic) outpatient counseling cases as well as for hospitalized schizophrenics.

So far as depth of self-exploration is concerned, the assessment of its connection with CPC was carried out by correlating the two; the actual correlation found was +.57 ($p < .05$), confirming the expectation that the amount of such self-exploration would be positively related to improvement. Truax and Carkhuff (1964b) have also pointed out that

A potentially even more exciting finding [was that] the level of patient depth of intrapersonal exploration, even during the initial stages of psychotherapy seems to be reasonably predictive of final case outcome. The rating of patient depth of intrapersonal exploration from the second interview was correlated with the final outcome of the patient's constructive personality change, yielding a Pearson correlation of .64 ($p < .05$). Thus, it would seem that very early in the therapeutic encounter a reasonably adequate prediction could be made of the final case outcome, based upon the patient's depth of intrapersonal exploration. (1964b, p. 139)

Truax (1963) gives a somewhat fuller account of the analysis of the relation between combined ratings of the therapist variables, TSC, UPR and AE, and the outcome measure or CPC score. In this part of the study he added fourteen control patients, who presumably received no treatment but were given the same tests as the treated subjects, and, like them, were given these tests on two occasions.

After a mean value on the therapist variables had been obtained for each treated patient, it was judged—on the basis of this score—that eight of the fourteen had received a relatively low level of these conditions combined, and that, presumably, six had received relatively high levels. The expectation was that patients receiving a high level of these conditions would show greater constructive personality change, while patients receiving low levels of these conditions in treatment—together with the patients in the control group—would show a low degree of constructive personality change.

The principal measures of CPC comprised "blind" judgments, on a number of tests, by two independent diagnosticians. Presumably, their overall judgments were then combined and calibrated in such a way that a "score" of 5.0 meant "no change" (i.e., pre- to posttreatment). Truax has described this result in the following way.

Patients receiving high levels of conditions showed an overall gain in psychological functioning (mean change of 6.0 where 5.0 represents no change) whereas patients who received relatively low levels of accurate empathy, unconditional positive regard, and self-congruence showed a *loss* in psychological functioning. Control patients evidenced moderate gains. These differences proved statistically significant ($p < .05$).

In terms of number of patients at or above the median change ratings, the control group had a rough 50–50 split while *all* patients in the group receiving low levels of conditions were below the median. Those patients receiving relatively high levels of conditions from the therapist are six of the eight patients at or above the median of positive change in psychological functioning.

Thus, the data suggest that high conditions facilitate constructive personality change as predicted. However, the findings also say that patients who received relatively low conditions showed negative personality change. (1963, p. 260)

These and similar findings have led Truax and Carkhuff (1964b) to the view that psychotherapy can therefore be either for better or for worse. The data collected by Truax's group suggest that a good therapist—who by definition is one who can display to his patients high levels of self-congruence, unconditional positive regard, and accurate empathy, and who can elicit from them deep self-exploration—will be likely to make them better. Conversely, a therapist low on these abilities may actually make his patients *worse*. Truax and Carkhuff believe that this may explain why surveys of the outcome of psychotherapy that, like Eysenck's (1952a), have neglected process variables, may have in general failed to find a difference between treated and untreated groups. The "treated" groups might, in fact, have been made up of some patients who had been improved by psychotherapy and others who had been made worse by it. If these subgroups were to be lumped together, the positive and negative results might cancel out, leaving the total treated group no better off than the untreated controls.

In Truax and Carkhuff's words:

> These findings also seem to be a step toward explaining the very puzzling mass of evidence which has indicated that psychotherapy is not, on the average, superior to no psychotherapy. The present findings suggest that these findings were sound, but misleading. High therapist-offered conditions in therapy lead to constructive change, while low conditions lead to negative personality change in the patient. An overall effect, determined by combining both high and low conditions, is quite similar to the results of a control or no-therapy group. Thus, if at one point we could eliminate low therapist conditions in psychotherapy, then the constructive value of psychotherapy would be markedly enhanced. (1964b, p. 153)

The generality of the positive effects of high conditions of the crucial therapist variables has also been explored by Truax and his associates. It has been found that, with minor variations, these conditions do indeed also have a beneficial effect in group therapy (Truax, 1961; Truax, Carkhuff, and Kodman, 1965) as well as in individual treatment. The kinds of patient or client improved by them have included hospitalized schizophrenics and out-patient neurotics (Truax, 1963) and depressed and mixed hospitalized groups (Truax, 1961). These circumstances have even been found to aid the adjustment of preschool children (Truax, 1965a).

Truax and his associates have claimed, and have produced evidence to show, that their findings have still wider implications than the descriptive and predictive ones considered above. Thus Truax and Carkhuff have contended that

> . . . research findings identifying elements of effective psychotherapy are directly applicable to the training of psychotherapists.

The evidence that therapists do not always practice what they preach implies that the therapist in training could perhaps profit from less theoretical and intellectual training and more specific training of how to make operational the effective ingredients in psychotherapy. Specifically, measuring instruments used in current research could be directly applied to training programs. Thus, tape-recordings of psychotherapy rated very high in the known elements of effective psychotherapy could be selected to provide concrete examples for beginning therapists, and such scales could also be used to evaluate the trainee's own early therapy behavior to give him immediate and concrete informational feedback telling him how well he is learning to operate with his concepts. (1964a, p. 147)

The means for implementing this suggestion have been outlined by Truax, Carkhuff, and Douds (1964). They have called this the "experiential" approach, which should, they believe, be integrated with the more usual "didactic" mode of training in counseling and psychotherapy. Since the training of the therapist involves making changes in *his* behaviour, it may be assumed that such change will best take place in an atmosphere in which he is exposed to high conditions of self-congruence, unconditioned positive regard, and accurate empathy. This will facilitate his own self-exploration and hence the desired change. At the same time, by being trained in rating the desirable therapeutic qualities in tape-recordings of both himself and other therapists in action, the trainee should be brought to a closer understanding of how these conditions may be fostered and developed.

Truax, Carkhuff, and Douds (1964) have described six possible stages in this training process. First, the student might be taught didactically about the nature and importance of the crucial variables. Second, he would be trained in the use of the relevant rating scales to ensure that he could discriminate between different levels. Third, he would be given a specific training; for example, his accurate empathy would be nurtured by supervised practice on recorded statements from patients. Fourth, he would practice "therapy" with another trainee, and then be required to rate his performance on the scales; this would provide him with necessary feedback on his own capacities. Fifth, he would undertake single sessions with selected patients, which would again be recorded and self-rated. Sixth, Truax, Carkhuff, and Douds have suggested

. . . after, and only after, the trainee has achieved moderately high levels of conditions with a variety of patients in single interviews and has also demonstrated an ability to facilitate moderately high levels of patient self-disclosure and self-exploration (determined by application of the research scales designed to measure patient self-exploration or depth of intrapersonal exploration) would a trainee begin to see patients in "psychotherapy." At that point he would begin supervised experience in the more usual continuing psychotherapeutic contact with a patient . . . . The trainee would continue to tape-record and continue to rate himself from randomly selected samples of the cases which he has been assigned. Comparison ratings would periodically be made by trained raters, evaluating both conditions provided in therapy and extent of self-exploration in the patient. (1964, p. 246)

The actual effect of such a procedure has now been reported upon in two further studies. The first of these, reported by Carkhuff and Truax (1965a), was concerned to see if, by these means, trainees could be brought to evince levels of competence with the therapeutic variables that would be at all commensurate with those shown by experienced therapists. Two differently composed trainee groups, one of twelve graduate students of psychology and the other of five hospital-employed volunteers (including three aides, one volunteer worker, and one industrial therapist), were trained in accordance with the scheme outlined above for about four hours a week over a period of sixteen weeks. Then, in order to evaluate the effects of this procedure on the therapist skills learned, in the last week each trainee had a single tape-recorded interview with each of three hospital patients. From these three tapes for each trainee, six four-minute excerpts were randomly selected, two from each tape. For purposes of comparison, excerpts were also chosen from tapes made by experienced therapists (including, for example, Truax and Rogers themselves) treating similar patients. Two trained raters then assessed all the coded productions for therapist self-congruence (TSC); two different raters assessed unconditional positive regard (UPR); two other raters rated accurate empathy (AE); and two other raters evaluated the patients depth of self-exploration (DSE). The reliability coefficients thus secured were: TSC = .62 and UPR = .48; AE ranged from .24 to .50, and DSE from .47 to .60.

The means and standard deviations of the ratings accorded the different groups (two trainee and one experienced) on the four scales are shown in Table 8.1. From a *t* test analysis of the difference between the separate mean values for each scale, Carkhuff and Truax were able to conclude that

. . . with the notable exception of the critical (depth of self-exploration) variable, where the lay therapists' mean scores were approximately equal to those of the students and the experienced therapists, the groups consistently performed in the following rank order: (*a*) the experienced therapists; (*b*) the graduate students; and (*c*) the lay personnel. While a hierarchy of performance was established, the experienced therapists did not effect significantly better process levels than the graduate students on any dimensions, and the latter were not significantly higher than the lay group on any indexes. The only significant difference was found in the comparison of the experienced and the lay groups on the therapist self-congruence dimension, . . . The results suggest that in a relatively short training period, i.e., approximately 100 hours, both graduate students and lay hospital personnel can be brought to function at levels of therapy nearly commensurate with those of experienced therapists. (1965a, p. 335)

TABLE 8.1
Mean Scale Values of Therapy Process Variables for Groups of Trainees and Experienced Therapists[a]

	TRAINEE THERAPISTS				EXPERIENCED THERAPISTS ($N = 15$)	
	Lay Trainees ($N = 5$)		*Student Trainees* ($N = 12$)			
SCALES	$\overline{m}$	σ	$\overline{m}$	σ	$\overline{m}$	σ
TSC	4.86	0.35	5.23	0.48	5.51	0.45
UPR	2.82	0.62	3.05	0.32	3.16	0.40
AE	4.58	0.30	5.14	0.69	5.22	0.84
DSE	4.66	0.30	4.56	0.60	4.86	0.56

[a] After Carkhuff and Truax, 1965a.

It seems a great pity that, in this study, no control group of therapists who were both untrained *and* inexperienced was rated, since only a comparison with such a group could show whether either training or experience had, indeed any effect at all.

One further encouraging, if not decisive, test of the effect of such training has, however, been reported by Carkhuff and Truax (1965b), in which treatment by the five lay trainees of eighty mental hospital patients in group therapy was compared with no treatment at all in another seventy patients. In this study, three of the trained lay personnel were given two groups of ten patients each to meet and treat; the two others were given one group of ten each. The patients spanned the range of psychiatric diagnosis, except that mental retardation and organic involvement were ruled out. They were seen twice a week for a total of twenty-four sessions over a period of three months; six patients in the treatment groups dropped out before the study was completed.

Carkhuff and Truax (1965b) have pointed out that

> In the treatment process, the lay counselors were oriented only toward providing high levels of therapeutic conditions. They had no cognitive map of where they were going except to attempt to elicit a degree of self-exploration relating to the problems and concerns which the patients brought to the sessions. The therapists' role was to communicate a warm and genuine concern and depth of understanding. (1965b, p. 428)

The final evaluation of patient improvement was based upon nurses' and attendants' opinions about changes in ward behavior as expressed on a rating scale devised by Carkhuff and De Burger (1964). The four behavior areas rated and the comparative results for the treated and the untreated groups are shown in Table 8.2.

TABLE 8.2
Direction of Changes of Gross Ratings of Patient Behavior by Ward Personnel[a]

	PATIENT GROUPS			
RATINGS	*Treatment*	*Control*	χ^2	*p*
Overall Improvement (Post Ratings Only)				
Improved	38	19	21.47	<·001
Deteriorated	1	12		
Unchanged	35	39		
	N = 74	N = 70		
Psychological Disturbance (Pre & Post Ratings)				
Improved	28	8	17.28	< ·001
Deteriorated	19	5		
Unchanged	27	37		
	N = 74	N = 50		
Interpersonal Concerns (Pre & Post Ratings)				
Improved	33	16	11.23	< ·01
Deteriorated	14	2		
Unchanged	27	32		
	N = 74	N = 50		
Intrapersonal Concerns (Pre & Post Ratings)				
Improved	28	15	6.79	< ·05
Deteriorated	16	4		
Unchanged	30	31		
	N = 74	N = 50		

[a] From Carkhuff and Truax, 1965b.

Carkhuff and Truax have concluded from these results that

. . . all scale differences between treatment and control groups were statistically significant by chi-square. It is notable that only one of the treatment group patients was rated as deteriorated in his overall behavior over the previous three months while thirty-eight were judged improved. Twelve of the control group members were rated behaviorally deteriorated overall while nineteen were rated improved. Furthermore, it is clear from the other scale values that control group members tended to remain unchanged while there was a greater variability in the treatment group ratings. (1965b, p. 430)

This study would appear to have two unfortunate flaws, both of them recognized by Carkhuff and Truax, who have acknowledged, for example, that the ward ratings were not done "blind." In other words, the ward personnel knew which patients were being treated and which were not. These authors admit that this fact might have contaminated their results. Their main inference, however, is still that the effect achieved in the treated group was due to the brief training accorded the lay therapists. In order to reinforce this conclusion, however, they assent that it would really have been necessary to have had another control group of patients seen in group therapy by untrained and inexperienced therapists. Lacking this control, it could easily be argued that the training as such was irrelevant; thus treated patients could have been responding merely to the increased attention and interest shown in them during group meetings.

The possibility not only exists, of course, of training therapists to higher levels on the therapist variables, it has also been found both possible and profitable to train patients to higher levels on the significant patient variable of depth of self-exploration. This technique has been labeled "vicarious therapy pretraining," or VTP; and Truax and Carkhuff (1965a) have described its use.

VTP simply involves presentation to prospective patients of a 30-minute tape-recording of excerpts of "good" patient therapy behavior. The tape itself illustrates in a very concrete manner how clients often explore themselves and their feelings, and thus allows for a vicarious experiencing of group psychotherapy prior to the patient's introduction into group psychotherapy. (1965a, p. 266)

Part of the Truax and Carkhuff (1965a) study involved two groups of ten patients in group psychotherapy, one group having had VTP, the other not. The MMPI (Hathaway and McKinley, 1951) was used as a measure of personality change. Each group received a total of twenty-four sessions with an experienced therapist. Analysis of variance of the difference between pre- and posttherapy testing led to the conclusion that

In general, the data modestly support the therapeutic value of vicarious therapy pretraining in group psychotherapy. The mean value for improvement on the MMPI scores indicate generally greater constructive personality change for patients receiving VTP in comparison to patients who have not received VTP. The statistical analysis lends only moderate support for the hypothesis but does indicate a significant superiority of the patients receiving vicarious therapy pretraining in improvement of schizophrenic symptoms, social introversion, and anxiety as measured by the psychasthenia subscale. (1965a, pp. 227–228)

Granted that we may be persuaded that Truax and his colleagues have come nearer to a specification of the necessary and sufficient conditions for changing behavior in and through this kind of person-to-person interaction, at least two further and important questions spring to mind, both of which have begun to be attacked by this indefatigable group.

In the first place, we might ask with regard, say, to the so-called "therapist variables," are these really antecedents of the patient's behavior? Might they not, in fact, be the consequents? When, for example, a therapist shows accurate empathy, is this really because of some quality he possesses or is it better conceived as a result of some characteristic of the patient he is treating?

In the second place, we might ask, what may be the mode of operation of the administration of, say, unconditional positive regard? Does it merely provide a general ambience within which the patient will improve, whenever and however it is administered, or, on the other hand, must it be used as a kind of reinforcement to be judiciously applied so as to increase the rate of emission of particular adjustive responses by the patient?

Two kinds of studies have been conducted in an effort to answer the first of these questions. One kind of study involves a statistical analysis of therapist-patient relationships, and has been described by Truax (1963) as follows.

> one way of answering this question is to have a group of therapists see each member of a group of patients and have each patient see all therapists. If the level of accurate empathy (for example) is different for different patients, this would show that patients determine accurate empathy levels offered by the therapists. If the level of accurate empathy is different for different therapists, this would show that therapists determine levels of accurate empathy. (1963, p. 258)

The data used in this study were again tape-recordings, this time obtained from the interaction of a set of eight therapists with a set of eight patients in a balanced incomplete-block analysis of variance design. It proved that different therapists tend to produce significantly different levels of accurate empathy ($p < .01$), even when interacting with the same set of patients. In contrast, different patients did not tend to produce significantly different levels of accurate empathy ($p < .40$) when interacting with the same set of therapists. In other words—for accurate empathy, at least—these data suggested that the main variance was indeed therapist-produced.

The second kind of study to answer the same general question seems more satisfactory since it involved the actual experimental manipulation of therapist conditions as independent variables and the observation of the patient's reaction as the dependent variable. Truax and Carkhuff (1965b) have experimentally varied the factors of unconditional positive regard and accurate empathy, while trying to hold therapist self-congruence constant, and they observed the effects of such alteration on depth of self-exploration by the patient.

They carried out this study with three female patients diagnosed as schizophrenic. Each patient was seen separately for one hour, this being covertly divided into three parts, each about twenty minutes long. For the first and third periods, the therapist tried to achieve and maintain high levels on all three therapist variables (TSC, UPR, and AE); for the middle period, he tried to reduce the amount of UPR and AE provided, while holding TSC fairly constant. The question was whether this change would have a significant effect on the patient variable, DSE.

It had, of course, first to be decided whether the therapist had succeeded in his intention of lowering two of the crucial variables. This was determined by having fifteen samples of three-minute periods of the whole tape-recorded hour assessed for the three therapist variables on the relevant rating scales. Each variable was rated by different small groups of raters to prevent any cross-contamination. As usual, the tapes were coded and were mixed in such a way that the raters could not know from which segment of the interview the samples had come. The average ratings of four raters on the UPR variable are shown in Figure 8.2.

It can be seen that the ratings for UPR in the middle section are lower, the experimenter having succeeded in reducing the level of this quality evinced by him during this time. The difference in question was also found to be statistically significant ($p < .01$).

Similarly, the average ratings of three different raters for the AE variable are shown in Figure 8.3. This figure again reflects the success of the experimenter in significantly ($p < .01$) reducing the level of accurate empathy in the middle period.

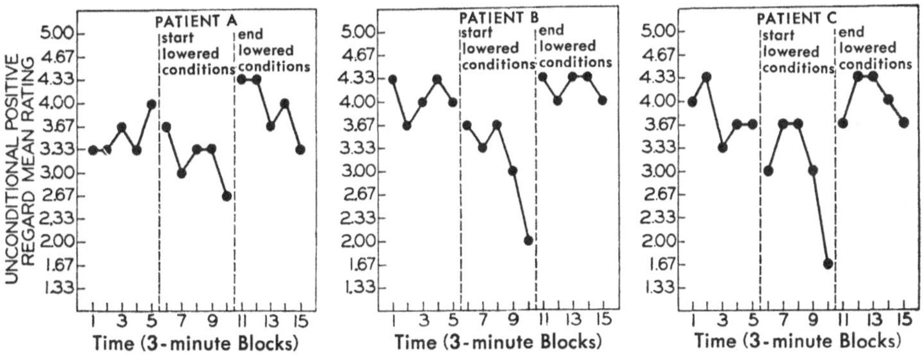

Fig. 8.2. Changes in ratings of the experimentally changed therapist variable, unconditional positive regard (UPR). (From Truax and Carkhuff, 1965b)

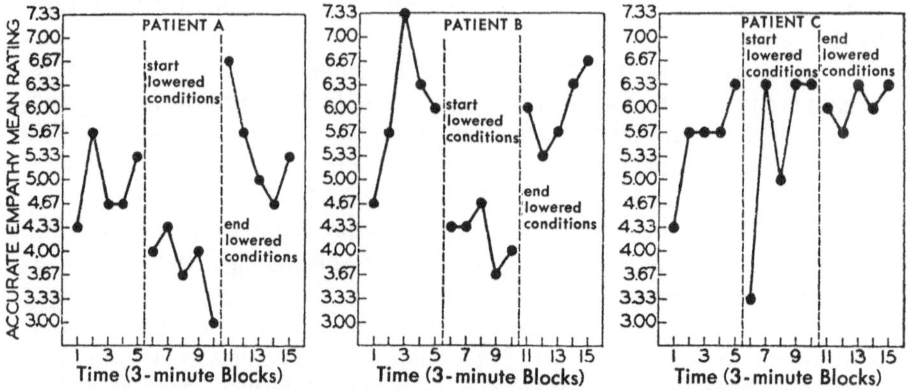

Fig. 8.3. Changes in ratings of the experimentally changed therapist variable, accurate empathy (AE). (From Truax and Carkhuff, 1965b)

The average ratings of three more raters, for TSC, are shown in Figure 8.4. The efforts of the experimenter *not* to lower this condition apparently resulted in some overcompensation, and hence a slightly significant *increase* ($p < .01$) in this condition in the middle period.

In general, the experimenters had succeeded in reducing two crucial independent therapist variables. What, then, was the effect on the dependent, patient variable of self-exploration? The result is shown in Figure 8.5. In Truax and Carkhuff's words

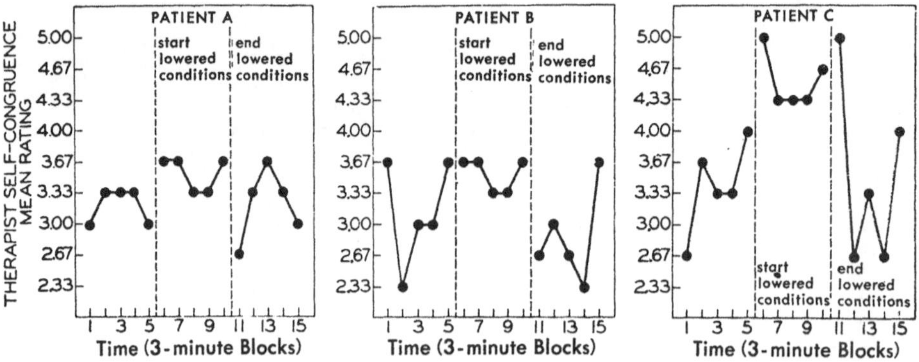

Fig. 8.4. Changes in ratings of the experimentally unchanged therapist variable, therapist self-congruence (TSC). (From Truax and Carkhuff, 1965b)

Here it can be seen that with all three patients there was the predicted consequent drop in patient depth of intrapersonal exploration during the period when conditions were lowered. The differences in patient depth of self-exploration predicted to occur as a consequence of lowered conditions of empathy and unconditional warmth proved statistically significant using both analysis of variance tests ($p < .01$) and t tests ($p < .05$). Also, the patients' level of process or depth of intrapersonal exploration returned to its previous higher level when the lowered conditions levels were removed . . . [and the] . . . higher levels of therapist conditions were reinstated. (1965b, p. 123)

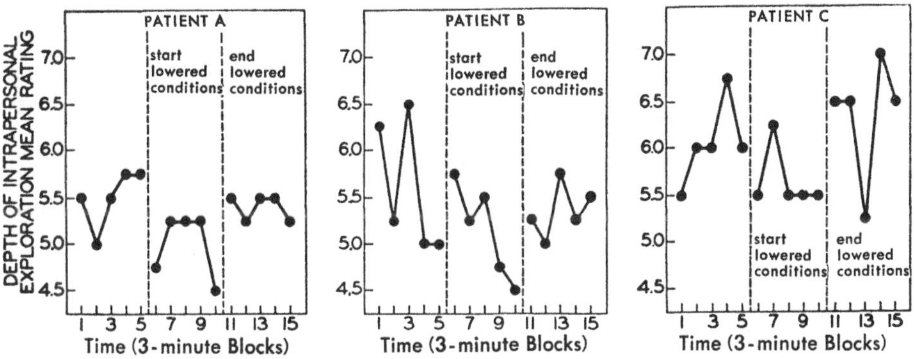

Fig. 8.5. Changes in ratings of the dependent patient variable, depth of self-exploration (DSE). (From Truax and Carkhuff, 1965b)

As these authors have noted, this result does not mean that the patients' reactions had no effect on the therapist-offered conditions; it does, however, serve to sort out one part of the antecedent-consequent concomitance of the conditions. It is, perhaps, curious that therapists self-congruence could seem to be maintained, or even increased, during the time that the therapist was consciously manipulating other conditions. Truax and Carkhuff have concluded, however, that

perhaps the most significant methodological finding of the present research is that therapist-offered conditions can be varied experimentally in the natural setting of therapy, with predictable ensuing consequences. (1965b, p. 124)

The final question to be considered here, then, is concerned with the possible mode of action of the therapist-offered conditions. Must the patient be bathed in as much warmth and empathy as possible during the therapeutic hour, or do these qualities work in a discrete fashion when offered intermittently as reinforcers for the emission of specific, desired behaviors? The second alternative would seem to be the more attractive hypothesis to the behavioral psychologist since it would serve to tie the data on therapy back to work on operant and verbal conditioning (briefly considered in two previous chapters).

Truax (1966), again, has begun to explore this question. He has represented the alternative points of view in this way.

> Support for the position exemplified by Rogers, viewed from the findings on empathy and warmth, rests upon the assumption that the therapist offers levels of conditions that do not systematically covary with the verbalizations or behavior emitted by the patient. If this were true (if, say, the level of therapist empathy or warmth did not systematically covary with patient response classes) then differential reinforcement could not account for the research findings of relationships between therapist behavior and patient outcome. On the other hand, if the therapist, in this case Rogers, does systematically vary his level of warmth or his level of empathy depending on the behavior, then Rogers' position would not be supported. (1966, p. 2)

Truax thereupon submitted this question to a most stringent test by analyzing recordings of some eighty-five of Rogers' own therapeutic sessions for concomitance of therapeutic variables with a particular behavior class!

> Five clinical psychologists rated an unbiased sample of 40 typewritten interaction units [i.e., two from each of 20 taken from the 85 sessions] consisting of (a) a therapist statement, (b) a succeeding patient statement, (c) the succeeding therapist statement. These interaction units (TPT, Therapist–Patient–Therapist) were designated by code numbers prior to the ratings, and were then assigned in random order to the five clinical psychologists who served as judges. Each judge rated separately each of the nine patient scales [referring to the behavior classes: learning discrimination, ambiguity, insight, similarity in expression to therapist, problem orientation, high catharsis, blocking, anxiety, and negative feeling expression] and the three therapist scales [empathy, UPR, and directiveness] in different order, so as to minimize rating biases. The ratings were then decoded, and the ratings of the three classes of "reinforcers" were simply correlated separately with the nine classes of patient behavior under examination. The presence of significant correlations would then be positive evidence to indicate systematic, nonrandom use of reinforcers with particular classes of patient behavior. Thus, the question became, for example, "Does the therapist's degree of acceptance significantly covary with the patient's degree of discrimination learning?" If a positive correlation was found, this would indicate that the therapist systematically was most accepting and unconditionally warm where the patient was engaged in discrimination learning and was least accepting and warm when the patient engaged in very little discrimination learning. (1966, p. 2).

The judges were, of course, unaware of the hypotheses being tested.

The upshot of this experiment was that a relationship was indeed found between the appearance of "reinforcement" accorded by the therapist and some of the different kinds of patient-emitted response-classes. Truax has summarized the correlations in the form shown in Table 8.3., which illustrates the fact that Rogers, as a therapist, did in fact respond selectively to patient behavior. His "reinforcements" have in this way been shown to be principally aimed at (1) the patient's learning of discriminations, (2) a *lack* of ambiguity (i.e., clarity), (3) expressions of insight, (4) problem orientation, and (5) similarity of expression to his own.

TABLE 8.3
Interrelationships between the Level of Therapist Reinforcement and Levels of Patient Behavior[a]

CLASSES OF PATIENT BEHAVIOR		REINFORCERS		
		Therapist Empathy	*Therapist Acceptance (UPR)*	*Therapist Directiveness*
	Reliability Coefficient	.48	.59	.68
Patient learning of discriminations	.59	.47	.37	n.s.
Patient ambiguity	.35	−.35	−.38	.33
Patient insight	.32	.46	.37	n.s.
Similarity of patient style of expression to that of therapist	.57	.48	.32	−.31
Problem orientation	.64	n.s.	.35	n.s.
Catharsis	.44	n.s.	n.s.	n.s.
Blocking	.54	n.s.	n.s.	n.s.
Anxiety	.26	n.s.	n.s.	n.s.
Patient negative feeling expression	.29	n.s.	n.s.	n.s.

[a] From Truax, 1966.

Truax has further pointed out that if the crucial therapist variables acted as reinforcers, the behavior that they reinforced should have then been emitted, as rated, with greater frequency in later as compared with earlier therapeutic sessions. In order to test this notion, the ratings of the forty samples for each patient-behavior class were grouped into five blocks across time-in-therapy, and the Grant (1956) orthogonal polynomial trend test analysis of variance was used to examine the significance of the trend with time. In addition, *t* tests were used to test for the significance of the difference between early and late ratings for all nine behavior classes. The results of these analyses are shown in Table 8.4.

TABLE 8.4
Analyses of Changes over Time in Patient Response Classes[a]

PATIENT RESPONSE CLASS	HIGHEST SINGLE CORRELATION WITH THERAPIST'S "REINFORCERS"	GRANT ORTHOGONAL POLYNOMIAL ANALYSIS OF VARIANCE FOR TREND: *F* Linear Trend	*p*	*F* Quadratic Trend	*p*	*F* Cubic Trend	*p*	*t*-TEST BETWEEN FIRST AND ALL LATER BLOCKS	*p*
Similarity of patient style of expression to that of therapist	.48	7.899	<.01	1.20	n.s.	0.85	n.s.	2.84	< .01
Patient learning of discriminations	.47	3.10	n.s.	0.79	n.s.	1.05	n.s.	2.94	< .01
Patient insight	.46	4.73	<.05	1.70	n.s.	0.75	n.s.	2.73	< .01
Patient ambiguity	−.38	3.04	n.s.	1.50	n.s.	0.91	n.s.	1.35	n.s.
Problem orientation	.35	3.28	<.07	1.61	n.s.	2.10	n.s.	1.76	< .05
Catharsis	n.s.	6.10	<.05	2.13	n.s.	1.20	n.s.	2.03	< .05
Blocking	n.s.	1.80	n.s.	6.01	<.05	1.50	n.s.	1.29	n.s.
Anxiety	n.s.	2.00	n.s.	0.98	n.s.	1.70	n.s.	0.93	n.s.
Patient negative feeling expression	n.s.	1.17	n.s.	0.65	n.s.	0.89	n.s.	0.75	n.s.

[a] From Truax, 1966

Truax summarized the import of these findings in the following terms.

Of the classes of patient behavior to which the therapist selectively responded (i.e., reinforced), four out of five showed changes in patient behavior over time-in-therapy. Thus, the data agree with the predictions in seven out of the nine classes of patient behaviors (78 per cent correct predictions).

Considering the probability that the therapist also used other types of rewards or reinforcers and also rewarded other related patient behavior classes, considering the unknown differential complexity levels of the patient response classes, and considering the crudity of measurement, the findings strongly suggest that important reinforcement effects do indeed occur even in client-centered therapy. (1966, p. 6)

Truax's findings in this study, in fact, act as a means of uniting the tough- and tender-minded views of psychotherapy. As he himself has concluded:

The present data, by demonstrating the role of empathy and warmth as positive reinforcers, suggest that the available evidence relating levels of these therapeutic conditions to patient outcome in therapy does not argue against a reinforcement interpretation of psychotherapy. On the contrary, the finding that empathy and warmth act as reinforcers suggests that the evidence relating empathy and warmth to patient outcome is open to a behavioristic interpretation, based in part on the therapist's use of differential reinforcement. (1966, p. 7)

The work of Truax and his associates, then, suggests that the examination of the effects of psychotherapy may legitimately be brought within the scope of the objective study of experimental behavior change. It also suggests that we cannot profitably look at either "process" or "outcome" in isolation, but we must, as in other areas of experimental inquiry, look at the interrelations of both of these as independent and dependent variables. The last study cited provides an extremely interesting link with the material in the previous two chapters in showing how the reinforcers that affect human behavior may, after all, be both more subtle and more complex than the standardized grunts of the verbal conditioners.

The scope of research opened by Truax's work is staggering; he makes no pretense that all the powerful variables in his linear equation have yet been conceived, let alone considered. One could, for example, imagine a vast range of inquiry in which a whole spectrum of therapist variables, including those already specified by Truax, could be even more systematically studied for their reinforcing power by the conjugate reinforcement techniques devised and developed by Lindsley and Nathan.

Another implication of Truax's work, which leads into the work to be considered in the next chapter, is broached by the return to the experimental study of the single case.

9

THE STUDY OF *The Single Case*

AN INTERESTING and recurrent theme in the work described in previous chapters has been sounded by those who have advocated and attempted scientific studies of the single case.

In the past, the supporters of the single case study in abnormal psychology have commonly preferred intuitive and subjective means of investigation, whereas those who have believed in public and objective methods have usually been more concerned with studying group phenomena. These two approaches, labeled the ideographic and the nomothetic by Allport (1937), have often been identified—respectively—with the nonscientific and the scientific view of psychology (Eysenck, 1952b). It may well prove, however, that the association of the study of groups with science and of the study of individuals with nonsense is contingent rather than necessary.

More than a century ago, Claude Bernard voiced his disbelief in one kind of group study in the following terms.

> If we collect a man's urine during twenty-four hours and mix all this urine to analyze the average, we get an analysis of a urine which simply does not exist; for urine, when fasting, is different from urine during digestion. A startling instance of this kind was invented by a physiologist who took urine from a railroad station urinal where people of all nations passed, and who believed he could thus present an analysis of *average* European urine! (1957, pp. 134–135)

In modern experimental psychology, Sidman (1952), for example, has also warned of the fallacious conclusions that may be drawn from the averaging of group data.

Dukes (1965), on the other hand, has reminded us of what distinguished and seminal research has come from the study of individuals. In at least two major areas in experimental psychology, studies of individual subjects have had lasting and influential effects. In the field of learning, the studies carried out by Ebbinghaus (1885) upon his own performance in memorizing nonsense syllables have been characterized by McGeogh and Irion (1952) as landmarks in the history of psychology. In the field of perception, Stratton's (1897a, 1897b) investigations of the effects of inverting lenses on his own visual perception have been described—by Taylor (1962)—as the most important experiments in the history of psychology. The question of the scientific usefulness of the single case study in abnormal psychology, therefore, cannot simply be ruled out of court.

One of the most consistent advocates of the need for the experimental study of the single case has been Dr. M. B. Shapiro of the Institute of Psychiatry of the University of London, who has, in effect, been the principal founder of one British school of experimental-clinical psychology (Shapiro, 1951b, 1957, 1961b, 1963, 1966; Payne, 1953, 1957; Jones, 1958, 1960;Inglis,1963).

In addition to his long-sustained interest in the investigation of the individual psychiatric patient, Shapiro has also been very actively engaged in parametric studies of various kinds of behavior abnormality. He has, for example, been involved in the experimental study of perceptual anomalies (Shapiro, 1951a, 1952, 1953, 1954, 1960; Shapiro and Tizard, 1958; Shapiro, Brierley, Slater, and Beech, 1962; Shapiro and Beech, 1965), of psychomotor defects (Shapiro, Kessell, and Maxwell, 1960; Shapiro, Slater, and Campbell, 1962), and of the behavioral effects of senile deterioration (Shapiro, Post, Löfving, and Inglis, 1956; Inglis, Shapiro, and Post, 1956; Shapiro, Field, and Post, 1957). For the purpose of this chapter, however, these contributions will be neglected in favor of a description of his work on the systematic investigation of the abnormalities of individual psychiatric patients.

In his earliest published formulation of the principles of experimental-clinical psychology, Shapiro (1951b) considered mainly those aspects of the single case that could be dealt with by the use of group-standardized and group-validated tests. He pointed out that, given a knowledge of the score distributions, reliability, practice-effect, and of the intercorrelations between tests, conclusions can usefully be reached, for example, about the statistical abnormality of differences between scores, and about the changes in scores between different occasions of testing, for given individuals. He argued that even by using data collected from groups, hypotheses could be made about individual performance and could be tested in a statistically rigorous fashion.

Some of the actual procedures involved in such testing, as well as their associated calculations, have been brought together, with examples, by two of Shapiro's former students and colleagues, Payne and Jones (1957). They have provided statistical solutions, for example, to the problems involved in assessing both the reliability and the abnormality of discrepancies between two test scores and in testing clinical predictions about changes in scores from occasion to occasion of testing in single case studies.

An example of the use of this kind of descriptive investigation of abnormality in a single case has been provided by Shapiro and Nelson (1955a), who found that some of the symptomatic difficulties of a young psychotic patient could be referred to an abnormal slowness of cognitive functioning, this patient's *speed* of reasoning being quite discrepant with his *level* of ability. These two investigators also conducted group studies that confirmed the importance of intellectual slowness in some kinds of behavior disorder (Shapiro and Nelson, 1955b). Shapiro, however, later came to the view that this method gave only an "indirect approach" to the investigation of problems in abnormal psychology because it depended, in essence, on the assumption that various aspects of psychological function interact with each other so that the understanding of one aspect of psychological function should be able to throw light on other aspects (Shapiro, 1957).

An unfortunate outcome of this view, however, is that some psychologists have chosen to consider only those aspects of behavior that they have been able to measure, often at the expense of those aspects that they should have explored. One is reminded by some of these studies of the old joke about the drunk man looking for his keys under the street lamp because that was where it was light—not in the doorway, where he had lost them, because there it was too dark. This approach, Shapiro said, has resulted in one kind of failure of clinical research that

> ... consists of the fact that the phenomena which are chosen for investigation appear, at first sight, to have little relationship to the disorders which bring psychiatric patients into the hospital: Psychiatric patients suffer from a variety of disorders of affect, cognition and volition. A large number, if not the majority, of papers published by psychologists do not deal with these phenomena. Instead, they report upon the performance, by psychiatric patients, of a variety of tasks which might be described, without much loss of accuracy, as puzzles and indoor games. Examples are such tests as the pursuit rotor, the mirror drawing test, the block design test, the Rorschach Test and the Thematic Apperception Test, and the rotation effect. (Shapiro and Ravenette, 1959, p. 296)

It should perhaps be noted that by the "rotation effect" Shapiro refers to his own extensive series of studies of perceptual anomalies in patients with organic brain disorders.

His first fully documented and published study that directly attacked the measurement and manipulation of a symptomatic abnormality in a single case involved the investigation and treatment of a nine-year old boy with a reading disability and severe psychiatric disturbances (Bartlet and Shapiro, 1956). This patient was tested on the Wechsler Intelligence Scale for Children

(Wechsler, 1949) and was found to have a Verbal Scale IQ of 80, a Performance Scale IQ of 78, and a Full Scale IQ of 75. He was dull, but he was not defective, and yet he had been completely unable to learn to read, despite much special coaching and tuition. He made no score at all on any standard reading test he was given. In addition to the administration of a number of psychometric tests, an experimental program was therefore initiated, divided here into four stages that involved both descriptive and manipulative elements and phases.

(1) *Investigation of visual perception.* To ensure that the patient could actually discriminate letters of the alphabet, he was asked to "post," in appropriately labeled slots, a pack of randomly distributed cards that contained thirty *M*'s, thirty *W*'s, and thirty abstract shapes similar to *M* and *W*. This he did without error, thus ruling out any crucial visual defect.

(2) *Investigation of the formation and retention of visual-auditory connections.* This stage of the program required the patient and a literate control subject (matched for age, sex, and IQ) to learn, relearn, and retain three series of three paired associates, all of which involved a design that had to be associated with a sound. The criterion of learning was five correct, successive repetitions. Learning trials took place over three days, and retention was tested after a five-day interval. The results of this part of the investigation are shown in Table 9.1.

TABLE 9.1
Comparisons of Patient (P) and Control Subject (C) on Learning and Retaining Visual Auditory Paired-associate Tests[a]

LEARNING AND RETENTION	*M*	*S.D.*	*C.R.*	1-TAIL *t*-TEST *p*
1st day of Learning				
P	17.33	5.51	7.224	.0005
C	2.89	1.10		
2nd day of Learning				
P	3.67	2.91	1.740	.05
C	1.38	0.75		
3rd day of Learning				
P	Difference between means infinitesimal		Not calculated	n.s.
C				
Retention after 5-day Interval				
P	Both identical		Not calculated	n.s.
C				

[a] From Bartlet and Shapiro, 1956.

From these results, the authors concluded that

. . . in the initial formation of associations with this kind of material [the patient] had much greater difficulty than the control subject. Nevertheless, once his initial learning had been accomplished, [the patient] was able to re-learn the same material almost as quickly as the control subject. He was also able to retain the material once learned as well as the control subject. (1956, p. 183)

If the control subject had *not* been different from the patient, the notion of a visual-auditory association difficulty as the basis of the patient's reading difficulty would not have been upheld. Since the results, however, confirmed this possibility—at least so far as initial learning was concerned—the investigators thought it wise to examine ten more children on the same kind of task. These were also of the same age and IQ as the patient, being taken from a school for the educationally subnormal. The experimenters had asked the school only for children who could read; it transpired, however, that some could read (group I) and some could not (group II). The results of testing these groups are shown in Table 9.2.

TABLE 9.2
Scores of Readers and Nonreaders on Paired Associates[a]

Readers	*Paired-associate Scores*	*Nonreaders*	*Paired-associate Scores*	*t*	*p*
1	5.3	6	4.3		
2	3.6	7	24.0		
3	4.6	8	12.0		
4	5.0	9	24.6		
5	5.3	10	9.3		
Mean	4.63	Mean	13.25	1.866	.05

[a] After Bartlet and Shapiro, 1956.

The results could be interpreted to mean that the associative difficulty experienced by the patient was also suffered by other nonreaders of his age. Bartlet and Shapiro concluded from this part of the study that

whilst there was some overlap between the reader and nonreader groups on the experimental test score, our control's score placed him outside the nonreader range, and [the patient's] score was well outside the range for readers.... These results indicate that our patient's difficulty in initial learning was abnormal and was probably related to his reading difficulty. On the other hand, we had the observation that his retention of material, once it was learned, was normal. These two observations meant that if he could overcome the initial learning difficulty, our patient would learn to read. The scope of these generalizations was limited by the fact that we had so far only investigated the efficiency of forming connections between uttered sounds and sights. If our remedial program were to have a rational basis, we needed to know the patient's efficiency in making connections between and within other modalities. (1956, p. 184)

At this time, for expedient reasons, remedial teaching (strictly speaking, the fourth of the phases described here) was begun. The investigation, however, continued as planned.

(3) *Investigation of the generality of the learning difficulty.* Since only visual-auditory (V–A) associations had been investigated, it was thought necessary to examine a number of the other possible combinations of association between visual (V), auditory (A), and tactile-kinaesthetic (TK) stimuli. If the patient proved relatively unimpaired on any of these, this might provide a further guide to the development of an optimal remedial teaching plan. The patient (*P*) was again compared with the control subject (*C*) used in the first phase of the investigation. Seven of the many possible cross-modality learning situations were chosen. The comparative results are shown in Table 9.3, and scores—on this occasion—were taken in terms of the number of trials required to reach two consecutively correct responses.

TABLE 9.3
Comparisons of Patient (P) and Control (C) on the Learning and Recall of Cross-modal Paired Associates[a]

	LEARNING SCORES						RECALL SCORES					
PAIRED ASSOCIATES	P		C				P		C			
	$\overline{m}$	σ	$\overline{m}$	σ	t	p	$\overline{m}$	σ	$\overline{m}$	σ	t	p
V–V	2.12	0.36	2.00	0.00	0.96	n.s.	2.12	0.36	2.25	0.45	0.63	n.s.
TK–TK	4.75	1.48	2.25	0.45	4.50	<.001	2.88	0.52	2.50	1.07	0.68	n.s.
A–A	6.50	3.54	2.10	0.35	4.37	<.001	3.50	1.13	2.63	0.52	1.51	n.s.
TK–V	3.00	0.76	2.25	0.45	2.39	<.05	2.38	1.03	2.00	0.00	2.05	.05
TK–A	5.50	1.57	2.60	0.74	4.57	<.001	3.75	1.55	2.30	0.53	3.03	<.01
V–A	5.60	2.39	3.10	0.83	2.78	<.02	4.13	1.35	2.63	0.52	2.29	<.05
VTK–A	5.12	2.47	3.00	0.53	2.36	<.05	3.25	0.89	2.00	0.00	3.99	<.005

[a] After Bartlet and Shapiro, 1956.

These results have been summarized by Bartlet and Shapiro as follows.

[The patient's] learning ability is markedly worse than that of the control subject in all spheres, with the exception of visual-visual (V–V). Visual learning is easiest for [the patient], as shown by the fact that he differs less from the control where visual cues enter into the learning situation than when they are absent [see Table 9.3] .... With one exception (VTK–A) [the patient] differs less from the control as regards retention than as regards learning. In fact, where only one type of cue enters into the recall of associates (i.e., V–V, A–A and TK–TK), ... [the patient's] performance is much the same as the control's. It is in the situation involving cues of more than one type that [the patient's] performance is significantly poorer than that of his control. (1956, p. 188)

The main conclusion from the descriptive stages of the investigation, then, was that the patient would have greater than usual difficulty in the acquisition of the associations to be learned in reading, but that, once he had formed them, they would be adequately retained; overlearning, therefore, was desirable. The results also suggested that, in teaching him the necessary associations, the main weight should be put upon the visual modality.

(4) *Remedial teaching.* Fortunately, the method of tuition (in fact chosen before stage 3), devised by a Mr. C. Moxon, a London County Council school teacher (for details see Bartlet and Shapiro, 1956), involved a predominantly visual approach—with, of course, a necessarily phonic component. After six months of coaching along the lines suggested by the descriptive explorations, the patient's "Reading Age" on a standard test (Schonell, 1951) had gone from below the baseline (four years) to just over seven years. Since he was by then about ten years of chronological age, his new Reading Quotient (if $RQ = \frac{RA}{CA} \times 100$) would be about seventy, which, since his Full Scale IQ was 75, would put his reading achievement at or about the "expected" level. This was quite evidently more than could have been anticipated from a child who had initially been referred to the hospital diagnosed as "a prepsychotic child who is ineducable." It is heartening to know that Bartlet and Shapiro were able to conclude their paper as follows,

An inquiry was made about [P's] subsequent progress at an ordinary school, one year after his discharge from the Maudsley Hospital. The inquiry elicited the following response, which is quoted in full. "Though childish in speech and slightly effeminate in manner, maintains intelligent conversation. Quiet and thoughtful and of a kindly disposition, [P] seems to have made a successful adjustment to the society of boys of his own age. He has overcome his solitary behavior largely as a result of a conscious effort to take his place in normal school life, having definitely made up his mind to do so. Scholastically, his chief progress continues to be in reading, which may be due to the fact that he obviously enjoys this activity. In this, his attainment is almost average for his age. Comprehension is good and oral expression is good. Arithmetic, however, remains elementary and halting. He may be regarded as competent in handicraft." (1956, p. 190)

It is, however, one of the undeniable difficulties of the single case study that, in examples such as this, the fallacy of *post hoc ergo propter hoc* may go undetected, if not unsuspected. How can we know that this boy did not simply "mature," over the time involved, to a degree that made reading come more easily to him? Or, it may be asked, how can we be sure that the "therapeutic contact" was not the powerful agent in the change rather than the specific remedial procedures adopted? These are very real problems. Shapiro has argued that one of the possible answers lies in the tracing of *repeatable* functional relationships.

The essential requirement for the use of the single case in fundamental research would seem to be that of predictive experimental control. The phrase "predictive experimental control" means that one knows enough about a phenomenon to be able to predict how it will appear in situations in which it has not yet been observed. If one is in a position to do this, then one is in possession of observations about a process, and an observed process is unlikely to be peculiar to only one individual. One would expect to repeat such observations in other individuals. (1963, pp. 123–124)

A rather similar view has of course been documented in greater detail by Sidman (1960).

With the aim of developing techniques of predictive experimental control over more serious abnormalities of behavior, a start was first made on the treatment of paranoid delusions by Shapiro and Ravenette (1959), the hope being that, by the use, turn, and turn about of measurement and manipulation, such functional relations could be detected and described even in very disordered subjects.

The patient involved in this experiment was a thirty – eight year-old man of relatively high intelligence, his Wechsler (1944) Verbal Scale IQ being 130, Performance Scale IQ 118, and Full Scale IQ 126. He was diagnosed as having had a paranoid illness of five years' duration, his main symptoms being (*a*) a fixed, unfounded belief that some association or organization was trying to change and punish him, and (*b*) guilt, which was mainly concerned with a number of sexual misdemeanors he believed he had committed. The patient also seemed to be depressed and hostile.

The main problems the psychologists set for themselves were, first, to obtain some measure of his symptoms (i.e., to quantify the dependent variable), and, second, by some means to gain control over them (i.e., to secure an independent variable). So far as their search for an independent variable was concerned, Shapiro and Ravenette (1959), perhaps too puritanically, denied themselves any of the advantages claimed for the more usual forms of the "talking cure" (see Chapter 8). They maintained, instead, that

The statement that the patient's paranoid beliefs were abnormally resistant to modification is . . .a statement that required confirmation. It seemed, therefore, that, at the risk of looking foolish, we had to begin with the systematic observation of the reaction of the patient's beliefs to such processes of modification. The process which could be provided by us most easily was the process of discussion. It was, therefore, decided to hold a series of discussions with the patient. (1959, pp. 299–300)

So far as the nature of these discussions was concerned, they were shared by the two investigators, who

. . . decided not to lay down rules about how the discussions should be tackled and what topics should be raised. It was left to each experimenter to conduct the discussion in the manner he thought best. The only restrictions were related to (1) the topic, which was either that of guilt or paranoid delusions, and (2) the commitment to discuss these topics on as rational grounds as we could muster. All one could say, therefore, is that the two discussers provided two complex forms of stimulation, the content of which could be identified as the rational and humanist approach to problems arising from intense guilt and from palpably false beliefs about the actions of other people. . . . Both of the discussers were verbally fluent people who normally enjoyed a rational and friendly argument. (1959, p. 300)

Twenty interviews were held in all. The first sixteen of these lasted one hour each, and were conducted four times a week. The dependent variables took the form of four short questionnaires.

(*a*) *The Depression scale (D)* included ten statements and contained such items as "I sometimes feel dead inside" and "I feel miserable today."

(*b*) *The Guilt score (G)* was a scale that also involved ten items, such as "I feel that I am an unworthy man" and "People would despise me if they really knew me."

(*c*) *The Hostility scale (H)* also had ten items, such as "I am very touchy" and "I feel I get a raw deal out of life."

(*d*) *The Paranoid belief scale (PB)* had twenty items, such as "I believe that a minority group is secretly organizing a campaign against me" and "I believe 'they' want to influence me."

Each question was printed on a 5 × 3 -inch index card. The pack, of fifty cards, was shuffled before each interview, and, either before (B) or after (A) the interview, the subject was asked to place each card under one of five headings. These varied from the maximum belief ("This is definitely the case"), with a score of four points, to outright rejection of belief ("This is definitely not the case"), with a score of zero. The maximum score on the D, G, and H scales was 40; the maximum score on the PB scale was eighty. The main results for the sixteen experimental and four postexperimental testing occasions are shown in Table 9.4.

The investigators decided not to analyze the hostility and depression scales because of misapprehensions by the patient about some of the questions. They carried out analyses of variance, and they constructed graphs

TABLE 9.4
"Before" and "After" Total Scores Made by Patient on Various Scales for Different Interviews (Interviewers: R = Ravenette; S = Shapiro)[a]

	EXPERIMENTAL SESSIONS																POSTEXPERIMENTAL SESSIONS			
Session	1	2	3	4	5	6	7	8	9	10	11	12	13	14	15	16	17	18	19	20
Content of Discussion	*Guilt*				*Paranoid Beliefs*								*Guilt*				*No Discussion*		*Guilt*	
	R		*S*		*R*		*S*		*S*		*R*		*S*		*R*		*R*	*S*	*S*	
Testing	*B*	*A*	*A*	*B*	*B*	*A*	*A*	*B*	*B*	*A*	*A*	*B*	*A*	*B*	*B*	*A*				
D	11	19	11	15	10	9	0	0	0	0	0	0	0	0	0	0	0	0	0	0
G	39	36	32	40	40	36	40	40	36	40	40	40	38	38	36	40	40	40	36	35
H	12	14	16	10	7	8	6	4	3	9	9	6	0	0	0	0	8	3	9	9
PB[b]	57	46	52	54	54	53	48	50	50	47	39	41	40	40	44	41	37	43	39	42
Day of Week	W	Th	M	T	W	Th	M	T	W	Th	M	T	W	Th	M	T	+14 days	+36 days	+46 days	+47 days

[a] After Shapiro and Ravenette, 1959.
[b] Score based on 18 items.

of the results of both the G and PB scales. These graphs are shown in Figure 9.1. So far as the G scale was concerned, no change was detected by the analysis of variance, which conclusion agrees with the almost horizontal line shown on the graph in Figure 9.1.

Shapiro and Ravenette were able to conclude, however, that

> . . . there is an apparent fall in the strength of the paranoid delusions (PB scale) with an occasional fluctuation. An analysis of variance was carried out which resulted in the differences between the sixteen occasions giving an *F* ratio of 5.74 which is significant at beyond the .001 level. This result indicates that the downward trend is probably significant. [Furthermore, they have stated that] to check the downward trend more precisely, a regression line was fitted, giving the regression of paranoid delusional strength upon occasions. This line is shown as a straight line in the graph [Figure 9.1]. The variance accounted for in this way gave an *F* of 19.3 which was significant at beyond the .001 level. The residual variance was, however, significant between the .01 and .05 level. This implies that the fluctuations in delusional strength around the regression line are still significant. (1959, pp. 306–307)

One hypothesis—put forward by their colleague, Dr. P. Slater—that the authors tested as an explanation of these latter fluctuations was that the principal effect of the discussions upon the questionnaire answers took place not immediately but over the weekends, when *no* discussions took place. This interpretation received some support from further statistical analysis. The postexperimental testing showed an initial decrease in the paranoid beliefs, but again no change in guilt.

The conclusions that these investigators felt justified in drawing from these results were threefold. In the first place, the rational discussion of paranoid beliefs did, in fact, appear to diminish their strength, but—secondly—the discussions of guilt feelings had little effect on the expression of guilt. Finally, the effects of the discussion were, if anything, delayed rather than immediate, appearing only after a period in which there was no discussion.

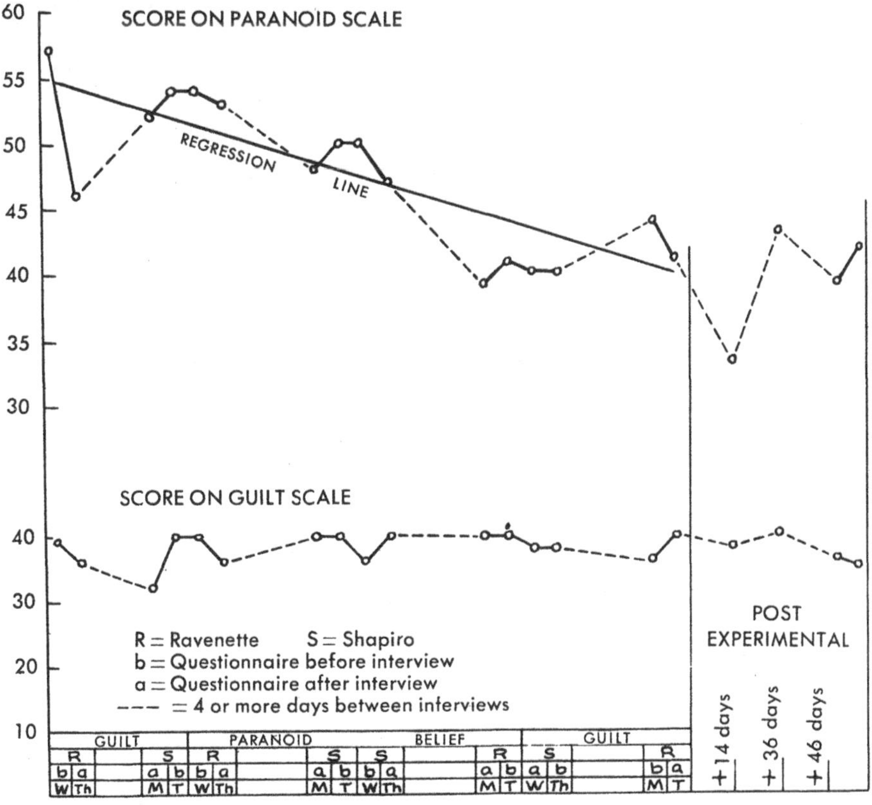

Fig. 9.1. Changes in paranoid and guilt scores. (From Shapiro and Ravenette, 1959)

These conclusions were regarded as tentative, and Shapiro and Ravenette have admitted that

> At best they can only be regarded as a starting point for further research. Our first objective is to put forward a point of view on research method. The experiment we carried out, with all its weaknesses, serves to illustrate the point of view which is being advanced. In addition, the results warrant the conclusion that the continued development of the direct experimental investigation of psychological disorder might produce useful results. It would seem to be worth our while, therefore, to carry out further experiments . . . in which more attention [would be] paid to the details of planning and of quantifying all the relevant variables. (1959, p. 311)

Shapiro then turned his main effort to the quantification of relevant dependent variables by means of a device he has called the Personal Questionnaire (Shapiro, 1961c). This technique was developed because he wanted to secure observations analagous to those made by the psychiatrist in his assessment of the patient, but he wanted to make them in as systematic, objective, and controlled a fashion as possible. He concluded that a questionnaire would permit this to be done, but that the form chosen would have to meet a number of criteria. In the first place, it was desired to eliminate irrelevant response sets, which are shown by some people when they answer questionnaire items; they may respond, for example, mainly to the categories of answer—"Yes," "No," or "?"—rather than to the content of the questions (Cronbach, 1950). Second, it was necessary to ensure that the questions would be thoroughly understood by the patient and that the items should be germane to the individual's own complaints. Third, the instrument had to be as reliable as possible.

Shapiro concluded that

> It followed, from all these considerations, that one required a technique which was based, as far as possible, upon the patient's own statements, and which required him to make two choices at a time. A controlled interview was, therefore, necessary in constructing the test, and paired comparisons seemed to be the most appropriate form for the actual test.
>
> There was a fourth point, on which no guidance could be found in the literature. It was necessary to have a method of comparing changes in any one symptom with changes in others. It had already been decided to make suffering, or unpleasantness of experience, the aspect of a patient's symptomatology we wished to investigate. It was therefore decided to make this aspect the "dimension" along which each symptom under investigation was to be measured.
>
> It was, therefore, necessary to devise a procedure for making the patient himself rate each statement for the unpleasantness it implied for him. Only statements implying certain degrees of unpleasantness were to be produced. In this aspect of the technique we were entering an uncharted field. (1963, pp. 134–135)

The construction of a Personal Questionnaire for each patient has been described in terms of five stages.

(1) The psychologist submits the patient to a standard form of interview in order to get from him a list of his symptoms—in the patient's own words.

(2) The psychologist and the patient's psychiatrist discuss the list obtained, and then, if necessary, they discuss it with the patient in order to clear up any discrepancies or obscurities in the catalog of complaints.

(3) For every symptom or "illness" statement the psychologist now tries to create two related statements. One of these, although still reflecting disorder, is meant to do so to a lesser degree; this is called the "improvement" statement. The second statement represents an even better state of affairs, and is called the "recovery" statement. Two examples have been given by Shapiro (1964a), and are shown in Table 9.5.

TABLE 9.5
Examples of the Three-stage Structure of Personal Questionnaire Items[a]

1. On the whole I have some energy.	*Recovery*
2. I have a little energy.	*Improvement*
3. I have not got any energy.	*Illness*
1. On the whole I do not feel I look peculiar.	*Recovery*
2. I feel it is possible I look peculiar.	*Improvement*
3. I feel certain I look peculiar.	*Illness*

[a] From Shapiro, 1964a.

(4) A scaling procedure is then undertaken so that the patient may himself calibrate each statement in terms of the unpleasantness of the implications it has for him. Shapiro has described this procedure in the following way.

> For this purpose a card is placed in front of the patient, and on it is written a list of nine hedonic phrases [see Table 9.6]. Each statement is placed before the patient, one at a time, and he is asked to say which of the nine phrases best describes the hedonic implications of the statement before him. We want each kind of statement to have roughly the same implication of unpleasantness. We aim to have all the illness statements rated by the patient as having implications which are very unpleasant or very greatly unpleasant, all the improvement statements as having moderately or slightly unpleasant implications, and all the recovery statements as having slightly or moderately pleasant implications. An additional aim of this method is that it might help to ensure comparability of changes in different symptoms.
>
> If the patient does not rate a statement in the intended manner, then we obtain his cooperation in arriving at a reformulation which he in fact would accept at the intended level. This procedure has the incidental effect of helping to ensure that the patient has the same understanding of the questionnaire as the psychologist. (1964a, pp. 247–248)

TABLE 9.6
List of Hedonic Phrases Used in the Patient's Calibration of the Personal Questionnaire[a]

Very great pleasure
Very pleasant
Moderately pleasant
Slightly pleasant
Indifferent
Slightly unpleasant
Moderately unpleasant
Very unpleasant
Very great displeasure

[a] From Shapiro, 1964a.

(5) At this stage, the actual test material that will be presented to the patient is prepared. For each symptom, all possible pairs of each of the three "illness," "improvement," and "recovery" statements are typed separately, on 5 × 3-inch index cards. The order of the two items on the card is balanced so as further to reduce the effect of any response set. In this way, three cards are prepared for each symptom. Examples are shown in Table 9.7.

TABLE 9.7
Examples of Paired Statements on Three Cards of the Personal Questionnaire[a]

Statements	Card
3. I have not got any energy. 2. I have a little energy.	Card one
2. I have a little energy. 1. On the whole I have some energy.	Card two
1. On the whole I have some energy. 3. I have not got any energy.	Card three

[a] From Shapiro, 1964a.

In using this test, these cards are presented to the patient one at a time, in random order, and for each card the patient is required to indicate which of the paired statements is closer to his actual state at that time. The eight different response patterns that could result from this forced-choice and paired-comparison technique are shown in Table 9.8.

The form of the response patterns provides a score *and* a check upon the reliability of the patient's responding. So far as reliability is concerned, for example, Shapiro has noted that

> A test of reliability, derived from Kendall (1948) is based upon the fact that, if the patient's responses are wholly random, then his response patterns will be equally divided among the eight response patterns [in Table 9.8] . . . . Appropriate tests of significance, such as x^2, can indicate the degree of reliability of the data. (1961a, p. 152)

TABLE 9.8
Possible Response Patterns on the Personal Questionnaire[a]

POSSIBLE RESPONSES	PATTERNS		
1.	1 ⟶2	1 ⟶3	2 ⟶3.
2.	1 ⟵2	1 ⟶3	2 ⟶3.
3.	1 ⟵2	1 ⟵3	2 ⟶3.
4.	1 ⟵2	1 ⟵3	2 ⟵3.
5.	1 ⟶2	1 ⟵3	2 ⟶3.
6.	1 ⟵2	1 ⟶3	2 ⟵3.
7.	1 ⟶2	1 ⟶3	2 ⟵3.
8.	1 ⟵2	1 ⟵3	2 ⟶3.

1 = Recovery statements ⟶ = "prefer"
2 = Improvement statements 1 ⟶2 = 1 is preferred to 2
3 = Illness statements 1 ⟵2 = 2 is preferred to 1
[a] From Shapiro, 1964a.

A more extended and technical discussion of this problem is to be found in a paper by Phillips (1964), who has worked with Shapiro on the scoring problems involved in this test.

Shapiro has stated that

> The scoring system is based on the assumption that when, during an actual test, a patient chooses a statement, that statement has for him not very different implications of unpleasantness [than] it did when he made his first judgments during the construction of the test. This assumption has to be checked experimentally, and, therefore, it is necessary to repeat the scaling experiment at least once. It is preferable to do this at the end of the experiment. A four-point scoring system can be used. Response patterns Nos. 1, 2, 3, and 4 can each be regarded as indicating a definite part of a continuum of increasing unpleasantness of experience; e.g., to produce response pattern 1 for a given symptom, the patient would have preferred the "recovery" statement to the "illness" and "improvement" statements, and the "improvement" to the "illness" statement. The four response patterns can be arbitrarily awarded scores, such as 1, 2, 3, and 4, in accordance with the numerical order above. Response patterns Nos. 5, 6, 7, and 8 are inconsistent with our dimension of illness. If they occur very rarely, they would presumably be the outcome of slips of the tongue or hand by either the patient or psychologist. (1961a, pp. 152–153)

Shapiro has also, from time to time, decided that some of these expressions pertaining to symptoms may be put together under broader labels; or, since he designed the test to be a measure along an "unpleasantness" dimension, he occasionally obtains only one score by lumping together all the scores obtained on all the patient's symptoms. He has confessed, however, that Claude Bernard might not have approved this procedure.

Shapiro and his associates have now published an account of the use of this test with four patients. In two cases, using the Personal Questionnaire as the dependent variable specifically tailored to the patient's complaints, they have (*a*) simply observed the spontaneous changes that have taken place over a brief period during the course of an illness; in two other cases they have (*b*) actually tried therapeutically to manipulate the symptom severity estimated by this test.

(*a*) *Observations of changes*. Shapiro (1961a) has described a case of a twenty-eight year-old unmarried woman, of dull intelligence, who was said to have suffered a depressive illness of three years' duration. Personal Questionnaire measurements were obtained from this lady on nine occasions, each about a week apart. Her symptom statements were divided into six groups (thinking difficulties, hostility, hypochondriacal delusions, delusions of reference, depressive, and somatic symptoms). Her response patterns fell into "reliable" patterns, and the scores she made over the period of testing are shown in Figure 9.2. Shapiro concluded from these observations that

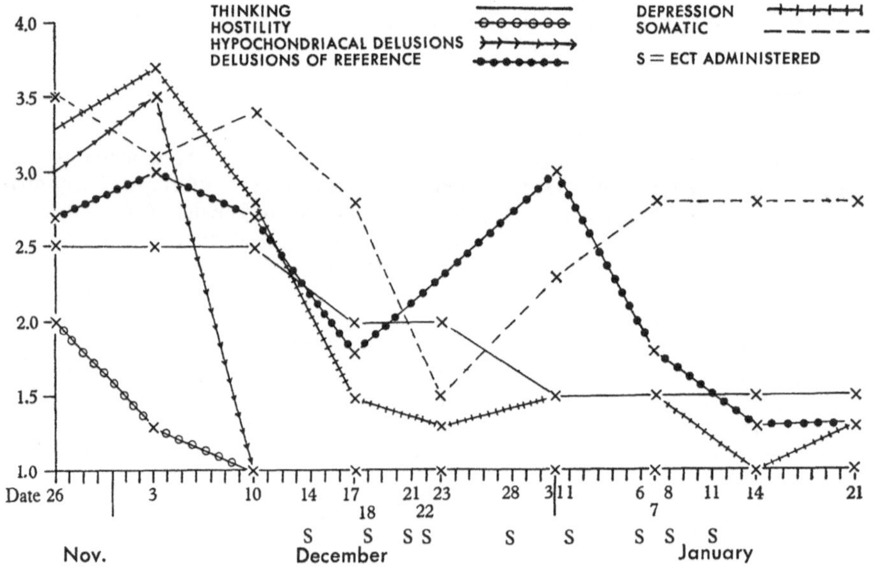

Fig. 9.2. Changes in grouped Personal Questionnaire scores over a period of about nine weeks. (From Shapiro, 1961a)

examination of the graph which plots changes in the average score for each class of symptoms shows that there are large fluctuations from occasion to occasion in the degree of illness, an analysis of variance producing an F of 15.96 ($p < 0.001$).

Two kinds of statistical comparison can be made between different classes of statements by means of analysis of variance. In the first place, the overall difference between the six classes of statement can be compared. This comparison yields an F ratio of 2.170, which does not reach the 0.05 level, for which an F of 2.96 would be necessary. The second way in which the classes can be compared is in the difference between their mode of fluctuation from occasion to occasion. According to the graph, there appear to be quite considerable differences in manner of fluctuation. For example, the hypochondriacal delusions rapidly recovered, whereas the somatic complaints, while fluctuating considerably during the illness, were still quite severe at the end of the period of measurement. The overall significance of difference in mode of fluctuation is indicated by the F ratio for the class-occasion interaction, which was 1.506. This was significant at the 0.001 level. We have here an indication of the validity of the initial classification of symptoms. One of the aspects of this finding is that the illness, during its course, appears to change its content quite considerably. The illness on December 31 is quite different from the illness on December 3. The changing character of an affective illness, if confirmed, might be a fact of some importance. (1961a, pp. 153–154)

The second case—without an attempt at manipulation—described by Shapiro (1963) was of a thirty-four-year-old married woman, again of dull intelligence, who was admitted to the hospital with a depressive illness and a mild obsessive compulsive reaction. Her symptom statements were divided into seven groups (thinking difficulties, depression, somatic complaints, social interests, work interests, fears or phobias, and obsessions or compulsions). Measurements were taken about once a week over a period of about two months (the scores obtained are shown in Figure 9.3), and statistical analysis showed there was a fairly rapid improvement in the illness as a whole ($p < .001$). There were, however, differences in the amount of improvement between the groups of symptoms ($p < .001$), as is evident from their graphical representation.

In these two cases, as has been noted, no independent variable was manipulated; however, an attempt was made to induce change in the next two cases.

(*b*) *Therapeutic manipulation.* The first of this second group of cases has so far been described only in a very brief note by Shapiro, Neufeld, and Post (1962). This involved a twenty-nine-year-old unmarried woman of bright intelligence. She had suffered from severe phobias since childhood, and had had a depressive illness of five years' duration. For a period of nine months, the unpleasant aspects of her illness had been measured by application of the Personal Questionnaire. At the same time, an attempt was made to manipulate treatment as the independent variable; and two forms of treatment were alternated. Each phobia was treated by a form of deconditioning,

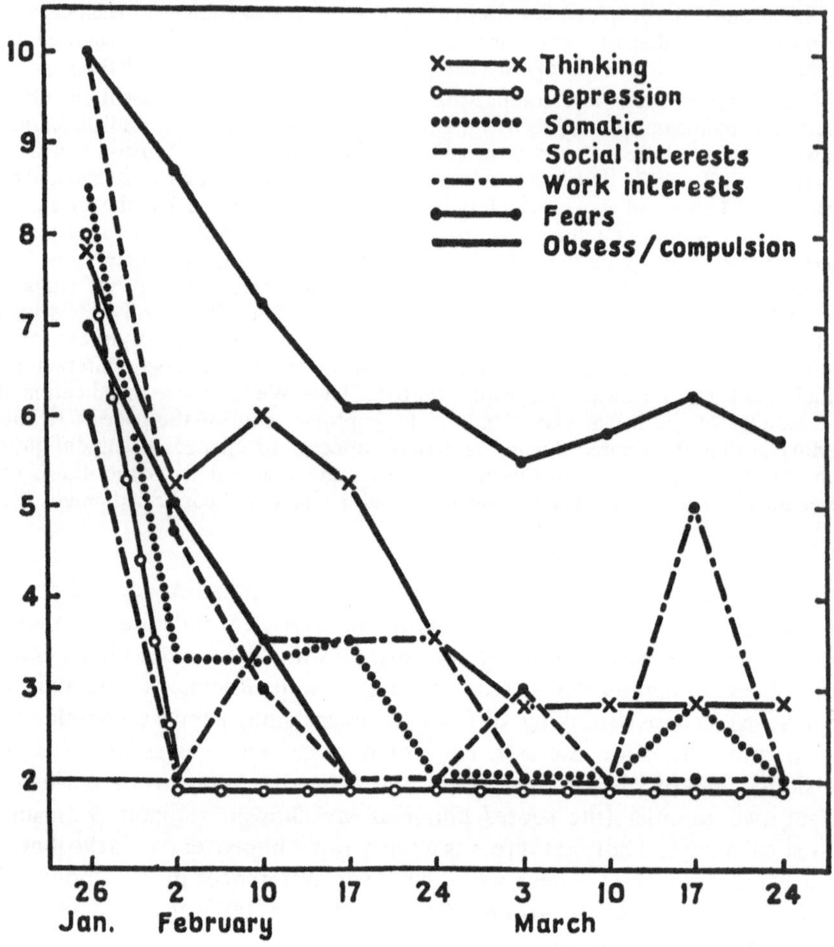

Fig. 9.3. Changes in grouped Personal Questionnaire scores over a period of about two months. (From Shapiro, 1963)

as described by Wolpe (1958), while her depressive symptoms were treated by a form of rational psychotherapy that had been derived from Ellis (1955). Shapiro, Neufeld, and Post (1962) concluded that most of the phobias had diminished but that many depressive symptoms remained, although some had remitted. Details of the Personal Questionnaire scores are not given in this note.

An extensive and detailed account of another single case, and one in which associations between the questionnaire (as the dependent variable) and treatment (as the independent variable) were investigated, has been reported by Shapiro, Marks, and Fox (1963). The patient in this case was a married woman of thirty-eight, of average to above-average intelligence, who suffered from phobias and depressive symptoms of about eight years' standing.

Two kinds of treatment were again used: sessions of "rational training" (T) and "nondirective therapy" (N), each form of treatment being given in blocks of two, for sixteen sessions in all, in the order NN, TT, TT, NN, NN, TT, TT, NN. The Personal Questionnaire was given on seventeen occasions; it was administered immediately (I) after the second treatment of each block of two sessions, and a delayed measure (D) was given *before* the first treatment of each block of two. In other words, the patient was tested *before* the first of two sessions and again *after* the second. Twenty-three symptoms were assessed, and the results were considered in terms of a total score. The consequent changes in the Personal Questionnaire were analyzed from occasions 2 to 17, inclusive, by means of a factorial analysis of variance (Maxwell, 1958). A graphical illustration of the changes in symptoms is given in Figure 9.4, and three main findings were derived.

(1) Both types of treatment produced beneficial effects so far as their immediate results were concerned.

(2) The delayed effect of "nondirective therapy" was also in the direction of improvement whereas the delayed effect of "rational training" seemed to be a relapse.

Shapiro (1964b) has provided tables that illustrate these conclusions, the first of which is Table 9.9. Since the "score difference" terms are obtained by subtracting each mean score from the preceding one, improvement (i.e., *decreases* in scores with time) produces a *positive* difference value and relapse produces a negative value. Given the array of differences shown in the table, it was now possible to compare the immediate and the delayed effects for nondirective and rational treatment, shown in Table 9.10.

One feature of these results is that the set of differences that reflect the immediate changes were found to be higher for the rational training sessions (+ 2.1, + 1.1, + 0.7, and + 1.1) than for the nondirective sessions (0.0, + 0.4, + 0.3 and + 2.0). This could suggest that the immediate effects of rational training were so to speak, "stronger" than the effects of nondirective therapy.

This finding, however, was actually *reversed* on the delayed measures, where the rational training produced nothing but relapse scores (− 0.3, − 1.3, − 1.0, and − 2.4) whereas the nondirective therapy—on the whole—produced greater improvement (0.0, − 0.8, + 0.6, and + 3.5). Shapiro has noted (1964b) that these results were also reflected in the statistical analyses carried out by Shapiro, Marks, and Fox (1963).

(3) The fluctuations of phobic and depressive symptoms were relatively

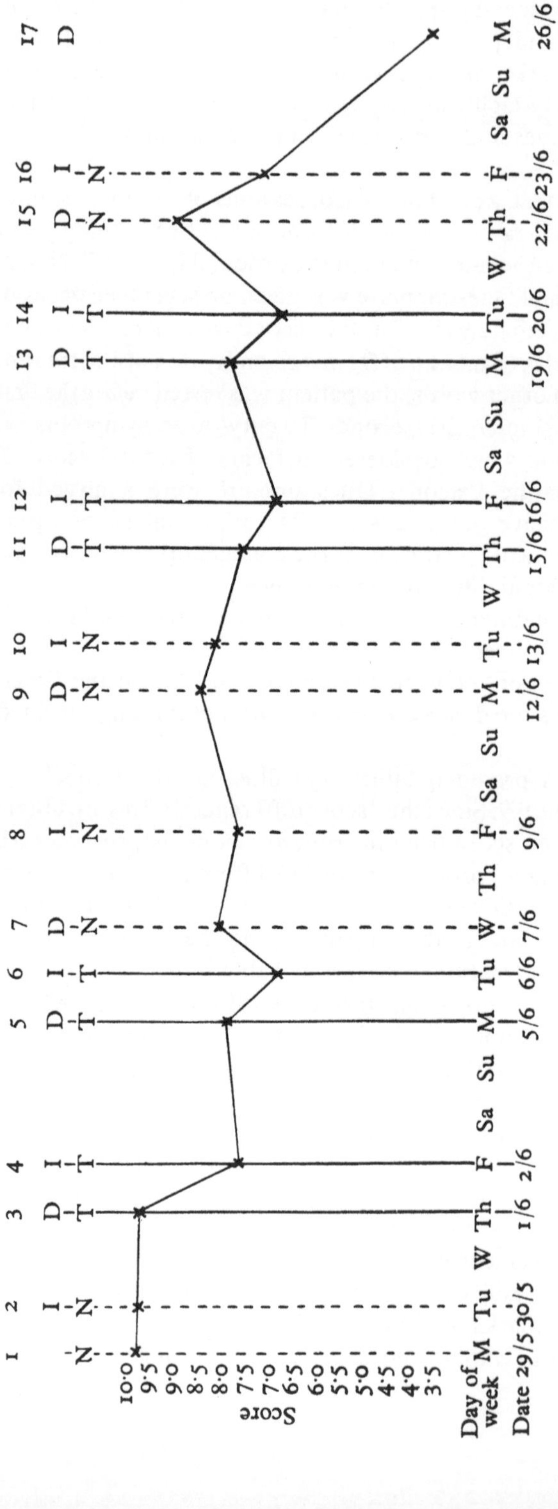

Fig. 9.4. Average scores on the Personal Questionnaire on seventeen occasions of testing I = immediate measure; D = delayed measure; T = rational training; and N = nondirective therapy. (From Shapiro, Marks, and Fox, 1963)

TABLE 9.9
Distribution of Treatments, Measures, and Mean Scores[a,b]

Occasion No.	1	2	3	4	5	6	7	8	9	10	11	12	13	14	15	16	17
Kind of Treatment	N	N	T	T	T	T	N	N	N	N	T	T	T	T	N	N	
Time of test	B	A	B	A	B	A	B	A	B	A	B	A	B	A	B	A	
Measures		I	D	I	D	I	D	I	D	I	D	I	D	I	D	I	D
Mean scores	9.9	9.9	9.9	7.8	8.1	7.0	8.3	7.9	8.7	8.4	7.8	7.1	8.1	7.0	9.4	7.4	3.9
Score differences	0.0	0.0	+2.1	−0.3	+1.1	−1.3	+0.4	−0.8	+0.3	+0.6	+0.7	−1.0	+1.1	- 2.4	+2.0	+3.5	

[a] From Shapiro, 1964b.
[b] Each score difference is obtained by subtracting each mean score from the preceding mean score.

Key: N = Non-directive therapy B = Before treatment
T = Rational training A = After treatment

I = Immediate measure
D = Delayed measure (24 to 72 hours after treatment).

TABLE 9.10
Immediate and Delayed Effects of Nondirective and Rational Training as Assessed by Score Differences[a]

IMMEDIATE		DELAYED		IMMEDIATE		DELAYED	
Occasion Nos.	*Difference*	*Occasion Nos.*	*Difference*	*Occasion Nos.*	*Difference*	*Occasion Nos.*	*Difference*
1–2	0.0	2–3	0.0	3–4	+2.1	4–5	−0.3
7–8	+0.4	8–9	−0.8	5–6	+1.1	6–7	−1.3
9–10	+0.3	10–11	+0.6	11–12	+0.7	12–13	−1.0
15–16	+2.0	16–17	+3.5	13–14	+1.1	14–15	−2.4

[a] From Shapiro, 1964b.

independent, which confirms findings made in the purely observational studies described above. Shapiro (1964a) presented the data in Table 9.11 to demonstrate how the phobic symptoms changed very little over time whereas the depressive symptoms changed a good deal in the period over which they were assessed.

Shapiro has shown a keen awareness of some of the unsolved problems of the technique he has devised. He has, in fact, said that

> The Personal Questionnaire cannot begin to be regarded as a fully developed technique of measurement. It presents many unresolved problems. For example, how do we know that different interviewers will produce the same list of illness statements? How do the responses to the questionnaire differ from responses to the same questions in a psychiatric interview? Can we accept the scaling procedure as a sufficient guarantee that a subject will operate the same scale every time he does the test? Such questions, and others, must be, and in fact are being, subjected to further research. (1963, pp. 140-141).

Elsewhere, Shapiro has admitted that

> There are two outstanding defects in the present form of the Personal Questionnaire. In the first place, one form of irrelevant response set, the set to make oneself appear more or less ill than one really is, has not been controlled. This is, of course, a difficulty which is inherent in all "question-answer" procedures. In the second place, it is not yet clear how far current methods of statistical analysis, which are based on the complete independence of all the relevant observations from each other, can be applied to observations made of the single case. (1961a, p. 155)

These problems, he adds, also require further investigation.

No claim is made, of course, that this—essentially a method of self-assessment—is the only kind of measure that may be applied to the individual case. Nor is the postulated underlying dimension of "unpleasantness" supposed to be the only dimension that is of any importance. Nevertheless, as

TABLE 9.11
Scores on Phobic and Depressive Symptoms from Personal Questionnaire[a]

THERE ARE FOUR POSSIBLE SCORES: 10 IS EQUIVALENT TO ILLNESS AND 2 TO RECOVERY

	Occasions																*Summary of Content*
No.	2	3	4	5	6	7	8	9	10	11	12	13	14	15	16	17	Mean	
1.	10	10	10	10	10	10	10	10	10	10	10	10	10	10	10	10	10·0	Shops-thinking
2.	10	10	10	10	10	10	10	10	10	10	10	10	10	10	10	10	10·0	Shops-running out
3.	10	10	10	10	10	10	10	10	10	10	10	7	10	10	10	10	9·9	Walks
4.	10	10	7	10	10	10	10	10	10	10	7	10	10	10	10	10	9·6	Garden
5.	10	10	10	10	10	10	10	10	10	10	10	10	7	7	7	7	9·2	Meeting people
6.	10	10	10	10	10	10	10	10	10	10	7	10	5	10	10	2	9·0	Falling fear
Mean	10	10	9.5	10	10	10	10	10	10	10	9.0	9.5	8.7	9.5	9.5	8.2		
20.	10	10	7	5	5	7	5	5	7	5	5	10	5	10	5	2	6·4	Guilt
21.	10	10	7	10	5	7	7	10	5	5	5	5	5	10	2	2	6·4	Interest
22.	7	10	5	5	2	5	7	10	7	5	5	5	7	7	7	2	6·0	Energy
23.	10	10	2	7	2	2	5	2	7	5	5	5	2	10	5	2	5·1	Future
Mean	9.2	10	5.2	6.7	3.5	5.2	6.0	6.7	6.5	5.0	5.0	6.2	4.0	9.2	4.7	2.0		

[a] From Shapiro, 1964a.

we have seen in the case of Truax's work on the processes and outcome of psychotherapy (Chapter 8), our current, usual tests of constructive personality change are, at best, but coarse—and at worst invalid. It would hardly seem overly optimistic to suggest that a technique such as the Personal Questionnaire may provide a means of focusing on the target symptoms of disordered individuals in order that we may more delicately detect crucial change.

Other regions of individual behavior that in the past have seemed inaccessible to measurement are also now beginning to be explored. For example, "the transference"—often held to be the potent factor in change, but which previously seemed insusceptible to calibration—has begun to be evaluated by Crisp (1964a, 1964b, 1964c; Crisp and Moldofsky, 1965), in both group and individual behavior, through the use of procedures derived from Kelly's (1955) theory of personal constructs and his repertory grid technique.

Perhaps the attempt to develop the scientific study of the individual case in abnormal psychology emphasizes—more forcefully than almost any other example—the need for the interdependent, oscillating study of the means of measurement and the means of manipulation. In this kind of study, the use of a "control group" may be difficult, impossible, or even irrelevant; we must seek, instead, for what Shapiro has labeled "predictive experimental control." We can secure this only through a persistent search for powerful independent variables, whose power, however, can be assessed only by dependent variables that are sensitive to the changes we manage to effect.

10

CONCLUSION – *Description and Change*

IT IS HOPED THAT the material reviewed in the foregoing chapters of this book can be seen as fitting, without too much distortion, into the general scheme of scientific activity that involves the two crucial components of description and manipulation.

The principal message to emerge from our consideration of these studies is that the problems of abnormal behavior can indeed profitably be tackled by a conjunction of skills and knowledge drawn from experimental *and* abnormal psychology. The precise determination of the contributions that each branch can most usefully make is facilitated by the explicit prior recognition of a number of dimensions of difference that exist between various kinds of psychologists (Inglis, 1964b).

In the first place, it must be admitted that—in the abnormal field—there are differences of opinion about what should properly be considered the rightful subject matter or content of psychology. For example, there are those who, covertly at least, still accept the dichotomy of the "ghost-in-the-machine" (Ryle, 1949), and most of these concern themselves with the misadventures of the "ghostly" component, usually in terms of some kind of psychodynamic discourse. Because these psychodynamic theorists and practitioners also tend to couch their systems in a form that is designed to be infallible, rather than testable, they are divided from other psychologists not only in terms of the content with which they choose to deal but also in terms of the canons of evidence they prefer to accept.

It may be maintained, however, on the evidence of the kinds of study considered in previous chapters, that the area covered by psychodynamic discourse does not by any means define the limits of the whole field of abnormal psychology. On the contrary, it serves rather to confine its advocates to an outflanked philosophical position in a way that actually prevents them from mounting a scientific attack upon human problems.

This latter group, then, is effectively split off from those who would hold that human activity, and even the so-called "mental disorders," may most profitably be handled within a *behavioral* frame of reference of the kind adopted in this book.

Even among those who would accept the behavioral approach, however, there is another dimension of difference, which relates to the choice of preferred method. Two broad classes of activity can be found here, and these, of course, are to some extent reflected in the division between the two parts of this volume. There are, on the one hand, those investigators who have been primarily concerned to devise and employ techniques of measurement, usually in the hope that their tests would prove to covary with other broad classes of behavior. There are, on the other hand, those investigators who have been interested mainly in the manipulation and alteration of behavior itself. The fact that both of these aspects of method may be abused does not prove that either should be left to stand alone.

This kind of division in psychology has of course been commented on before; for example, by Bindra and Scheier (1954), by Cronbach (1957), and by Inglis (1962c, 1964c). It has happened, in the past, that many psychologists in the abnormal field have principally employed the first aspect of method; the "pure" experimentalists have mainly used the second. It is evident from the illustrations offered in previous chapters, however, that this association between method and field of specialization is neither inevitable nor necessary. These examples have shown that, even in abnormal psychology, interest is now coming to bear more and more upon the force of experiment or manipulation as well as upon the power of observation and measurement.

It has, indeed, been one of the main aims of this book to demonstrate that each method can be used to inform and complement the other, since adequate measurement is absolutely essential for the proper assessment of change. Perhaps one might even risk a paraphrase and conclude that, in the study of abnormal behavior, change without measurement is blind whereas measurement without change is empty.

Many of the investigations that have been cited emphasize and reinforce the contention that the problems of abnormal behavior must be explored *directly*—and not just by the indirect means so often employed. One kind of indirect investigation is sometimes pursued by the experimental psychologist in the belief that human disorders may best be dealt with in terms of analogues manufactured in laboratory animals. Broadhurst (1960), however, has reminded us of the great length of the chain of inference from rat to man, and also how weak are its many links. Another kind of indirect investigation is often conducted by the clinical psychologist, who may study human abnormalities only after they have been refracted through the diagnostic hypotheses of psychiatry. Such workers would do well to remember that the help that bacteriology has given to surgery did not spring from a more refined understanding of orthodox views on "spontaneous generation" but that it came from a direct confrontation of the problems of fermentation and infection with the methods of science.

The material we have reviewed, it is hoped—if only by the sequence of the chapters—will have shown that the variables involved in the scientific study of abnormal behavior can cover a very wide span: they may range from the effects of neurosurgical interference with the structural elements underlying behavior to the influence of social, psychotherapeutic interaction. Moreover, some preliminary results show that the scientific approach need not be applied only to the behavior of groups of people: a courageous return is being made to the systematic and objective study of the single case.

It seems likely, then, that future advances in knowledge that is related to abnormal human behavior will be made by those experimental-clinical psychologists who can comprehend both the skills necessary for the development of sensitive, objective measures of behavior and the knowledge needed for the creation of significant, repeatable change. Their reach will have to be wide enough to encompass a broad range of relevant variables, their grasp must be fine enough to fasten directly upon individual disorder.

Proposals have come from a number of sources about how such psychologists should train (Shapiro, 1955, 1962; Maher, 1965) and practice (Jones, 1960; Goldiamond, Dyrud and Miller, 1965). It is certain that there are now far too few psychologists of this persuasion. For a multitude of problems in abnormal psychology, the application of scientific procedure remains more a future hope than a present reality.

As students of abnormal behavior, we must continue to strive, over the entire range of our inquiries, toward the discovery and description of powerful and specifiable independent variables and of relevant and measurable dependent variables. Until we succeed, we will be caught in a crossfire from the academics, who will properly accuse us of imprecision, and from clinicians, who will justifiably accuse us of triviality.

Examples are before us and the onus is upon us: but the opportunity is also ours.

REFERENCES

Adorno, T. W., Frenkel-Brunswik, Else, Levinson, D. J., and Sanford, R. N. *The authoritarian personality*. New York: Harper, 1950.

Alcorn, D. E. Some experiences in sensory deprivation experiments. *Med. Services J.*, 1960, *16*, 955–962.

Allport, G. W. *Personality: a psychological interpretation*. New York: Holt, 1937.

Ammons, R. B., Larson, W. L., and Shearn, C. R. The full-range picture vocabulary test V. Results for an adult population. *J. consult. Psychol.*, 1950, *14*, 150–155.

Arnhoff, F. N., and Leon, H. V. Bibliography of sensory deprivation, isolation and confinement. Unpublished bibliography, Dept. of Psychiatry, University of Miami School of Medicine, August, 1962.

Ayllon, T. Intensive treatment of psychotic behavior by stimulus satiation and food reinforcement. *Behav. Res. Ther.*, 1963, *1*, 53–62.

Azima, H., Vispo, R., and Azima, Fern J. Observations on anaclitic therapy during sensory deprivation. In P. Solomon *et al.* (Eds.), *Sensory Deprivation*. Cambridge, Mass.: Harvard Univ. Press, 1961.

Azrin, N. H., and Lindsley, O. R. The reinforcement of cooperation between children. *J. abnorm. soc. Psychol.*, 1956, *52*, 100–102.

Babcock, Harriet, and Levy, Lydia. *Manual of directions for the revised examination of the measurement of efficiency of mental functioning*. Chicago: Stoelting, 1940.

Bailey, P., Green, J. R., Amador, L., and Gibbs, F. A. Treatment of psychomotor states by anterior temporal lobectomy: report of progress. *Proc. Assoc. Res. nerv. ment. Dis.*, 1953, *31*, 341–346.

Balint, M. *The doctor, his patient and the illness*. New York: Internat. Univ. Press, 1957.

Barrett, Beatrice H. Reduction in rate of multiple tics by free operant conditioning methods. *J. nerv. ment. Dis.*, 1962, *135*, 187–195.

Bartlet, Deone, and Shapiro, M. B. Investigation and treatment of a reading disability in a dull child with severe psychiatric disturbances. *Brit. J. educ. Psychol.*, 1956. *26*, 180–190.

Bartlet, J. E. A. A case of organized visual hallucinations in an old man with cataract and their relation to the phenomena of the phantom limb. *Brain*, 1951, *74*, 363–373.

Benjamin, J. D. A method for distinguishing and evaluating formal thinking disorders in schizophrenia. In J. S. Kasanin (Ed.), *Language and thought in schizophrenia.* Berkeley, Calif.: Univ. of Calif. Press, 1946.

Berlyne, D. E. Knowledge and stimulus-response psychology. *Psychol. Rev.*, 1954, *61*, 245–254.

Bernard. C. *An introduction to the study of experimental medicine* (Trans. H. C. Green) New York: Dover, 1957.

Bexton, W. H., Heron, W., and Scott, T. H. Effects of decreased variation in the sensory environment. *Canad. J. Psychol.*, 1954, *8*, 70–76.

Bindra, D., and Scheier, I. H. The relation between psychometric and experimental research in psychology. *Amer. Psychologist*, 1954, *9*, 69–71.

Bleuler, E. *Dementia praecox or the group of schizophrenias.* New York: Internat. Univ. Press, 1950.

Brady, J. P., and Lind, D. L. Experimental analysis of hysterical blindness: operant conditioning techniques. *Arch. gen. Psychiat.*, 1961, *4*, 331–339.

Brierley, J. B. Clinico-pathological correlations in amnesia. *Geront. Clin.*, 1961, *3*, 97–109.

Broadbent, D. E. Successive responses to simultaneous stimuli. *Quart. J. exp. Psychol.*, 1956, *8*, 145–162.

——Immediate memory and simultaneous stimuli. *Quart. J. exp. Psychol.*, 1957, *9*, 1–11.

—— *Perception and communication.* London: Pergamon Press, 1958.

——, and Gregory, Margaret. Some confirmatory results on age differences in memory for simultaneous stimulation. *Brit. J. Psychol.*, 1965, *56*, 77–80.

Broadhurst, P. L. Abnormal animal behavior. In H. J. Eysenck (Ed.), *Handbook of abnormal psychology.* London: Pitman Med. Pub., 1960.

Bromley, D. B. Notes on the Shaw test. *Brit. J. Psychol.*, 1955, *46*, 310–311.

Brownfield, C. A. Sensory deprivation: a comprehensive survey. *Psychologia*, 1964, *7*, 63–93.

Bruner, J., Goodnow, Jaqueline J., and Austin, G. A. *A study of thinking.* New York: Wiley, 1956.

Caird. W. K., and Inglis, J. The short-term storage of auditory and visual two-channel digits by elderly patients with memory disorder. *J. ment. Sci.*, 1961, *107*, 1062–1069.

——, Sanderson, R. E., and Inglis, J. Cross-validation of a learning test for use with elderly psychiatric patients. *J. ment. Sci.*, 1962, *108*, 368–370.

Cameron, D. E. Studies in senile nocturnal delirium. *Psychiat. Quart.*, 1941, *15*, 47–53.

Cameron, N. Reasoning, regression and communication in schizophrenics. *Psychol. Monogr.*, 1938a, *50*, 1–30 (Whole No. 221).

——A study of thinking in senile deterioration and schizophrenic disorganization. *Amer. J. Psychol.*, 1938b, *51*, 650–664.

——— Deterioration and regression in schizophrenic thinking. *J. abnorm. soc. Psychol.*, 1939a, *34*, 265–270.

——— Schizophrenic thinking in a problem-solving situation. *J. ment. Sci.*, 1939b, *85*, 1012–1035.

——— *Personality development and psychopathology: a dynamic approach.* Boston: Houghton Mifflin, 1963.

———, and Magaret, Ann. Experimental studies in thinking. 1. Scattered speech in the responses of normal subjects to incomplete sentences. *J. exp. Psychol.*, 1949, *39*, 617–627.

———, and Magaret, Ann. Correlates of scattered speech in the responses of normal subjects to incomplete sentences. *J. gen. Psychol.*, 1950, *43*, 77–84.

Carkhuff, R. R., and Deburger, R. Gross ratings of patient behavior. Mimeographed rating sheet, Univ. of Massachusetts, 1964.

———, and Truax, C. B. Training in counseling and psychotherapy: an evaluation of an integrated didactic and experiential approach. *J. consult. Psychol.*, 1965a, *29*, 333–336.

———, and Truax, C. B. Lay mental health counseling: the effects of lay group counseling. *J. consult. Psychol.*, 1965b, *29*, 426–431.

Cattell, R. B. The measurement of adult intelligence. *Psychol. Bull.*, 1943, *40*, 159–193.

——— *Factor analysis: an introduction and manual for the psychologist and social scientist.* New York: Harper, 1952.

Cleveland, S. E., and Dysinger, D. W., Mental deterioration in senile psychosis. *J. abnorm. soc. Psychol.*, 1944, *39*, 368 – 372.

———, Reitman, E. E.,and Bentinck, C. Therapeutic effectiveness of sensory deprivation. *Arch. gen. Psychiat.*, 1963, *8*, 455 – 460.

Cohen, B. D., Luby, E. D., Rosenbaum, G., and Gottlieb, J. S. Combined Sernyl and sensory deprivation. *Comprehensive Psychiat.*, 1960, *1*, 345 – 348.

———, Rosenbaum, G., Dobie, Shirley I., and Gottlieb, J. S. Sensory isolation: hallucinogenic effects of a brief procedure. *J. nerv. ment. Dis.*, 1959, *129*, 486 – 491.

Cohen, D. J. Justin and his peers: an experimental analysis of a child's social world. *Child Develpm.*, 1962, *33*, 697 – 717.

———, and Lindsley, O. R. Catalysis of controlled leadership in cooperation by human stimulation. *J. child Psychol. Psychiat.*, 1964, *5*, 119 – 137.

Cooper, G. D., Adams H. B., and Gibby, R. G. Ego strength changes following perceptual deprivation: report on a pilot study. *Arch. gen. Psychiat.*, 1962, *7*, 213 – 217.

Cosin, L. Z., Mort, Margaret, Post, F., Westropp, Celia, and Williams, Moyra. Persistent senile confusion: a study of 50 consecutive cases. *Internat. J. soc. Psychiat.*, 1957, *3*, 195 – 202.

———, Mort, Margaret, Post, F., Westropp, Celia, and Williams, Moyra. Experimental treatment of persistent senile confusion. *Internat. J. soc. Psychiat.*, 1958, *4*, 24 – 42.

Craik, F. I. M. The nature of the age decrement in performance on dichotic listening tasks. *Quart. J. exp. Psychol.*, 1965, *17*, 227 – 240.

Crisp, A. H. An attempt to measure an aspect of "transference." *Brit. J. med. Psychol.*, 1964a, *37*, 17 – 30.

—— Development and application of a measure of "transference." *J. Psychosom. Res.*, 1964b, *8*, 327–335.

—— Transference and behavior therapy. Paper read at 6th International Congress of Psychotherapy, London, August, 1964c.

——, and Moldofsky, H. A psychosomatic study of writer's cramp. *Brit. J. Psychiat.*, 1965, *111*, 841–858.

Cronbach, L. J. Further evidence on response sets and test design. *Educ. Psychol. Measmt.*, 1950, *10*, 3–31.

—— The two disciplines of scientific psychology. *Amer. Psychologist*, 1957, *12*, 671–684.

Doane, B. K., Mahatoo, W., Heron, W., and Scott, T. H. Changes in perceptual function after isolation. *Canad. J. Psychol.*, 1959, *13*, 210–219.

Dukes, W. F. N = 1. *Psychol. Bull.*, 1965, *64*, 74–79.

Ebbinghaus, H. *Über das Gedächtnis: Üntersuchungen zur experimentellen Psychologie.* Leipzig: Duncker & Humblot, 1885.

Edwards, A. L. *Experimental design in psychological research.* New York: Holt, Rinehart & Winston, 1960.

Ellis, A. Rational psychotherapy. *J. gen. Psychol.*, 1955, *59*, 35–44.

Ellis, N. R., Barnett, C. D., and Pryer, M. W. Operant behavior in mental defectives: exploratory studies. *J. exp. Anal. Behav.*, 1960, *3*, 63–69.

Epstein, S. Overinclusive thinking in a schizophrenic and a control group. *J. consult. Psychol.*, 1953, *17*, 384–388.

Esquirol, J. E. D. *Des maladies mentales: considérées sous les rapports médicaux, hygiéniques, et medico-légaux.* Brussels: Tircher, 1838.

Eysenck, H. J. The effects of psychotherapy: an evaluation. *J. consult. Psychol.*, 1952a, *16*, 319–324.

—— *The scientific study of personality.* London: Routledge & Kegan Paul, 1952b.

—— *The dynamics of anxiety and hysteria; an experimental application of modern learning theory to psychiatry.* London: Routledge & Kegan Paul, 1957.

——The effects of psychotherapy. In H. J. Eysenck (Ed.), *Handbook of abnormal psychology.* London: Pitman Med. Pub., 1960.

Falconer, M. A. Discussion on the surgery of temporal-lobe epilepsy: surgical and pathological aspects. *Proc. Roy. Soc. Med.*, 1953, *46*, 971–974.

——, Hill, D., Meyer, A., Mitchell, W., and Pond, D. A. Treatment of temporal-lobe epilepsy by temporal lobectomy. *Lancet*, 1955, *1*, 827–835.

Feldman, M. J., and Drasgow, J. A visual-verbal test for schizophrenia. *Psychiat. Quart. Suppl.*, 1951, pt. 1, 1–10.

Ferster, C. B. Positive reinforcement and behavioral deficits of autistic children. *Child. Develpm.*, 1961, *32*, 437–456.

——, and Skinner, B. F. *Schedules of reinforcement.* New York: Appleton-Century-Crofts, 1957.

Finney, D. J. The Fisher-Yates tests of significance in 2 × 2 contingency tables. *New statistical table No. VII.* Cambridge, Eng.: Cambridge Univ. Press, 1948.

Ford, D. H., and Urban, H. B. *Systems of psychotherapy: a comparative study.* New York: Wiley, 1963.

Fuller, P. R. Operant conditioning of a vegetative human organism. *Amer. J. Psychol.*, 1949, *62*. 587–590.

Furneaux, W. D. *The Nufferno Manual of Speed and Level Tests*. London: Nat. Found. Educ. Res., 1956.
Gastaut, H. So called "psychomotor" and "temporal" epilepsy. A critical study. *Epilepsia*, 1953, *2*, 59–76.
Gibbs, E. L., Gibbs, F. A., and Fuster, B. Psychomotor epilepsy, *Arch. neurol. Psychiat.*, 1948, *60*, 331–339.
Gibby, R. G., Adams, H. B., and Carrera, R. N. Therapeutic changes in psychiatric patients following partial sensory deprivation. *Arch. gen. Psychiat.*, 1960, *3*, 33–42.
Goldberger, L., and Holt, R. R. Experimental interference with reality contact: individual differences. In P. Solomon *et. al* (Eds.) *Sensory Deprivation.* Cambridge, Mass.: Harvard Univ. Press, 1961.
Goldiamond, I., Dyrud, J. E., and Miller, M. D. Practice as research in professional psychology. *Canadian Psychologist*, 1965, *6a*, 110–128.
Goldstein, K. The significance of special mental tests for diagnosis and prognosis in schizophrenia. *Amer. J. Psychiat.*, 1939, *96*, 575–578.
———, and Scheerer, M. Abstract and concrete behavior: an experimental study with special tests. *Psychol. Monogr.*, 1941, *53*, No. 2.
Graham, J. R., Hunter, R. C. A., and Inglis, J. The effects of psychotherapy in depression. Unpublished Research Design Scheme, Queen's University, Kingston, Ontario, 1964.
Grant, D. A. Analysis of variance tests in the analysis and comparison of curves. *Psychol. Bull.*, 1956, *53*, 141–154.
Greenspoon, J. The effect of verbal and non-verbal stimuli on the frequency of members of two verbal response classes. Unpublished Ph. D. dissertation, Indiana Univ., 1951.
———The reinforcing effect of two spoken sounds on the frequency of two responses. *Amer. J. Psychol.*, 1955, *68*, 409–416.
Halstead, W. C. *Brain and intelligence: a quantitative study of the frontal lobes.* Chicago: Univ. of Chicago Press, 1947.
Harris, A. Sensory deprivation in schizophrenia. *J. ment. Sci.*, 1959, *105*, 235–237.
Hathaway, S. R., and McKinley, J. C. *The Minnesota Multiphasic Personality Inventory (rev. ed.).* New York: Psychol. Corp., 1951.
Hebb, D. O. Man's frontal lobes. *Arch. neurol. Psychiat.*, 1945, *54*, 10–24.
———*The organization of behavior: a neuropsychological theory.* New York: Wiley, 1949.
———Alice in wonderland or psychology among the biological sciences. In H. F. Harlow and C. N. Woolsey (Eds.) *Biological and biochemical bases of behavior.* Madison, Wis.: Univ. of Wisconsin Press, 1958a.
———*A textbook of psychology.* Philadelphia: Saunders, 1958b.
———Introduction to Heron's "Cognitive and physiological effects of perceptual isolation." In P. Solomon *et al.* (Eds.), *Sensory deprivation.* Cambridge, Mass: Harvard Univ. Press, 1961.
———, and Morton, N. W. The McGill Adult Comprehension Examination: Verbal Situation and Picture Anomaly Series. *J. educ. Psychol.*, 1943, *34*, 16–25.
Heron, W. The pathology of boredom. *Scient. American*, 1957, *196*, 52–56.
———Cognitive and physiological effects of perceptual isolation. In P. Solomon *et al.* (Eds.), *Sensory deprivation.* Cambridge, Mass.: Harvard Univ. Press, 1961.

———, Doane, B. K., and Scott, T. H. Visual disturbances after prolonged perceptual isolation. *Canad. J. Psychol.*, 1956, *10*, 13–18.
Hill, D. Discussion on the surgery of temporal lobe epilepsy: The clinical study and selection of patients. *Proc. Roy. Soc. Med.*, 1953, *46*, 965–971.
Hull, C. L. The formation and retention of associations among the insane. *Amer. J. Psychol.*, 1917, *28*, 419–435.
———*The principles of behavior*. New York: Appleton-Century-Crofts, 1943.
Huxley, A. *Heaven and hell.* London: Chatto & Windus, 1956.
Inglis, J. An experimental study of learning and "memory function" in elderly psychiatric patients. *J. ment. Sci.*, 1957, *103*, 796–803.
———Psychological investigations of cognitive deficit in elderly psychiatric patients. *Psychol. Bull.*, 1958, *55*, 197–214.
———A paired, associate learning test for use with elderly psychiatric patients. *J. ment. Sci.*, 1959a, *105*, 440–442.
———Learning, retention and conceptual usage in elderly patients with memory disorder. *J. abnorm. soc. Psychol.*, 1959b, *59*, 210–215.
———On the prognostic value of the Modified Word Learning Test in psychiatric patients over 65. *J. ment. Sci.*, 1959c, *105*, 1100–1101.
———Dichotic stimulation and memory disorder. *Nature*, 1960a, *186*, 181–182.
———Abnormalities of motivation and "ego-functions." In H. J. Eysenck (Ed.), *Handbook of abnormal psychology* London: Pitman Med. Pub., 1960b.
———Effect of age on responses to dichotic stimulation. *Nature*, 1962a, *194*, 1101.
———Dichotic stimulation, temporal-lobe damage and the perception and storage of auditory stimuli—a note on Kimura's findings. *Canad. J. Psychol.*, 1962b, *16*, 11–17.
———Psychological practice in geriatric problems. *J. ment. Sci.*, 1962c, *108*, 669–674.
———Experimental-clinical method and the cognitive disorders of the senium. In R. H. Williams, C. Tibbits, and W. Donahue (Eds.), *Processes of aging: social and psychological perspectives.* New York: Atherton Press, 1963.
———Influence of motivation, perception, and attention on age-related changes in short-term memory. *Nature*, 1964a, *204*, 103–104.
———A preface to discussion concerning the training of psychologists. *Canadian Psychologist*, 1964b, *5a*, 88–90.
———A case-history of one approach to the study of behavior change. In B. T. Wigdor (Ed.), *Recent advances in the study of behavior change.* Montreal: McGill Univ. Press, 1964c.
———Immediate memory, age and brain function. In A. T. Welford and J. E. Birren (Eds.), *Behavior, aging and the nervous system.* Springfield, Ill.: Thomas, 1965a.
———Dichotic listening and cerebral dominance. *Acta Otolaryngol.*, 1965b, *60*, 231–238.
———Sensory deprivation and cognitive disorder. *Brit. J. Psychiat.*, 1965c, *111*, 309–315.
———, and Ankus, Mary N. Effects of age on short-term storage and serial rote learning. *Brit. J. Psychol.*, 1965, *56*, 183–195.
———, and Caird, W. K. Age differences in successive responses to simultaneous stimuli. *Canad. J. Psychol.*, 1963, *17*, 98–105.

———, and Sanderson, R. E. Successive responses to simultaneous stimulation in elderly patients with memory disorder. *J. abnorm. soc. Psychol.*, 1961, *62*, 709–712.

———, Shapiro, M. B., and Post, F. "Memory function" in psychiatric patients over sixty: the role of memory in tests discriminating between "functional" and "organic" groups. *J. ment. Sci.*, 1956, *102*, 589–598.

Isaacs, B. A preliminary evaluation of a paired-associate verbal learning test in geriatric practice. *Geront. clin.*, 1962, *4*, 43–55.

———, and Walkley, F. A. A simplified paired-associate test for elderly hospital patients. *Brit. J. Psychiat.*, 1964, *110*, 80–83.

Isaacs, W., Thomas, J., and Goldiamond, I. Application of operant conditioning to reinstate verbal behavior in psychotics. *J. speech hear. Disorders*, 1960, *25*, 8–12.

Jackson, D. D. (Ed.), *The etiology of schizophrenia.* New York: Basic Books, 1960.

James, I. P. Temporal lobectomy for psychomotor epilepsy. *J. ment. Sci.*, 1960, *106*, 543–558.

Jones, H. G. Neurosis and experimental psychology. *J. ment. Sci.*, 1958, *104*, 55–62.

———Applied abnormal psychology. In H. J. Eysenck (Ed.), *Handbook of abnormal psychology.* London: Pitman Med. Pub., 1960.

Kelly, G. A. *The psychology of personal constructs.* New York: Norton, 1955.

Kendall, M. G. *Rank correlation methods.* London: C. Griffin, 1948.

Kendrick, D. C., Parboosingh, Rose-Cecile, and Post, F. A synonym learning test for use with elderly psychiatric patients: a validation study. *Brit. J. soc. clin. Psychol.*, 1965, *4*, 63–71.

Keschner, M., Bender, M. B., and Strauss, T. Mental symptoms in cases of tumor of the temporal lobe. *Arch. Neurol. Psychiat.*, 1936, *35*, 572–596.

Kimura, Doreen. Some effects of temporal-lobe damage on auditory perception. *Canad. J. Psychol.*, 1961, *15*, 156–165.

———Perceptual and memory functions of the left temporal lobe—a reply to Dr. Inglis. *Canad. J. Psychol.*, 1962, *16*, 18–22.

———Right temporal-lobe damage: perception of unfamiliar stimuli after damage. *Arch. Neurol.*, 1963, *8*, 264–271.

King, G. F., Armitage, S. G., and Tilton, J. R. A therapeutic approach to schizophrenics of extreme pathology: an operant-interpersonal method. *J. abnorm. soc. Psychol.*, 1960, *61*, 276–286.

King, H. E. *Psychomotor aspects of mental diseases.* Cambridge, Mass.: Harvard Univ. Press, 1954.

Klopfer, B., and Kelley, D. McG. *The Rorschach Technique: a manual for a projective method of personality diagnosis.* New York: World Book Co., 1946.

Kohs, S. C. *Intelligence measurement: a psychological and statistical study based upon the block-design tests.* New York: Macmillan, 1923.

Kolodny, A. The symptomatology of tumors of the temporal lobe. *Brain*, 1928, *51*, 385–417.

Kral, V. A., Grad, B., Cramer-Azima, Fern, and Russell, L. Biologic, psychologic and sociologic studies in normal aged persons and patients with senile psychoses. *J. Amer. geriat. Soc.*, 1964, *12*, 21–37.

Krasner, L. The use of generalized reinforcers in psychotherapy research. *Psychol. Rep.*, 1955, *1*, 19–25.

—— Studies of the conditioning of verbal behavior. *Psychol. Bull.*, 1958, *55*, 148–170.

——, and Ullmann, L. P. (Eds.), *Research in behavior modification: new developments and implications.* New York: Holt, Rinehart & Winston, 1965.

Kretschmer, E. *Körperbau und Charakter.* Berlin: Springer, 1951.

Kubie, L. S. Theoretical aspects of sensory deprivation. In P. Solomon *et al.* (Eds.), *Sensory deprivation.* Cambridge Mass.: Harvard Univ. Press, 1961.

Lawes, T. G. G. Schizophrenia, "Sernyl" and sensory deprivation. *Brit. J. Psychiat.*, 1963, *109*, 243–250.

Leiderman, P. H., Mendelson, J. H., Wexler, D., and Solomon, P. Sensory deprivation: clinical aspects. *Arch. Intern. Med.*, 1958, *101*, 389–396.

Leiter, R. G., and Partington, J. *Examination manual for the Leiter – Partington Adult Scale.* Washington, D. C., Psychol. Service Center Press, 1950.

Lilly, J. C. Mental effects of reduction of ordinary levels of physical stimuli on intact, healthy persons. *Psychiat. Res. Reports*, 1956, *5*, 1–9.

Lindsley, D. B. Common factors in sensory deprivation, sensory distortion and sensory overload. In P. Solomon *et al.* (Eds.), *Sensory deprivation.* Cambridge, Mass.: Harvard Univ. Press, 1961.

Lindsley, O. R. Operant conditioning methods applied to research in chronic schizophrenia. *Psychiat. Res. Reports*, 1956, *5*, 118–139.

—— Operant behavior during sleep: a measure of depth of sleep. *Science*, 1957, *126*, 1290–1291.

—— Reduction in rate of vocal psychotic symptoms by differential positive reinforcement. *J. exp. Anal. Behavior*, 1959, *2*, 269.

—— Characteristics of the behavior of chronic psychotics as revealed by free-operant conditioning methods. *Dis. nerv. System*, 1960, *21*, 66–78.

—— Direct measurement and functional definition of vocal hallucinatory symptoms in chronic psychosis. In *Proceedings of the Third World Congress of Psychiatry.* Montreal: McGill Univ. Press, 1961.

—— Operant conditioning methods in diagnosis. In J. H. Nodine and J. H. Moyer (Eds.), *Psychosomatic medicine: the first Hahnemann symposium.* Philadelphia: Lea & Febiger, 1962a.

—— Operant conditioning techniques in the measurement of psychopharmacologic response. In J. H. Nodine and J. H. Moyer (Eds.), *Psychosomatic medicine: the first Hahnemann symposium.* Philadelphia: Lea & Febiger, 1962b.

—— A behavioral measure of television viewing. *J. advertising Res.*, 1962c, *2*, 2–12.

—— Direct measurement and functional definition of vocal hallucinatory symptoms. *J. nerv. ment. Dis.*, 1963a, *136*, 293–297.

—— Free-operant conditioning and psychotherapy. In J. H. Masserman (Ed.), *Current Psychiatric Therapies*, Vol. III. New York: Grune & Stratton, 1963b.

—— Experimental analysis of social reinforcement. *Amer. J. Orthopsychiat.*, 1963c, *33*, 624–633.

—— Direct measurement and prosthesis of retarded behavior. *J. Educ.*, 1964a, *147*, 62–81.

—— Geriatric behavioral prosthetics. In R. Kastenbaum (Ed.), *New thoughts on old age.* New York: Springer, 1964b.

———, and Conran, P. Operant behavior during EST: a measure of depth of coma. *Dis. nerv. System*, 1962, *23*, 407–409.

———, Hobika, J. H., and Etsten, B. E. Operant behavior during anesthesia recovery: a continuous and objective method. *Anesthesiology*, 1961, *22*, 937–946.

Lovaas, O. I., Freitag, G. Gold, Vivian, J., and Kassorla, Irene C. Experimental studies in childhood schizophrenia: analysis of self-destructive behavior. *J. exp. Child Psychol.*, 1965. *2*, 67–84.

———, Freitag, G., Kinder, M. I., Rubenstein, D. B., Schaeffer, B., and Simmons, J. B. Experimental studies in childhood schizophrenia. Developing social behavior using electric shock. Paper read at American Psychological Association, Los Angeles, September, 1964.

Lucero, R. J., and Meyer, B. F. A behavior rating scale suitable for use in mental hospitals. *J. clin. Psychol.*, 1951, *7*, 250–254.

Luchins, A. S. Mechanization in problem solving: the effect of Einstellung. *Psychol. Monogr.*, 1942, *54*, No. 6.

Mackay, H. A. Operant techniques applied to disorders of the senium. Unpublished Ph.D. dissertation, Queen's University, 1965.

———, and Inglis, J. The effect of age on a short-term auditory storage process. *Gerontologia*, 1963, *8*, 193–200.

———, and Inglis, J. The reinforcement of simple responses in elderly psychiatric patients with and without memory disorder. Paper read at the Eastern Psychological Association, Atlantic City, N.J., April, 1965.

Maher, B. A. Training for professional psychology. *Canadian Psychologist*, 1965, *6a*, 129–142.

Matarazzo, J. D. The interview. In B. B. Wolman (Ed.), *Handbook of clinical psychology*. New York, McGraw-Hill, 1965.

Maxwell, A. E. *Experimental design in psychology and the medical sciences*. London: Methuen, 1958.

McGeoch, J. A., & Irion, A. L. *The psychology of human learning* (2nd ed.) New York: Longmans, Green, 1952.

McNemar, Q. *Psychological statistics*. New York: Wiley, 1949.

Mednick, Martha, T., & Lindsley, O. R. Some clinical correlates of abnormal behavior. *J. abnorm. soc. Psychol.*, 1958, *57*, 13–16.

Meyer, J. S., Greifenstein, F., and Devault, M. A new drug causing symptoms of sensory deprivation. *J. nerv. ment. Dis.*, 1959, *129*, 54–61.

Meyer, V. Critique of psychological approaches to brain damage. *J. ment. Sci.*, 1957a, *103*, 80–109.

——— Cognitive changes following temporal lobectomy for the relief of focal temporal lobe epilepsy. Unpublished Ph.D. dissertation, University of London, 1957b.

——— Cognitive changes following temporal lobectomy for relief of temporal lobe epilepsy. *Arch. neurol. Psychiat.*, 1959, *81*, 299–309.

———, and Falconer, M. A. Defects of learning ability with massive lesions of the temporal lobe. *J. ment. Sci.*, 1960, *106*, 472–477.

———, and Jones, H. G. Patterns of cognitive test performance as functions of the lateral localization of cerebral abnormalities in the temporal lobe. *J. ment. Sci.*, 1957, *103*, 758–772.

——, and Yates, A. J. Intellectual changes following temporal lobectomy for psychomotor epilepsy: Preliminary communication. *J. neurol. neurosurg. Psychiat.*, 1955, *18*, 44–52.

Miller, G. A., Galanter, E., and Pribram, K. H. *Plans and the structure of behavior.* New York: Holt, 1960.

Milner, Brenda. Intellectual effects of temporal-lobe damage in man. Unpublished Ph. D. dissertation, McGill University, 1952.

—— Intellectual function of the temporal lobes. *Psychol. Bull.*, 1954, *51*, 42–62.

—— Psychological defects produced by temporal lobe excision. *Proc. Ass. Res. nerv. ment. Dis.*, 1958, *36*, 244–257.

—— The memory defect in bilateral hippocampal lesions. *Psychiat. Res. Reports,* 1959, *11*, 43–58.

—— Laterality effects in audition. In V. B. Mountcastle (Ed.), *Interhemispheric relations and cerebral dominance.* Baltimore: Johns Hopkins Press, 1962.

——, and Penfield, W. The effect of hippocampal lesions on recent memory. *Trans. Amer. Neurol. Assoc.*, 1955, *80*, 42–48.

Murray, H. A. *Thematic Apperception Test.* Cambridge, Mass.: Harvard Univ. Press, 1943.

Nathan, P. E., Schneller, P., and Lindsley, O. R. Direct measurement of communication during psychiatric admission interviews. *Behav. Res. Ther.*, 1964, *2*, 49–57.

Newcombe, Freda, and Steinberg, B. Some aspects of learning and memory function in older psychiatric patients. *J. Gerontol.*, 1964, *19*, 490–493.

Orlando, R., and Bijou, S. W. Single and multiple schedules of reinforcement in developmentally retarded children. *J. exp. Anal. Behav.*, 1960, *3*, 339–348.

Osgood, C. E., Suci, G. J., and Tannenbaum, P. H. *The measurement of meaning.* Urbana, Ill.: Univ. of Illinois Press, 1957.

Pavlov, I. P. *Conditioned reflexes: an investigation of the physiological activity of the cerebral cortex.* (Trans. G. V. Anrep). London: Oxford Univ. Press, 1927.

Payne, R. W. The role of the clinical psychologist at the Institute of Psychiatry. *Rev. Psychol. App.*, 1953, *3*, 150–160.

—— An investigation into the possibility of defining "dissociation" as a personality trait by means of objective tests. Unpublished Ph.D. dissertation, Univ. of London, 1954.

—— Experimentelle Untersuchung zum Spaltungsbegriff von Kretschmer. *Z. f. d. exp. u. angew. Psychol.*, 1955, *3*, 65–97.

—— Experimental method in clinical psychological practice. *J. ment. Sci.*, 1957, *103*, 189–196.

—— Diagnostic and personality testing in clinical psychology. *Amer. J. Psychiat.*, 1958a, *115*, 25–29.

—— Thought processes, normal and abnormal. Proceedings of the XIII Congress, Internat. Assoc. Applied Psychol., Rome, April, 1958b.

—— Some aspects of perception and thought disorder in schizophrenic subjects. *Swiss Rev. Psychol. Appl.*, 1958c, *17*, 300–308.

—— Cognitive abnormalities. In H. J. Eysenck (Ed.), *Handbook of abnormal psychology.* London: Pitman Med. Pub., 1960.

—— Thought disorder and retardation in schizophrenia. *Canad. Psychiat. Assoc. J.*, 1961, *6*, 75–78.

——— An object classification test as a measure of overinclusive thinking in schizophrenic patients. *Brit. J. soc. clin. Psychol.*, 1962, *1*, 213–221.

——— The measurement and significance of overinclusive thinking and retardation in schizophrenic patients. In P. H. Hoch and J. Zubin (Eds.), *Psychopathology of schizophrenia*. New York: Grune & Stratton, 1966.

———, Ancevich, Singrida S., and Laverty, S. G. Overinclusive thinking in symptom-free schizophrenics. *Canad. Psychiat. Assoc. J.*, 1963, *8*, 225–234.

———, Caird, W. K., and Laverty, S. G. Overinclusive thinking and delusions in schizophrenic patients. *J. abnorm. soc. Psychol.*, 1964, *68*, 562–566.

———, Friedlander, D., Laverty, S. G., and Haden, P. Overinclusive thought disorder in hospitalized chronic schizophrenic patients and its response to "Proketazine." *Brit. J. Psychiat.*, 1963, *109*, 523–530.

———, & Hewlett, J. H. G. Thought disorder in psychotic patients. In H. J. Eysenck (Ed.), *Experiments in personality*, (Vol. II). London: Routledge & Kegan Paul, 1960.

———, and Inglis, J. Testing for intellectual impairment–some comments reconsidered. *J. ment. Sci.*, 1960, *106*, 1134–1138.

———, and Jones, H. G. Statistics for the investigation of individual cases. *J. clin. Psychol.*, 1957, *13*, 115–121.

———, Matussek, P., and George, E. I. An experimental study of schizophrenic thought disorder. *J. ment. Sci.*, 1959, *105*, 627–652.

Penfield, W. The interpretive cortex. *Science*, 1959, *129*, 1719–1725.

———, and Baldwin. M. Temporal lobe seizures and the technique of sub-total temporal lobectomy. *Ann. Surg.*, 1952, *136*, 625–634.

———, and Flanigin, H. Surgical therapy of temporal lobe seizures. *Arch. neurol. Psychiat.*, 1950, *64*, 491–500.

———, Lende, R. A., and Rasmussen, T. Manipulation hemiplegia: an untoward complication in the surgery of epilepsy. *J. Neurosurg.*, 1961, *18*, 760–776.

———, and Milner, Brenda, Memory deficit produced by bilateral lesions in the hippocampal zone. *Arch. neurol. Psychiat.*, 1958, *79*, 475–497.

Phillips, J. P. N. Techniques for scaling the symptoms of an individual psychiatric patient. *J. Psychosom. Res.*, 1964, *8*, 255–271.

Portnoy, Stephanie, and Salzinger, K. The conditionability of different verbal response classes: positive, negative and non-affect statements. *J. gen. Psychol.*, 1964, *70*, 311–323.

Raven, J. C. *Guide to using the Mill Hill Vocabulary Scale with the Progressive Matrices Scale*. London: Lewis, 1958.

Rey, A. D'un procédé pour évaluer l'éducabilité. *Arch. Psychol. Geneve.*, 1934, *24*, 297–337.

Riddell, Sylvia A. The performance of elderly psychiatric patients on equivalent forms of tests of memory and learning. *Brit. J. soc. clin. Psychol.*, 1962a, *1*, 70–71.

——— The relationships between tests of organic involvement, memory impairment and diagnosis in elderly psychiatric patients. *Brit. J. soc. clin. Psychol.*, 1962b, *1*, 228–231.

Rogers, C. R. *Counseling and psychotherapy*. Boston: Houghton Mifflin, 1942.

——— *Client-centered therapy*. Boston: Houghton Mifflin, 1951.

——— The necessary and sufficient conditions of therapeutic personality change. *J. consult. Psychol.*, 1957, *21*, 95–103.

——— *On becoming a person: a therapist's view of psychotherapy.* Boston: Houghton Mifflin, 1961.

Rokeach, M. Generalized mental rigidity as a factor in ethnocentrism. *J. abnorm. soc. Psychol.*, 1948, *43*, 259–278.

Rosenzweig, S. A transvaluation of psychotherapy: a reply to Hans Eysenck. J. *abnorm. soc. Psychol.*, 1954, *49*, 298–304.

Rubin, L. S. The psychopharmacology of lysergic acid diethylamide (LSD–25). *Psychol. Bull.*, 1957, *54*, 479–489.

Ruff, G. E., Levy, E. Z., and Thaler, V. H. Factors influencing reactions to reduced sensory input. In P. Solomon *et al.* (Eds.), *Sensory deprivation.* Cambridge, Mass.: Harvard Univ. Press, 1961.

Ryle, G. *The concept of mind.* London: Hutchinson, 1949.

Salzinger, K. Experimental manipulation of verbal behavior: a review. *J. gen. Psychol.*, 1959, *61*, 65–94.

——— The experimental analysis of the interview. In J. Zubin (Ed.), *Experimental abnormal psychology,* Vol. II: New York: Columbia Univ. Bookstore, 1960.

——— Some problems of response measurement in verbal behavior: the response unit and intraresponse relations. Paper read at a Conference on Methods of Measurement of Change in Human Behavior, Montreal, September, 1962.

———, Feldman, R. S., Cowan, Judith E., and Salzinger, Suzanne. Operant conditioning of verbal behavior of two young speech-deficient boys. In L. Krasner and L. P. Ullman (Eds.), *Research in behavior modification: new developments and implications.* New York: Holt, Rinehart & Winston, 1965.

———, and Pisoni, Stephanie. Reinforcement of affect responses of schizophrenics during the clinical interview. *J. abnorm. soc. Psychol.*, 1958, *57*, 84–90.

———, and Pisoni, Stephanie. Reinforcement of verbal affect responses of normal subjects during the interview. *J. abnorm. soc. Psychol.*, 1960, *60*, 127–130.

———, and Pisoni, Stephanie. Some parameters of the conditioning of verbal affect responses in schizophrenic subjects. *J. abnorm. soc. Psychol.*, 1961, *63*, 511–516.

———, and Portnoy, Stephanie. Verbal conditioning in interviews: application to chronic schizophrenics and relationship to prognosis for acute schizophrenics. *J. psychiat. Res.*, 1964, *2*, 1–9.

———, Portnoy, Stephanie, and Feldman, R. S. Experimental manipulation of continuous speech in schizophrenic patients. *J. abnorm. soc. Psychol.*, 1964, *68*, 508–516.

Salzinger, Suzanne, Salzinger, K., Portnoy, Stephanie, Eckman, Judith, Bacon, Pauline M., Deutsch, M., and Zubin, J. Operant conditioning of continuous speech in young children. *Child Developm.*, 1962, *33*, 683–695.

Sanderson, R. E., & Inglis, J. Learning and mortality in elderly psychiatric patients. *J. Gerontol.*, 1961, *16*, 375–376.

Sandler, J. A test of the significance of the difference between the means of correlated measures based on a simplification of Student's *t*. *Brit. J. Psychol.*, 1955, *46*, 225–226.

Scheflen, A. E. The significance of posture in communication systems. *Psychiatry*, 1964, *27*, 316–331.

Schonell, F. J. *The psychology and teaching of reading* (3rd ed.) Edinburgh: Oliver & Boyd, 1951.

Scott, T. H., Bexton, W. H., Heron, W., and Doane, B. K. Cognitive effects of perceptual isolation. *Canad. J. Psychol.*, 1959, *13*, 200–209.

Scoville, W. B., and Milner, Brenda. Loss of recent memory after bilateral hippocampal lesions. *J. neurol. neurosurg. Psychiat.*, 1957, *20*, 11–21.

Shalman, D. C. The diagnostic use of the McGill picture anomaly test in temporal lobe epilepsy. *J. neurol. neurosurg. Psychiat.*, 1961, *34*, 220–222.

Shapiro, M. B. Experimental studies of a perceptual anomaly. I. Initial experiments. *J. ment. Sci.*, 1951a, *97*, 90–110.

——— An experimental approach to psychological diagnostic testing. *J. ment. Sci.*, 1951b, *97*, 748–764.

——— Experimental studies of a perceptual anomaly. II. Confirmatory and explanatory experiments. *J. ment. Sci.*, 1952, *98*, 605–617.

——— Experimental studies of a perceptual anomaly. III. The testing of an explanatory theory. *J. ment. Sci.*, 1953, *99*, 394–409.

——— An experimental investigation of the block design rotation effect. *Brit. J. med. Psychol.*, 1954, *27*, 84–88.

——— Training of clinical psychologists at the Institute of Psychiatry. *Bull. Brit. Psychol. Soc.*, 1955, No. *26*, 15–20.

——— Experimental method in the psychological description of the individual psychiatric patient. *Internat. J. soc. Psychiat.*, 1957, *3*, 89–103.

——— The rotation of drawings by illiterate Africans. *J. soc. Psychol.*, 1960, *52*, 17–30.

——— A method of measuring psychological changes specific to the individual psychiatric patient. *Brit. J. med. Psychol.*, 1961a, *34*, 151–155.

——— The single case in fundamental clinical psychological research. *Brit. J. med. Psychol.*, 1961b, *34*, 355–364.

——— *The personal questionnaire: an abbreviated manual.* Unpublished mimeograph, Institute of Psychiatry, University of London, 1961c.

——— A two-year course for the training of clinical psychologists at the Institute of Psychiatry, Maudsley Hospital, Denmark Hill, London. *Bull. Brit. Psychol. Soc.*, 1962, No. *48*, 30–32.

——— A clinical approach to fundamental research with special reference to the study of the single patient. In P. Sainsbury and N. Kreitman (Eds.), *Methods of psychiatric research: an introduction for clinical psychiatrists.* London: Oxford Univ. Press, 1963.

——— The measurement of clinically relevant variables. *J. Psychosom. Res.*, 1964a, *8*, 245–254.

——— The single case in psychological research: a reply. *J. Psychosom. Res.*, 1964b, *8*, 283–291.

——— The single case in clinical psychological research. *J. gen. Psychol.*, 1966, *74*, 3–23.

———, and Beech, H. R. General implications of the Block Design Rotation effect. *Percept. Mot. Skills*, 1965, *20*, 306.

———, Brierley, J., Slater, P., and Beech, H. R. Experimental studies of a perceptual anomaly. VII. A new explanation. *J. ment. Sci.*, 1962, *108*, 655–688.

———, Field, J., and Post, F. An enquiry into the determinants of a differentiation between elderly "organic" and "non-organic" patients on the Bender Gestalt Test. *J. ment. Sci.*, 1957, *103*, 364–374.

———, Kessell, Rose, and Maxwell, A. E. Speed and quality of psychomotor performance in psychiatric patients. *J. clin. Psychol.*, 1960, *16*, 266–271.

———, Marks, I. M., and Fox, B. A therapeutic experiment on phobic and affective symptoms in an individual psychiatric patient. *Brit. J. soc. clin. Psychol.*, 1963, *2*, 81–93.

———, and Nelson, Elizabeth H. An investigation of an abnormality of cognitive function in a cooperative young psychotic: an example of the application of experimental method in a single case. *J. clin. Psychol.*, 1955a, *11*, 344–351.

———, and Nelson, Elizabeth H. An investigation of the nature of cognitive impairment in cooperative psychiatric patients. *Brit. J. Psychol.*, 1955b, *28*, 239–256.

———, Neufeld, I., and Post, F. Note: experimental study of depressive illness. *Psychol. Rep.*, 1962, *10*, 590.

———, Post, F., Löfving, Barbro, and Inglis, J. "Memory function" in psychiatric patients over sixty: some methodological and diagnostic implications. *J. ment. Sci.*, 1956, *102*, 233–246.

———, and Ravenette, E. T. A preliminary experiment on paranoid delusions. *J. ment. Sci.*, 1959, *105*, 295–312.

———, Slater, P., and Campbell, D. The effects of distraction on psychomotor slowness in cooperative depressed and schizophrenic subjects. *Brit. J. soc. clin. Psychol.*, 1962, *1*, 121–126.

———, and Tizard, Barbara. Experimental studies of a perceptual anomaly. VI. The application of the "peephole" analogy to the perception of organic psychiatric patients. *J. ment. Sci.*, 1958, *104*, 792–801.

Shurley, J. T. Profound experimental sensory isolation. *Amer. J. Psychiat.*, 1960, *117*, 539–545.

Sidman, M. A note on functional relations obtained from group data. *Psychol. Bull.*, 1952, *49*, 263–269.

——— *Tactics of scientific research: evaluating experimental data in psychology.* New York: Basic Books, 1960.

Siegel, S. *Nonparametric statistics for the behavioral sciences.* New York: McGraw-Hill, 1956.

Skinner, B. F. *The behavior of organisms.* New York: Appleton-Century-Crofts, 1938.

——— A case history in scientific method. *Amer. Psychologist*, 1956, *11*, 221–233.

——— *Verbal behavior.* New York: Appleton-Century-Crofts, 1957.

——— *Cumulative record.* New York: Appleton-Century-Crofts, 1959.

Slater, P. Canonical analysis of discriminance. In H. J. Eysenck (Ed.), *Experiments in personality.*, (Vol. II.) London: Routledge & Kegan Paul, 1960.

Smith, S., Thakurdas, H., and Lawes, T. G. G. Perceptual isolation and schizophrenia. *J. ment. Sci.*, 1961, *107*, 839–844.

Solomon, P., Kubzansky, P. E., Leiderman, P. H., Mendelson, J. H., Trumbull, R., and Wexler, D. (Eds.) *Sensory deprivation.* Cambridge, Mass.: Harvard Univ. Press. 1961.

Sommer, R., and Ross, H. Social interaction on a geriatrics ward. *Internat. J. soc. Psychiat.*, 1958, *4*, 128–133.

Spradlin, J. E. Effects of reinforcement schedules on extinction in severely mentally retarded children. *Amer. J. ment. Defic.*, 1962, *66*, 634–640.

Stephenson, W. *The study of behavior.* Chicago: Univ. Chicago Press, 1953.

Stratton, G. M. Vision without inversion of the retinal image. *Psychol. Rev.*, 1897a, *4*, 341–360.

——— Vision without inversion of the retinal image. *Psychol. Rev.*, 1897b, *4*, 463–481.

Taffel, C. Conditioning of verbal behavior in an institutionalized population and its relation to "anxiety level." Unpublished Ph.D. dissertation, Indiana Univ., 1952.

——— Anxiety and the conditioning of verbal behavior. *J. abnorm. soc. Psychol.*, 1955, *51*, 496–501.

Taylor, J. G. *The behavioral basis of perception.* New Haven, Conn.: Yale Univ. Press, 1962.

Thurstone, L. L. A factorial study of perception. *Psychometr. Monogr.*, No. *4*, 1944.

——— *Multiple factor analysis.* Chicago: Univ. Chicago Press, 1947.

Truax, C. B. The process of group psychotherapy. *Psychol. Monogr.*, 1961, 75, *7* (Whole No. 511).

——— A tentative scale for the measurement of therapist genuineness or self-congruence. *Discussion Papers,* Wisconsin Psychiatric Institute, University of Wisconsin, 1962a, *35.*

——— A tentative scale for the measurement of unconditional positive regard. *Psychiatric Institute Bulletin,* Wisconsin Psychiatric Institute, University of Wisconsin, 1962b, 2, *1.*

——— A scale for the measurement of accurate empathy. *Psychiatric Institute Bulletin,* Wisconsin Psychiatric Institute, University of Wisconsin, 1962c, 2, *1.*

——— A scale for the measurement of depth of intrapersonal exploration (DX). *Discussion Papers,* Wisconsin Psychiatric Institute, University of Wisconsin, 1962d, *29.*

——— Effective ingredients in psychotherapy: an approach to unraveling the patient-therapist interaction. *J. counsel. Psychol,* 1963, *10,* 256–263.

——— Antecedent conditions to constructive personality change in preschool children. Mimeographed manuscript, Univ. of Kentucky, 1965a.

——— Reinforcement and non-reinforcement in Rogerian psychotherapy. *J. abnorm. Psychol.*, 1966, *71*, 1–9.

———, and Carkhuff, R. R. Client and therapist transparency in the psychotherapeutic encounter. Paper read at a Symposium on the Transparent Self. American Psychological Association, Philadelphia, August, 1963.

———, and Carkhuff, R. R. Significant developments in psychotherapy research. In L. E. Abt and B. F. Riess (Eds.), *Progress in clinical psychology* (Vol. VI). New York: Grune & Stratton, 1964a.

———, and Carkhuff, R. R. For better or for worse: the process of psychotherapeutic personality change. In B. T. Wigdor (Ed.), *Recent advances in the study of behavior change.* Montreal: McGill Univ. Press, 1964b.

———, and Carkhuff, R. R. Concreteness: a neglected variable in research in psychotherapy. *J. clin. Psychol.*, 1964c, *20*, 264–267.

———, and Carkhuff, R. R. Personality change in hospitalized mental patients during group psychotherapy as a function of the use of alternate sessions and vicarious therapy pretraining. *J. clin. Psychol.*, 1965a, *21*, 225–228.

——, and Carkhuff, R. R. Experimental manipulation of therapeutic conditions. *J. consult. Psychol.*, 1965b, *29*, 119–124.

——, Carkhuff, R. R., and Douds, J. Toward an integration of the didactic and experiential approaches to counseling and psychotherapy. *J. counsel. Psychol.*, 1964, *11*, 240–242.

——, Carkhuff, R. R., and Kodman, F. Relationships between therapist-offered conditions and patient change in group psychotherapy. *J. clin. Psychol.*, 1965, *21*, 327–329.

Vernon, J. A. *Inside the black room.* New York: Clarkson N. Potter, 1963.

——, McGill, T. E., Gulick, W. L., & Candland, D. K. The effect of human isolation upon some perceptual and motor skills. In P. Solomon *et al.* (Eds.), *Sensory deprivation.* Cambridge, Mass.: Harvard Univ. Press, 1961.

Verplanck, W. S. The control of the content of conversation: reinforcement of statements of opinion. *J. abnorm. soc. Psychol.*, 1955, *51*, 668–676.

—— The operant conditioning of human motor behavior. *Psychol. Bull.*, 1956, *53*, 70–83.

Vigotsky, L. S. Thought in schizophrenia. *Arch. Neurol. Psychiat.*, 1934, *31*, 1063–1077.

Wada, J., and Rasmussen, T. Intracarotid injection of sodium amytal for the lateralization of cerebral speech dominance. Experimental and clinical observations. *J. Neurosurg.*, 1960, *17*, 266–282.

Walton, D., and Black, D. A. The validity of a psychological test of brain damage. *Brit. J. med. Psychol.*, 1957, *30*, 270–279.

Wechsler, D. *The measurement of adult intelligence* (3rd ed.) Baltimore: Williams and Wilkins, 1944.

——A standardized memory scale for clinical use. *J. Psychol.*, 1945, *19*, 87–95.

—— *Manual of the Wechsler Intelligence Scale for Children.* New York: Psychol. Corp., 1949.

——*The Wechsler Adult Intelligence Scale.* New York: Psychol. Corp., 1955.

Welford, A. T. Age and learning: theory and needed research. In *Symposium on experimental gerontology.* Basel: Birkhauser, 1956.

——*Aging and human skill.* London: Oxford Univ. Press, 1958.

Wilcoxon, F. *Some rapid approximate statistical procedures.* New York: American Cyanamid, 1949.

Willett, R. A. The effects of psychosurgical procedures on behavior. In H. J. Eysenck (Ed.), *Handbook of abnormal psychology.* London: Pitman Med. Pub., 1960.

Wittenborn, J. R. Symptom patterns in a group of mental hospital patients. *J. consult. Psychol.*, 1951, *15*, 290–302.

Wolpe, J. *Psychotherapy by reciprocal inhibition.* Stanford, Calif.: Stanford Univ. Press, 1958.

Zangwill, O. L. Clinical tests of memory impairment. *Proc. Roy. Soc. Med.*, 1943, *36*, 576–580.

—— Some clinical applications of the Rey-Davis performance test. *J. ment. Sci.*, 1946, *92*, 19–34.

Zilboorg, G., and Henry, G. W. *A history of medical psychology.* New York: Norton, 1941.

Zimmerman, J., and Grosz, H. J. "Visual" performance of a functionally blind person. *Behav. Res. Ther.*, 1966, *4*, 119–134.
Ziskind, E., Jones, H., Filante, W. and Goldberg, J. Observations on mental symptoms in eye-patched patients: hypnagogic symptoms in sensory deprivation. *Amer. J. Psychiat.*, 1960, *116*, 893–900.
Zubek, J. Effects of prolonged sensory and perceptual deprivation. *Brit. med. Bull.*, 1964, *20*, 38–42.
——, Aftanas, M., Kovach, K., Wilgosh, L., and Winocur, G. Effect of severe immobilization of the body on intellectual and perceptual processes. *Canad. J. Psychol.*, 1963, *17*, 118–133.
——, and Wilgosh, L. Prolonged immobilization of the body: changes in performance and in the electroencephalogram. *Science*, 1963, *140*, 306–308.

INDEX

Accurate empathy, (AE), 181, 183, 186, 188-193, 196-201, 203
Adams, H. B., 126
Adorno, T. W., 187
Aftanas, M., 120
After-effects, 114, 115
Aging, 41, 42, 57, 59, 60, 65, 67, 95, 124, 125
Alcorn, D. E., 119
Allport, G. W., 205
Amador, L., 74
Ambiguity, 200-202
Ammons, R. B., 140
Ammons Full Range Picture Vocabulary Test (APV), 140, 141
Analogies Test, 104, 109
Ancevich, S. S., 39
Animal studies, 74, 75, 230
Ankus, M. N., 61-64, 66, 67
Anxiety, 26, 200-202
See also Dysthymia, Phobia
Apostolic function of physician, 163
Apparent movement, 114, 115
Archimedes spiral, 115
Arithmetic tests, 104, 107, 108
Armitage, S. G., 152-157
Arnhoff, F. N., 119
Ascending reticular activating system (ARAS), 120, 121, 125, 128
Associative loosening, 18, 20
See also Overinclusion
Attention, 65, 66
See also Filter Mechanism
Auditory acuity, 61, 63, 65, 96, 168
Auditory perception, 94, 96
Austin, G. A., 19
Autism, 18, 162
Autokinetic effect, 115
Autonomic arousal, 71
Ayllon, T., 162
Azima, F. J., 121, 122, 125
Azima, H., 121, 122
Azrin, N. H., 151

Babcock, H., 37
Babcock-Levy Tests, 37, 38
Bacon, P. M., 175
Bailey, P., 74
Baldwin, M., 72
Balint, M., 163
Barnett, C. D., 162
Barrett, B. H., 158
Bartlet, D., 207-211
Bartlet, J. E. A., 124
Beech, H. R., 206
Behavior prosthetics, 151
Behavior therapy, 12, 151
Benactyzine, 144, 145
Bender, M. B., 75
Benjamin, J. D., 23
Benjamin Proverbs Test, 23-26, 28, 30, 31, 38
Bentinck, C., 126
Berlyne, D. E., 163
Bernard, C., 6, 205, 220
Bexton, W. H., 101, 102, 104-106, 108, 110-113
Bijou, S. W., 162
Bindra, D., 230
Biometrics Research Laboratory, New York State Department of Mental Hygiene, 164

Black, D. A., 49
Bleuler, E., 17, 18, 20
Blocking, 200-202
See also Thought blocking
Boredom, 102, 110, 121, 122
Brady, J. P., 158-161
Brain damage, 10, 19, 21, 41, 46, 48, 49, 74, 75, 97, 124, 139, 207
Brainwashing, 101
Brierley, J. B., 92n, 206
Brightness constancy, 115
Brightness contrast, 115
Broadbent, D. E., 49, 50, 55, 67, 68, 92, 94-97
Broadhurst, P. L., 230
Bromley, D. B., 26
Brownfield, C., 119
Bruner, J., 19

Caird, W. K., 37, 38, 48, 54, 57-59
Calibration, *see* Scaling
Cameron, D. E., 123, 124
Cameron, N., 19, 20, 39
Campbell, D., 206
Candland, D. K., 121
Canonical variate analysis, 33
Carkhuff, R. R., 182, 185, 186, 188, 190-199
Carrera, R. N., 126
Cataract, 124
Catharsis, 200-202
Cattell, R. B., 35, 45
Cell assemblies, 122
Cerebral Dominance, 75, 96
See also Laterality
Cleveland, S. E., 45, 126
Cohen, B. D., 127
Cohen, D. J., 151
Color adaptation, 115
Competition, 151
Concept formation, 20, 21, 23, 125
See also Overinclusion
Concreteness, 23-25, 30, 31, 186
Conran, P., 150
Constructive personality change (CPC), 181-183, 186-190, 195, 228
Contrast effects, 114
Cooper, G. D., 126
Cooperation, 151-155
Cosin, L. Z., 128
Counseling, *see* Psychotherapy
Cowan, J. E., 175
Craik, F. I. M., 67
Cramer-Azima, F., *see* Azima, F. J.
Crisp, A. H., 228
Criterion contamination, 10, 183, 195, 197
Critical flicker frequency, 115
Cronbach, L. J., 216, 230
Cross-validation, 48
Cumulative recording, 133–135, 150
Cumulative response curves, 130, 145, 167, 169, 174
See also Rate of responding

DeBurger, R., 194
Deconditioning, 222
Delayed auditory feedback, 120
Delayed recall, 89, 90
See also Memory
Delirious states, 124
See also Nocturnal delirium
Delta Blocks Test, 106, 110
Deluded behavior, 37, 38, 212, 213, 220, 221
See also Ideas of reference, Psychotic behavior, Schizophrenic patients
Dementia praecox, *see* Schizophrenia
Depressed patients, 26-29, 31, 33-36, 52, 71, 139, 142, 168, 190, 220-223, 226, 227
See also Psychotic patients
Depressive symptoms, *see* Depressed patients
Depth of self-exploration (DSE), 183, 186, 188-193, 195, 197-199
Deutsch, M., 175
Devault, M., 127
Diagnosis, 8, 9, 11, 13, 18, 48, 49, 139, 170, 175, 231
Dichotic listening performance, 49-67, 93-97
Digit span tests, 104, 109
See also Dichotic listening performance
Discriminant function analysis, 32
Discriminated operant, 132
See also Operant behavior
Dissociation, 20
Doane, B. K., 104-106, 108, 110, 111, 113-119
Dobie, S. I., 127
Douds, J., 191
Drasgow, J., 23
Dualism, 2, 229
See also Mind
Dukes, W. F., 205
Dyrud, J. E., 231
Dysinger, D. W., 45
Dysphasia, 75, 76, 78, 81-86
Dysthymia, 26
See also Anxiety, Phobia

Ebbinghaus, H., 206
Eckman, J., 175
Educational subnormality, 209
See also Reading disability
Edwards, A. L., 57
Ego strength, 121, 122
Electroconvulsive shock, 71, 142, 143, 150
EEG, 72, 74, 102, 111, 119
Ellis, A., 222
Ellis, N. R., 162
Epstein, S., 22
Epstein Test of Overinclusion, 22, 24, 26, 28
Esquirol, J. E. D., 41
Etsten, B. E., 150
Extinction, 21, 130, 144, 145, 164, 166-170, 172, 173

Resistance to, 135, 171, 172
Eysenck, H. J., 21, 180, 181, 190, 205

F-scale, 184, 187
Factor analysis, 27, 30, 35
Falconer, M. A., 72, 74, 75, 97-99
Feedback, negative, 122-125
positive, 126
Feldman, M. J., 23
Feldman, R. S., 173-176
Feldman-Drasgow Test, 23-25
Ferster, C. B., 130, 162
Field, J., 206
Filante, W., 124
Filter mechanism, 21, 125, 126
See also Attention
Finney, D. J., 140
Flanigin, H., 74
Flatness of affect, 18, 165, 169, 170
Ford, D. H., 179
Form discrimination, 115, 116
Fox, B., 223, 224
Freitag, G., 241
Frenkel-Brunswik, E., 187
Friedlander, D., 39
Frontal lobe patients, 74, 87, 89, 93, 94
Frontal lobectomy, 94, 97
Fuller, P. R., 131
Furneaux, W. D., 22, 75
Fuster, B., 72

Galanter, E., 123
Gastaut, H., 72
General linear equation, 182, 203
Genuineness, *see* Therapist self-congruence (TSC)
George, E. I., 21-26, 30
Ghost-in-the-machine fallacy, 3, 120-122, 229
See also Psychodynamic theory
Gibbs, E. L., 72
Gibbs, F. A., 72, 74
Gibby, R. G., 126
Gold, V. J., 241
Goldberg, J., 124
Goldberger, L., 121
Goldiamond, I., 176, 231
Goldstein, K., 23
Goldstein-Scheerer Tests, 23-26, 29-31, 39
Goodnow, J. J., 19
Gottlieb, J. S., 127
Grad, B., 125
Graham, J. R., 184
Grant, D. A., 201
Green, J. R., 74
Greenspoon, J., 164
Gregory, M., 67
Greifenstein, F., 127
Grosz, H. J., 162
Gulick, W. L., 121
Guys-Maudsley Neurosurgical Unit, 72, 75

Haden, P., 39
Hallucinations, 111-113, 119, 136, 137, 145, 146, 150, 151
See also Psychotic behavior
Halstead, W. C., 75
Harris, A., 125, 127
Harvard Medical School Behavior Research Laboratory, 131
Hathaway, S. R., 187, 195
Hebb, D. O., 5, 68, 74, 90, 101, 106, 122, 128
Hemianopia, 76, 85
See also Visuospatial defects
Henry, G. W., 17, 41
Heron, W., 101-119
Hewlett, J. H. G., 26, 27, 29-33, 35, 36, 39
Hill, D., 72, 74
Hippocampal structures, 92n
Hobika, J. H., 150
Holt, R. R., 121
Hull, C. L., 21, 42
Hunter, R. C. A., 184
Huxley, A., 126
Hydrohypodynamic environment, 119
Hyperactivity, 175
Hysteria, 26, 164
Hysterical blindness, 158

Ideas of reference, 37
See also Deluded behavior
Ideographic, 205
Immobilization, 120
Inglis, J., 41-64, 66, 67, 94, 122, 162, 163, 184, 206, 229, 230
Inhibition, 20-22
Insight, 200-202
Institute of Psychiatry, University of London, 206
Insulin, 142, 143
Intelligence, 6, 7, 22, 26, 30, 36-38, 42, 45, 47, 75, 76, 81, 84, 87, 89, 102, 104, 207
Intermittent reinforcement, *see* Schedules of reinforcement
Interview, 165-168, 170, 172, 178, 183, 184, 191, 216, 217
Iproniazid, 143, 144
Irion, A. L., 44, 206
Isaacs, B., 48
Isaacs, W., 176

Jackson, D. D., 18
James, I. P., 74
Jones, H., 124
Jones, H. G., 88, 206, 231

Kassorla, I. C., 241
Kelley, D. M. G., 187
Kelly, G. A., 228
Kendall, M. G., 218
Kendrick, D. C., 49
Keschner, M., 75
Kessell, R., 206
Kimura, D., 91-97

Kinder, M. I., 241
King, G. F., 152-157
King, H. E., 140
Klopfer, B., 187
Kodman, F., 190
Kohs, S. C., 106
Kohs Block Design Test, 75, 104, 106, 110, 207
Kolodny, A., 75
Kovach, K., 120
Kraepelin, E., 17
Kral, V. A., 125
Krasner, L., 176, 177
Kretschmer, E., 20
Kubie, L., 121, 122
Kubzansky, P. E., 101

Larson, W. L., 140
Laterality, ear, 61, 64, 93, 95
 hand, 75, 81, 86
 See also Cerebral dominance
Laverty, S. G., 37-39
Lawes, T. G. G., 126, 127
Learning, 42, 44-47, 49, 55, 68, 71, 75, 77, 84, 88, 92
 See also Learning defect, Memory
Learning defect, 209, 210
 auditory, 77, 82, 84, 86, 90, 92, 96
 verbal, 86-90
 visual, 92
 See also Learning, Memory, Memory disorder
Learning discrimination, 200-202
Leiderman, P. H., 101, 124
Leiter, R. G., 22
Leiter-Partington Pathways Test, 22, 24, 26, 28
Lende, R. A., 72
Leon, H. V., 119
Levinson, D. J., 187
Levy, E. Z., 119
Levy, L., 37
Lilly, J. C., 119
Lind, D. L., 158-161
Lindsley, D. B., 120, 121
Lindsley, O. R., 131-152, 158, 162, 172, 176, 203
Lindsley manipulandum, 132, 133, 147
Löfving, B., 206
Lovaas, O. I., 162
Luby, E. D., 127
Lucero, R. J., 140
Luchins, A. S., 27
Luchins Test, 27, 29

Mackay, H. A., 51, 57, 60, 162
Magaret, A., 39
Mahatoo, W., 113-119
Maher, B. A., 231
Mania, 126
Marks, I. M., 223, 224
Matarazzo, J. D., 11
Matussek, P., 21-26, 30
Maxwell, A. E., 206, 223
McGeogh, J. A., 44, 206
McGill, T. E., 121
McGill Picture Anomalies Test, 74, 75, 90, 91, 106, 110
McGill University, 101, 102, 112, 119, 120, 125
McKinley, J. C., 187, 195
McNemar, Q., 53
Mednick, M. T., 139-141
Memory, 42, 49, 71, 75, 77, 88
 registration (acquisition), 42–50, 53, 55, 57, 60, 65, 67, 68, 77, 82, 94–96, 123, 124, 208, 209
 retention, 42, 44, 46, 48, 49, 68, 77, 89, 208, 209
 retrieval, 42, 49
 See also Delayed recall, Learning, Learning defect, Relearning, Retained members
Memory disorder, 10, 41-68, 75, 92, 127
 See also Learning defect
Memory-disordered patients, 44-50, 52-56, 162
 See also Senile patients
Mendelson, J. H., 101, 124
Mentally defective patients, 131, 151, 162
Mental events, *see* Mind
Meyer, A., 74
Meyer, B. F., 140
Meyer, J. S., 127
Meyer, V., 72, 75-88, 90, 96-99
Mill Hill Vocabulary Test, 22, 26, 37, 38, 75, 76, 81-86
Miller, G. A., 123
Miller, M. D., 231
Milner, B., 72-75, 86-92, 96
Mind, 2, 3, 18, 163
 See also Dualism
Minnesota Multiphasic Personality Inventory (MMPI), 187, 195
Mirror Drawing Test, 106, 110, 207
Mitchell, W., 74
Modified Word Learning Test, 49
Moldofsky, H., 228
Monotony, *see* Boredom
Montreal Neurological Institute, 72-74, 86, 92
Morel, B., 17
Mort, M., 128
Mortality, 49
Morton, N. W., 74, 90, 106
Motivation, 56, 57, 60
Moxon, C., 211
Multiple Operant Problem Solving Apparatus (MOPSA), 152, 153
Murray, H. A., 187

Nathan, P. E., 148, 149, 203
Necker Cube Reversal, 115
Negative feeling expression, 200-202
Negative induction, *see* Inhibition
Nelson, E. H., 75, 81, 207

Neologisms, 22
Neufeld, I., 221, 222
Neurotic patients, 22-26, 28, 29, 31-37, 188, 190
New Word Learning and Retention Test, 75, 77, 81-86, 98, 99
Newcombe, F., 48
Nocturnal delirium, 123
See also Delirious states
Nomothetic, 205
Nonpossessive warmth, *see* Unconditional positive regard (UPR)
Nufferno Tests, 22, 75, 76
Number-series Test, 104, 107, 108

Obsessive compulsive reaction, 26, 221
Operant behavior, 129-177, 200
See also Discriminated operant
Operant level, 165-170, 172
Opinion stating, 165
Organic (cerebral) disorder, *see* Brain damage
Orlando, R., 162
Orthopedic surgery, 124
Osgood, C. E., 171, 172
Overinclusion, 19-30, 35-39, 125-127
See also Associative loosening, Concept formation, Sensory overload

Paired associate learning tests, 42, 44-49, 104, 208
auditory recall, 42, 43, 45-49, 75, 77, 78, 82-86, 96, 98, 211
auditory recognition, 42, 44, 45, 78, 81-86, 96, 98, 99
cross-modality, 208-211
tactile recognition, 80-86, 98, 211
visual recall, 42, 44, 45, 78, 79, 82-86, 98, 99, 211
visual recognition, 42, 44, 45, 78, 79, 81-86, 98
Paired comparisons, method of, 216, 218
Patient self-disclosure, *see* Depth of self-exploration (DSE)
Parboosingh, R. C., 49
Parietal lobe patients, 74, 87, 89
Partington, J., 22
Passage copying test, 106, 110
Patterned stimulation, 111, 119
visual, 101, 112, 113
Pavlov, I. P., 21
Payne, R. W., 8, 18-27, 29-33, 35-39, 41, 206
Payne Object Classification Test, 22, 24, 26, 28, 38, 39
Penfield, W., 72, 74, 75, 92n
Perceptual anomalies, 206, 207
Perseveration, 172
Personal construct theory, 228
Personal Questionnaire, 216-224, 226-228
Phase sequences, 122
Phi-phenomenon, 115
Phillips, J. P. N., 219
Phobia, 221-223, 226, 227
See also Anxiety, Dysthymia

Pisoni, S., 165-169, 171-176
Poliomyelitis, 124
Pond, D. A., 74
Portnoy, S., *see* Pisoni, S.
Post, F., 49, 128, 206, 221, 222
Prediction, 7, 8, 189, 190, 207
See also Prognosis
Predictive control, 212, 228
Preschool children, 190
Pressure of ideas, 20
Pribram, K. H., 123
Primary processes, 121
Princeton University, 119
Problem orientation, 200-202
Problem solving, 122, 123, 125
Prognosis, 8, 38, 49, 172, 175
See also Prediction
Progressive Matrices, 75, 76, 81-86
Proketazine, 39
Propaganda, effects of, 101, 104, 106, 107, 110, 111
Pryer, M. W., 162
Psychical phenomena, belief in, 106, 111
Psychodynamic theory, 121, 183, 229
See also Ghost-in-the-machine fallacy
Psychology, content of, 1-3
method in, 1, 3, 6, 11, 71
relation to the other sciences, 2-6, 71
Psychomotor defects, 206
See also Speed
Psychomotor epilepsy, *see* Temporal lobe epilepsy
Psychotherapy, 12, 146-148, 158, 176, 177, 179-203, 212
client centered, *see* Nondirective
group, 190, 193-195
nondirective, 177, 223-226
outcome of, 12, 180-182, 185, 190, 203, 228
process in, 177, 181, 182, 190, 203, 228
psychoanalytic, 180
rational, 222-226
training in, 190-193, 195
See also Verbal therapy
Psychotic behavior, 135, 137
episodic, 135-137
phasic, 137, 138
Psychotic patients, 25, 33, 35, 139, 140, 143, 145, 168
See also Depressed patients, Schizophrenic patients
Psychotomimetic drugs, 126
Pursuit rotor, 207

Q-sort, 184, 187

Rasmussen, T., 72, 96
Rate of responding, 130, 131, 135, 137, 138-140, 150, 151
See also Cumulative response curves
Rating scales, 12, 132, 138, 139, 152, 185, 191, 193, 194, 197, 215
amount of verbalization, 152, 156

clinical improvement, 152, 155, 156
depression, 213, 214
extreme mental illness, 152, 155
Fergus Falls Behavior Sheet, 140, 141
guilt, 213-215
hostility, 213, 214
paranoid belief, 213-215
Tulane Psychological Test Performance Behavior Rating, 140, 141
ward behavior, 138, 152, 155
See also Personal Questionnaire
Raven, J. C., 22, 37, 75, 81
Ravenette, E. T., 212, 214-216
Reading Age (RA), 211
Reading disability, 207
Recreational therapy, 152, 155, 156
Regressed behavior, 19, 122
Reinforcement, 21, 27, 129-177, 196, 199-203
"altruistic", 135, 142
conditioned, 132-134
conjugate, 149, 150, 203
human, 176
impersonal, 173, 176
musical, 158
"sexual", 135
See also Schedules of reinforcement
Reitman, E. E., 126
Relearning score, 46-48, 209
See also Memory, retention
Remedial teaching, 210, 211
Repertory grid technique, 228
Respondent behavior, 129, 130, 132
Response set, 216, 226
Retained members score, 46-48
See also Memory, retention
Retardation, *see* Speed
Rey, A., 46
Rey-Davis Test, 46-48
Riddell, S. A., 48
Rogers, C. R., 177, 181-183, 188, 190, 192, 200, 201
Rokeach, M., 27
Rorschach Test, 10, 140, 141, 184, 187, 207
Rosenbaum, G., 127
Rosenzweig, S., 181
Ross, H., 128
Rotation effect, 207
Rubenstein, D. B., 241
Rubin, L. S., 126
Ruff, G. E., 119
Russell, L., 125
Ryle, G., 2, 3, 120, 229

Salzinger, K., 164-176
Salzinger, S., 175
Sanderson, R. E., 48, 49, 52-54
Sandler, J., 44, 47, 81
Sanford, R. N., 187
Scaling, 217-219, 226, 228
Schaeffer, B., 241
Schedules of reinforcement, 129, 154
differential reinforcement of low rate (DRL), 158
fixed interval, 130, 173
fixed ratio, 130, 150
variable interval, 130, 135, 139, 144
variable ratio, 130
See also Reinforcement
Scheerer, M., 23
Scheflen, A. E., 179
Scheier, I. H., 230
Schizophrenia, 17-20, 126, 175
Schizophrenic patients, acute, 38, 172
anergic, 158, 162
catatonic, 152
children, 162
chronic, 38, 39, 146-148, 157, 172
hebephrenic, 139, 152
paranoid, 37, 52, 139, 152
recovered, 39
undifferentiated, 19, 22-31, 33-37, 125-127, 152, 165-173, 187, 190, 197
See also Deluded behavior, Psychotic behavior, Psychotic patients
Schneller, P., 148, 149
Schonell, F. J., 211
Scott, T. H., 101, 102, 104-106, 108, 110-119
Scoville, W. B., 92
Secondary processes, 121
Self-referred affect, statements of, 165-174
Semantic differential, 172
Semmelweis, I. P., 11
Senile dementia, 41, 48, 55, 68, 95, 206
Senile patients, 19, 52, 125, 127, 151
See also Memory-disordered patients
Sensory overload, 120, 128
See also Overinclusion
Sernyl, 126, 127
Set, 23, 27
Shalman, D. C., 91
Shape distortion, 114, 115
Shape constancy, 115
Shapiro, M. B., 21, 75, 81, 206-228, 231
Shaw Test, 26, 29
Shearn, C. R., 140
Short-term (memory) storage, *see* Memory, registration
Shurley, J. T., 119
Sidman, M., 141, 205, 212
Siegel, S., 156, 170, 172
Similarity of expression of patient to therapist, 200-202
Simmons, J. B., 241
Simultaneous stimulation, *see* Dichotic listening performance
Single case, study of the, 158, 176, 203, 205-228, 231
Size constancy, 115
Skinner, B. F., 129, 130, 132, 141, 158, 163
Slater, P., 30, 32, 206, 215
Slowness, *see* Speed
Smith, S., 126
Sodium amytal, 96
Solomon, P., 101, 121, 124
Somaesthesia, 114, 115

Sommer, R., 128
Spatial orientation, 114, 116-118
Speech-deficient behavior, 175, 176
Speed, 23, 27, 29, 35-39, 71, 207
Spradlin, J. E., 162
Steinberg, B., 48
Stephenson, W., 187
Stratton, G. M., 206
Strauss, T., 75
Stroop Test, 184, 187
Subcortical patients, 93
Successive approximations, method of, 131, 176
Suci, G. J., 172
Symbols, 163

Tabo-paresis, 122
Tachistoscopic perception, 115
Tactile Formboard Test, 75
Taffel, C., 164, 165, 172
Tannenbaum, P. H., 172
Target symptoms, 228
Taylor, J. G., 206
Temporal lobe, 72, 73, 92
  epilepsy, 72, 74
  excision, 71, 72, 74
    bilateral, 92
    unilateral dominant, 75-77, 81-96
    unilateral nondominant, 75-77, 81-94
  growth or scar, 97-99
  patients, 74, 75, 81, 89, 93, 95
Temporal lobectomy, *see* Temporal lobe excision
Test-Operate-Test-Exit (TOTE), 123
Thakurdas, H., 126
Thaler, V. H., 119
Thematic Apperception Test (TAT), 184, 187, 207
Therapist activity level, 183
Therapist directiveness, 200, 201
Therapist-Patient-Therapist interaction units (TPT), 200
Therapist self-congruence (TSC), 181, 183, 185, 188-193, 196-199
Therapist sensitivity, *see* Accurate Empathy (AE)
Thomas, J., 176
Thought-blocking, 20, 126
  See also Blocking
Thought disorder, 17-39, 119, 125
Thurstone, L. L., 30, 187
Thurstone-Gottschaldt Figures, 106, 110
Tics, 158
Tilton, J. R., 152-157
Tizard, B., 206
Toilet training, 175, 176
Transference, 228
Transparency, *see* Therapist self-congruence (TSC)
Triangular Blocks Test, 75
Truax, C. B., 182-203, 228
Trumbull, R., 101
Two-point limen, 116, 117

Ullmann, L. P., 176
Unconditional positive regard (UPR), 181, 183, 185, 186, 188, 189-193, 196, 197, 199-201, 203
Unpleasantness, 216-219, 221, 226
Urban, H. B., 179
Urine, 205

Validity, 7, 132, 176, 187
Verbal therapy, 152, 155, 156
  See also Psychotherapy
Vernon, J. A., 119, 121
Verplanck, W. S., 165
Vicarious therapy pretraining (VTP), 195
Vigotsky, L. S., 19
Vigotsky Sorting Test, 19
Vispo, R., 121
Visual acuity, 115
Visual perception, 74, 88, 90-92, 102, 111-115, 119, 208
Visuospatial defects, 74-76, 82, 83, 85-88, 90, 92, 111, 208
See also Hemianopia

Wada, J., 96
Walkley, F. A., 48
Walton, D., 49
Wassermann Test, 8
Wechsler, D., 42, 44, 47, 52, 75, 78, 81, 87, 106, 140, 187, 208, 212
Wechsler Adult Intelligence Scale (WAIS), 47, 52-54, 184, 187
Wechsler Bellevue Intelligence Test, 44, 45, 75, 76, 81-87, 104, 106, 110, 140, 141, 212
Wechsler Intelligence Scale for Children (WISC), 207
Wechsler Memory Scale, 42, 75, 77, 78, 88-90
Welford, A. T., 49, 67
Westropp, C., 128
Wexler, D., 101, 124
Wilcoxon, F., 166
Wilgosh, L., 120
Willett, R. A., 97
William James Lectures, Harvard University, 163
Williams, M., 128
Winocur, G., 120
Wittenborn, J. R., 187
Wittenborn Rating Scales, 187
Wolpe, J., 222
Word-making tests, 104, 105, 108, 109

Yates, A. J., 75-77, 88

Z scores, 97, 98
Zangwill, O. L., 46
Zilboorg, G., 17, 41
Zimmerman, J., 162
Ziskind, E., 124
Zubek, J., 120
Zubin, J., 175